TEDDY HIT ME

SCATTERED STORIES OF MY SEARCH FOR ATTENTION

TED LEAVITT

CONTENTS

NAMES

*There are many people whose
names appear in the stories in these pages.*

Some of them have been changed.

Everyone else has given me permission.

DEDICATION

For Tina, Manda, Becca,
Jill, Holly, Luke
and
all of you who can relate

ONE

BEGIN WITH THE ENDING

WHO REALLY CARES about another memoir? I mean, it's one thing if the person you're reading about is famous or has done something really amazing, but why would people want to read someone's collection of stories and anecdotes and observations if they don't even know the person? Plus, it's a super fancy sounding word for something that could also be called, "Stuff I Remembered." Having said that, I've read lots of memoirs and biographies and historical fiction, plus all of the *Black Stallion* books by Walter Farley. Have you ever read those? If you haven't guessed, they're about a black stallion, lovingly named "The Black" by his adopted owner. Really? Not just Black or Blackie? The Black. I'm going to go and ride The Black. Has anyone seen The Black? The movie was all right, but it was a bit slow moving at first, so when I tried to watch it with my kids, they felt like they were being tortured with a hot poker, which is actually a pretty gruesome thing, if you think about it. Also, it's funny that a poker is called a poker. It's like someone said,

"What's that thing for?"

"Uh, it's for poking the fire."

"What's it called?"

"It doesn't have a name."

"Should we call it something?"

"Sure, any ideas?"

"Hmm, how about poker?"

"Do you mean, 'The Poker'?"

"No that's too fancy..."

Anyway, memoirs. I began my career in counselling working at a residential treatment centre for men struggling with substance abuse problems. I was naive and armed with good grades and thought I could make a difference by telling them what I had learned. I was repeatedly asked by the men, as they were about to explain their feelings and experiences to me, if I had ever struggled with substance abuse. I would defensively answer that I had not but that I didn't think it would be a barrier to my helping them. I asked if they had cancer, would they only see a doctor who had cancer, or would they trust the training and education of a doctor who was an expert in cancer treatment? While this simple argument won me some points, and over the years I was able to help many guys and their families, I was missing a fundamental aspect of helping, from both a professional and non-professional point of view. A big part of helping is relating. It wasn't until I began to relate my own addictive behaviour and tendencies to the addiction experiences of my clients that I began to really connect with their feelings of confusion, hopelessness, isolation, anger, and shame. It wasn't until I began to see myself reflected in my clients that they began to see themselves reflected in me. That's when I became able to give them something that a textbook or a grade on an exam could never give them: hope. They needed to see that what I was saying, what they were being taught, had roots in the real world. They had to know that they could overcome.

There is great power and relief in hearing someone else speak of your experiences, thoughts, and feelings with firsthand knowledge because he or she has shared them. It is especially liberating when those experiences, thoughts, and emotions had previously left you feeling like you didn't belong, like an outsider hiding on the inside. As my career has progressed and evolved, I have always made an effort to see myself in my clients and hope that they can see themselves in me. That's why I'm sharing some of the experiences that have brought me to where I am. My hope is that you will see yourself in me, and that if you do, you won't feel so alone. I grew up with an ADHD brain, without knowing I had one. It's kind of like growing up with a super-power disguised as a giant zit. It's embarrassing and painful and draws attention for all the wrong reasons, but when you finally understand it, actually... it's not really like a zit, because in order for that analogy to work, there would have to be an upside to having a giant zit. Having lived through puberty for a few decades, I can tell you there are virtually no upsides to having a giant zit. So come up with your own analogy then, if you think you're so smart.

It's like when I was 19 years old. I lived in a different city, and my roommate and I traveled everywhere on bikes because we couldn't afford any other way to get around. His bike was a high-quality ride, and he was an experienced rider. My bike was a piece of crap, and I had no idea what I was doing. My bike had a problem where the front brakes were almost always on, just a little bit. Because I had no idea what I was doing, rather than fix it, I just rode everywhere with the brakes on. I'm not sure why my roommate didn't offer to help me, but I imagine I must have mentioned the issue more than once as he would race off ahead of me and then wait for me to catch up, looking annoyed and bored. Anyway, one day a friend took us out for dinner, and I happened to mention this issue I was having with my bike, and he offered to get it fixed for me, since he knew a guy. I happily handed it over to him, and he brought it back the next day, good as new. I can tell you that all that time riding around with the extra resistance of the unwanted brakes had strengthened my legs to the point where now I was the one waiting impatiently for my roommate to catch up. Growing up with undiscovered ADHD was kind of like that. Things were harder for me than for other people, but all along I was nursing an inner strength that I didn't know I had. It wasn't until

I finally understood myself--why I was the way I was and did the things I did and forgot the things I forgot--that my strength became something I could use.

Those of us with ADHD have brains that can often remember conversations from decades ago but can't remember to flush the toilet, that can hear a slight ticking noise at the end of the hall when trying to watch a movie but can't hear the person who is standing right in front of us speaking, that generate ideas like popcorn poppers but follow through on those ideas like ... something that doesn't follow through at all. I want people who have been blessed and cursed with this brain to be able to laugh at our flaws instead of seeing them as evidence of inadequacy and unworthiness. I want us to be able to accept that because we are exceptional at some stuff, we are terrible at other stuff and that there is no shame in that. I want us to have the courage to proclaim to the world, "I'm a weirdo!" Now that's a funny word, if you think about it. We take an adjective and attach -o to the end of it to make it a noun. So if I am strong, then I am a strongo? Or if I'm hungry, then I'm a hungryo? Actually, that sounds like a real snack food or breakfast cereal or something, but apparently it's not, because I googled it and there isn't any type of food called HungryOs. I even tried different spellings. The closest I could come up with was a restaurant in Marshalltown, Iowa, called O'Hungry's. Uh, what the heck? Their menu says you can get a large pizza for $5 or a filet mignon for $12! Now that's a sweet deal.

In January of 2018, I had the opportunity to prepare and deliver a speech at a TEDx event in Langley, British Columbia, Canada. The title of my talk was "Giving Up and Getting Up." It was about the dual tendencies of people with ADHD to give in to learned helplessness, believing that failure is inevitable, but also to get back up and try something else. The video is on YouTube with a disappointingly small number of views. Anyway, I am no stranger to public speaking and teaching, and I thought the opportunity to give a talk on my ADHD experience in school and life would be fun and helpful. It turned out to be incredibly stressful. In fact, that was kind of what the talk was about, so I'm not going to spoil it by telling the story twice. If you want to know about it, go watch it. I bring it up because during the talk, something happened that is so quintessentially ADHD that I have to share it. It illustrates both the frustrating and the wonderful aspects of this complicated operating system that I have been given.

My talk ended with two stories back to back, with a small but important point made in between them. As I finished the first of these two stories, my mind went completely blank. I felt a surge of panic as I stared out into the combination of blinding spotlight and darkness where the audience was allegedly seated. I paused for a moment and tried to buy some time by repeating the last line of the story, hoping it would jog my memory. It didn't, and in that millisecond I decided to just move ahead with the concluding story. As I started to tell this story, I realized that the piece I had forgotten was actually critical to its ending, which allowed me to finally remember the missing piece. However, I had now started the final story and couldn't go back to the spot where I had gotten stuck without making the talk really choppy and lame. I debated whether I should just leave it out altogether and decided that this was not possible as the final line of the story wouldn't have nearly the impact without this principle. All the while I was having this internal dialogue, I was still telling the story, getting closer to the end, where the train would either pull into the station and stop or go crashing through and derail. Just as I approached the critical point, my brain found a way to wrestle the principle into the last line, allowing the story to make sense and drive the point home. I ended my talk with relief and turned to make my way off stage before the applause could even catch up.

I love this story because it illustrates so many aspects of the ADHD brain. Creativity, forgetfulness, resourcefulness, anxiety, risk-taking, and--to some degree--meta-cognition. I was telling a story while deciding how to tell the story and noticing that I was doing both while I was doing them. Is it any wonder that I had a hard time paying attention in school? Anyway, this book is full of these kinds of moments. Some of them were disastrous, and some of them were triumphant. Most of them were disastrous. But all of them count, which is something I try to get through to my clients. Nothing is all good or all bad. Our brains fall victim to the confirmation bias, which is the tendency to pay attention to and remember only the things that confirm what we already think. If we come to believe that we are stupid, awkward, or a failure, then we will compile a list of experiences that serve as evidence of this belief. We will also ignore all evidence to the contrary, and if we can't ignore it, we will twist it so that it still fits the belief. The only way to counteract this is to deliberately work on compiling contradictory evidence. It is not effective to counteract the belief that I am stupid by saying that I am not stupid, because there is evidence that I might be. Instead, I must acknowledge that sometimes I do some short-sighted, impulsive things, but—at the same time—I must acknowledge that I also have the ability to make good, well-reasoned decisions. I hope you enjoy this journey through my journey.

TWO

SIGNS OF THINGS TO COME

EVEN THOUGH MY dad grew up in fairly urban settings, he spent many summers at his Uncle Grant's farm with his brother Tom, playing cowboy. They helped out with farm chores but mostly spent a lot of time shooting gophers. Their grandparents were farmers and their parents had grown up on farms, and I think this led them to identify with the cowboy-farmer image. Not only that, but my dad's innate (probably genetic) thirst for adventure, hard work, and the great outdoors led him to always skirt the line of Beverly Hillbilly. What this meant for me was a childhood full of the same type of adventure, hard work (up to a certain point), and outdoor exploits. When my parents were still young, with only a couple of boys, they rented a farmhouse while my dad was a university student. The landlord was a guy named Ming Wong, whom my dad talked about sometimes, and I really liked the name Ming Wong. Because I was just a small kid and knew nothing about different cultures or languages, the name Ming Wong just sounded like a fun character. I think I might have met or seen him a few times, but I have no recollection of it beyond a passing impression. Years later, after we were long removed from the farmhouse, I remember hearing that Ming Wong was murdered in Vancouver. When I asked why, my dad hinted that Ming Wong was not always a person who was above-board. I like to say Ming Wong still. It sounds weird to refer to him as Wong, or just Ming, so I have to say Ming Wong every time. Also, is it kind of weird that my dad rented a house from someone he knew to be a bit shady?

The farmhouse was located in a little rural suburb of Surrey, British Columbia, called Cloverdale. Down the hill was an actual farm, where my dad tried his hand at hobby farming. I remember the barn had a swing, made from a barrel hung from the rafters. The barrel lay on its side with a hole cut out, making a perfect rocket-ship shape. Because the rafters were high up in the ceiling of the barn, when that swing got going it really went high. My mom swears it wasn't as high as I remember, but I have a distinct memory of going so high in that swing that I could see the farm cats scurrying around up in the hayloft. I had no fear of such things, focusing only on the thrill.

My dad tried to raise some pigs in his spare time, which is so typical of my dad. My only memory of this attempt was when I went gleefully marching through the pigpen in my shoes, glorying in the mud until it grabbed hold of my shoes and wouldn't let go, which led me to do the only logical thing: walk around in the mud in my socks. My dad also tried to raise a calf named Rosie. He must have bought her from someone or at the auction or something, but she lived down the road at the farm. I remember one day, however, my dad got a phone call telling him that Rosie had escaped the farm and was making her way down the road. My dad must have been watching us kids, because we all piled into the car to chase after her. Of course we eventually caught her, and then my dad was left with a dilemma. He had to lead the calf back to the farm, but he also had a couple of kids and a car. Of course, similar to my decision-making process with the pigpen, he did the most logical and efficient thing possible: he put the calf into the backseat of the car and drove her back to the farm. I remember thinking at the time that this was about the most awesome thing I had ever seen in my young life.

When I was four years old, living in a little place in the British

Columbia Kootenays called Castlegar, my mom's friend was over for a visit. She'd brought her son, another active four-year-old boy who I sometimes played with at church. We lived in a fairly rustic setting. Okay, that's an understatement. Our backyard was a steep hill, covered with trees and dense bush--the perfect place for four-year-old boys to play completely unsupervised. I remember standing above my playmate, slightly up the hill from where he was squatting, poking through the leaves and other foliage on the ground. Somehow, I ended up with a large rock in my hands. Yes, hands. It was big enough that it took two hands for me to lift. I don't remember if he looked at me at all, but there is a whisper of memory of him gazing up at me, where I stood holding the rock aloft. He had a puzzled look on his face, as if questioning whether I was actually going to do what I appeared to be set to do. The answer to his unspoken question came abruptly and painfully as I dropped the rock. On his head. Predictably, the scene shifts in my memory to the living room, with me standing in front of my mom and her friend. "Teddy hit me with the rock!" my friend cried. I remember my mom's look of disbelief (probably mingled with embarrassment) as she grasped for explanations as to why her sweet little boy would intentionally drop a rock on someone's head. "Teddy, why would you do that?" she asked, partly in reproach and partly out of curiosity. My answer left her wanting more, I suppose, as I came up with the best explanation I could think of: "I don't know."

I knew nothing of the surrounding geography of Castlegar at the time, so as far as I was concerned, the world consisted of our house, the surrounding houses, and the trees and the neighbours. Also, there was the river. We had moved to the Kootenays because my dad had got a job working for West Kootenay Power, a hydroelectric company that ran a few dams in the region. One of these dams was just down the railroad tracks from our house. I remember walking down there many times with my dad to stare at the incredible power of water as it poured through the open spillways. There were these big red-and-white balls suspended on the powerlines over the river, and I was never sure why they were there, but they sure made me want to eat candy.

There were a few kids in the neighbourhood that I played with. One in particular was known (by my parents) as a notorious liar. I didn't know what they were talking about, but every time I passed on a story this friend had told me, my parents would gently encourage me not to believe everything she said. One time she told me that she had seen a cougar down by the dam. Since I had no idea what a cougar was, my brain created the most fearsome creature it could think of, and--for some reason--it came up with a skunk the size of a bear.

As I mentioned, there were railroad tracks running in front of our house, and because it was the 1980s, there were no fences or gates or anything that would prevent us from playing or walking on the tracks. We appreciated this, because it was a fun place to play and walk. One day, however, a tragedy was narrowly averted. My dad was working on something in the backyard when he heard the train horn blast. For some reason that we can only ascribe to the divine, a distinct thought came into his mind: "Where's Stephen?" Luckily, he didn't hesitate and instead ran to the front of the house, where he saw my little one-year-old brother Stephen standing on the train tracks with a train coming fast. My dad sprinted the distance from the house to the tracks just in time to scoop Steve up and whisk him to safety. I'm sure that when he told my mom about it later he down-played its seriousness, but that incident could have changed our family forever.

Other memories I have from this house near the Brilliant Dam include our massive sandbox that my dad made, building gigantic (to us) snowmen for my dad to ram with the car when he came home from work (which he did), and the first pet I remember, a small grey tabby cat named Puddy, who came trotting out of the bushes behind our house one day and welcomed herself into our home and family. My next younger brother, Mike, was the one who named her after Puddy Tat from the Tweety cartoons on Looney Tunes, which is weird because we had no TV, and I have no idea where he would have ever heard of a cat named Puddy before that. Puddy fit right in to our crazy little family, one day falling out of the second story window and surviving, even though she had a bit of a limp for the rest of her life. Her closest brush with death, however, involved bath time. Of course, the stereotype of cats and water holds up in most cases, because that's how stereotypes come to be, and Puddy was no exception. However, one evening it was not the water that almost did her in but my good intentions. After Puddy mysteriously fell into the bathtub, I thought I would let her outside to dry off. However, it was the middle of winter, and the temperature must have been near freezing. My mom noticed that she hadn't seen the cat for a while and asked if anyone knew where she was. This was when I proudly announced my altruistic act, and my mom rushed to open the backdoor where she found a soaking wet, freezing-cold kitty who was probably wondering whether joining this family had been the best decision for her future. Like I said, though, she was made for us.

When I was little, I sucked my thumb, as I believe all my siblings did, too. I remember one day waking up from a good night's sleep in this little house and racing to my mom and yelling, "Mom, I didn't suck my thumb last night!" I was so proud and so relieved and so happy. I guess I must have been trying for a while. If you think about it, it's kind of a strange-sounding thing to be addicted to. How hard is it to not suck your thumb? It doesn't taste good, there are no commercials for it on TV, there's no peer pressure involved, but for some reason, it's very difficult to quit. The reason is the same as it is for any and all addictions. It provides soothing, and once a brain that craves soothing has been soothed, it is very difficult to convince it to stop the activity that has soothed it. Anyway, I stopped all on my own and felt proud of myself.

Another memory from this house is when my parents went away so that Mike could have corrective surgery on his eyes, since he was born with severely crossed eyes that couldn't be corrected just by glasses or patches. While he was gone, my Grandma and Grandpa

Leavitt came to stay with us, and this was when my grandma went too far and actually tried to parent me instead of just being a nice grandma who gave me candy and hugs. The result was that when it was time for her to leave, after my parents had come home, I refused to come out and say goodbye. Even when my mom tried to talk me into it. Even when my grandma came back into the house to talk to me. I refused to hug her or even talk to her. I remember her looking down at me and saying in her loud voice, with a big smile on her face, "You don't like me very much, do you?" It's funny because I loved my grandma my whole life, but I was not going to be bent or broken on this occasion. The irony is that the stubbornness that held me strong that day was probably inherited from her directly and passed down through my dad.

When I was in kindergarten at Kinnaird Elementary in Castlegar, I remember standing in line outside the classroom before the start of school. That day, I had proudly brought my hard-plastic dinosaur to school with me. It was a brown stegosaurus. I've always wondered if there is any scientific basis for the colors assigned to our reconstructions of dinosaurs or if they are just arbitrarily assigned based on the artist's imagination. Anyway, there was this girl in my class who had a little bit of something in the corner of her mouth. It reminded me of some food, like toast, stuck to her face. "She must not know that she has food on her face," I reasoned, because who would intentionally go to school, even kindergarten, with food stuck to her face? I also reasoned that it would be rude to outright tell her that she had food on her face or to ask what was stuck to her mouth. At the same time, my attention was magnetically drawn to the thing, and I couldn't just ignore it or let it be. So, being the benevolently clever lad that I was, I determined the best way to address the situation was to have my dinosaur friend "eat" whatever was stuck to her. "He's hungry!" I proclaimed loudly, and shoved the dinosaur into her face, using the hard, sharp teeth (curiously white for an herbivore that didn't brush) to scrape the stuff off. She recoiled with a look of shock and horror, which quickly transformed to the closed eyes and exaggerated frown of an incoming but still-silent burst of painful tears.

When she finally exploded, I was caught completely off guard. What had I done? I didn't think it was that rough. Was it too rough? Then I heard another little girl yell (with what seemed like great pleasure) to the teacher at the head of the line, "Teddy hit her in the face!" Then, the explanation came, not to me but to the teacher, as if I already knew the story. "She has stitches in her face and Teddy hit them with his dinosaur! ON PURPOSE!" Stitches? I was even more confused. This was the first time I had ever seen stitches, little brown threads tied into a knot in the corner of her lip. In my mind, I collected data from my short years on earth. That was the moment when I learned that stitches didn't look like they did in the comic books: little railroad tracks, standing out from the skin in clear relief. Unfortunately, there were layers of pain to this experience. First, the idea that I was being accused of intentionally hurting this girl, when I'd thought I was sparing her feelings. Second, the teacher not knowing the full story and me not having a voice to explain myself. Third, a deeper feeling of guilt that I hadn't known what stitches looked like. I remember thinking, "How does everyone else know what stitches look like, but I don't? Is this something that I should have known?" This question, in an infinite variety of iterations, repeated itself throughout my childhood and early adulthood. "How does everyone else seem to know this thing? Am I supposed to know this thing? How come I don't know this thing?" Of course, looking back now, I realize that there was no way I could have known what stitches looked like, because I had never seen them before.

THREE

MRS. ANDERSON IS NOT NICE

In Grade 2, my teacher was Mrs. Anderson. I'm not sure what she really looked like, but in my mind's eye, she looks and sounds like the granny who owns Tweety Bird on Looney Tunes. Sweet and old, but then she pulls out an umbrella and beats the living daylights out of the cat who is trying to get her bird. Our desks were arranged in groups of four, two on each side, facing each other. Seating assignments were changed periodically. I have no idea who my desk mates were during this incident, but I remember kneeling up on my chair and leaning way over my desk, reaching out towards the desk of the kid who was sitting kitty corner to me. I don't know why. I don't know if I was talking, helping, bugging, or just messing around. What I do know is that Mrs. Anderson did not like what I was up to and let me know, not with a gentle reminder or even a firm reprimand. Instead, she let me know with a hard smack across my butt. The smack hurt, the sound was loud, and everyone looked to see what had happened. The pain of the blow, however, was less than the pain of the humiliation--that my teacher, whom I'd had no previous bad experiences with, had betrayed me in such a terrible way.

Later that same day, we were sitting on the carpet together as

Mrs. Anderson read us a book. I don't know what the story was about, but I know that I sat in the front row and listened intently. At least until I became fascinated with the hem of Mrs. Anderson's dress. Absentmindedly, I began to twist it gently in my fingers. I guess it was not quite as gentle as I thought, because once again, for all to see, Mrs. Anderson stopped her reading, looked down, and said, "Why are you pulling on my dress?" Of course I had no explanation. What could I say? So I said nothing. "So, I give you a spank, and you pull my dress? Hmmm, I guess that makes us even," she said. She had a twinkle in her eye, and I seemed to recognize her lame attempt at an apology, but I remember thinking at the time, "Even? Not even close."

You know how sometimes you might be watching TV while eating chips with dip and absent-mindedly dip the remote into the dip and try to change the channel with your chip? No? I'm sure some of you know what I'm talking about. Last night, my son just about brushed his teeth with Polysporin because his mind was wandering somewhere else and reverted to its simple rule: squishy stuff in tubes goes on the toothbrush. Anyway, when I was in Grade 2, which seems to have been a fairly disastrous year, this tendency came back to bite me in a major way. There was this little girl, Gina, who sat in front of me and who, in retrospect, was seriously troubled. I remember being horrified one time as she turned around and said, "Hey, Teddy, look at this," and proudly displayed the thumbtack she had stabbed into her wrist. One day after school, Gina was being scolded by the teacher, Mrs. Anderson, that picture of warmth who had spanked me loudly in front of my class. I don't remember what Gina had allegedly done, but I'm sure that Mrs. Anderson was handling it with softness and all the compassion of a starving jackal. Outside the classroom, in the hallway, there was a little shelf where we hung our coats and backpacks and placed our outdoor shoes. It was the end of the day, and along with packing my bag and putting my coat back on, I needed to change from my indoor shoes to my outdoor shoes. I was distracted, though, eavesdropping as Mrs. Anderson ripped into Gina.

While I was occupied with my nosiness, my brain went into autopilot, pulling my shoes off and placing them on the shelf. This is where autopilot became a problem and threatened to derail my already disastrous year. When else might you take off your shoes, you might wonder? How about when getting changed for gym? Or having a bath? Or getting ready for bed? Any number of these situations involve taking off your shoes. Unfortunately, they also involve taking off your pants. Which is what I did. After placing my indoor shoes on the shelf, instead of putting on my outdoor shoes, I undid the button on my jeans, grabbed each side of my waistband and pulled them down to my ankles, revealing my tighty-whities to Mrs. Anderson and Gina, who was known for her discretion. I awoke from my eavesdropping trance as my pants hit my ankles and looked up in shock as Mrs. Anderson and Gina looked down and paused with their mouths hanging open. Quickly I yanked up my pants, abandoning all hope of appearing nonchalant. Mrs. Anderson, pillar of empathy, made an embarrassing comment that I can't remember and released Gina from her grasp. With her newfound freedom, Gina ran gleefully from our scene, straight out the double doors to the playground yelling, "Teddy pulled his pants down!" Thankfully, it was after school and most of the kids had gone home; otherwise, the story would have taken on much more life and followed me around for a while.

Around the same age, I remember standing, facing a few kids in my class and raising the scissors to my hair. On a tight budget with a million kids, my mom had learned the art of the bowl cut. As such, there was plenty of hair to work with. I'm not sure what I was trying to prove, but I proved it by snipping a big piece out of my bangs. With no mirror to check my aim, I guess I didn't realize the angle of the scissors or how much I was cutting. I just remember the looks of shock and horror on my classmates' faces as they saw what I had done. I immediately panicked, imagining getting in big trouble at home for doing it. My teacher did not manage to lessen my fears as she took me down to the principal's office where, racked with sobs, I was forced to call my mom on the principal's phone and tell her what I had done. She responded in the best possible way, telling me that it was no problem at all and wondering why they'd had me call her. Later, she took a picture in which I'm wearing a sweatshirt with the word "Calgary" written repeatedly down one side. The shirt definitely steals the show in the picture and distracts attention from my error, just like my mom did by not making a big deal out of it.

FOUR

HEY, LET'S KICK THE WINDOW

As you read through these stories, you might notice a few themes. Impulse control problems, forgetfulness, embarrassment, physical injuries and the like. Another recurring theme will be my brother Mike. While I had my share of impulsive adventures, we could fill volumes with Mike's near-misses, which is getting to be a more and more outdated expression. Filling volumes of things. I picture a large bookcase in a dark office, its shelves loaded with massive, leather-bound books, volumes of stories. Like volumes of encyclopedias. We had encyclopedias when I was younger; I remember on more than one occasion determining that I was going to read every volume and learn everything there was to know about stuff. I can't say that I remember any particular thing I learned, but that's probably because I never got through more than a few pages before something else grabbed my attention. I tried the same thing with the dictionary on more than one occasion, which is how I learned the word lugubrious, which means "excessively sad." I haven't had much opportunity to work that into my daily conversation, but I hold out hope that one day the right moment will present itself and I'll be ready. Anyway, Mike. Volumes.

This is just a small slice of Mike and me working together as a team. You know those little windows that appear beside front doors? I think they're called sidelights. They are often full of patterns and textures, which I imagine are designed to make it harder to see into the person's house--but I always just found them frustrating because, of course, I wanted to see into the person's house. Not seeing into their house was boring. I figured there must have been interesting things inside the house. Anyway, we had a window like this beside our own front door in Salmo. The glass was very frosted and had a bumpy texture, making it possible to only see a shadow of a person on the other side. One day, Mike was outside the window, on the front porch, and I was inside, in the front entryway. I'm not sure who started it or how, but I think for some reason I had locked Mike out of the house and wouldn't let him in the front door. I don't think it was mean-spirited--we were just playing a game or something. Mike dealt with this wrinkle in a very adaptive fashion, deciding (and I use that term generously as most of these types of actions are anything but calculated) that the best approach was to kick the door. Of course, this did not change my mind, so instead, Mike kicked the window. I thought this was great, so--from my safe perch inside the house--I kicked the window back. He then kicked it again, followed by my kick in response. I'm sure you can see where this is going. That's when my mom heard the noise and came and stopped us before anything bad could happen. No she didn't. She was probably busy keeping someone else from lighting themselves on fire, so she was not able to intervene as Mike and I increased the intensity and tempo of our window kicking, one from the inside, one from the outside. Finally, the predictable conclusion was reached, and the window shattered into little pieces. I remember feeling two things at the same time: terror at the reaction that was sure to come from our parents, Dad specifically, and shock that the window had broken. This is the stuff that low self-esteem is made of. Obviously, the window would break if we just kept kicking it, but that outcome had never even crossed my mind. Once it broke, my shock at this result only made me feel stupid, because OF COURSE the window would break. How could I not have known that? How could I not have seen how this would end? My explanation was one that would become my default for the next few decades: I was obviously a moron.

FIVE

I PROBABLY SHOULD HAVE WORN A HELMET

My good friend Tim lived far outside the village of Salmo in a little settlement called Nelway. I think it might have been technically classified as a ghost town. There were three hippie families there, and Tim didn't have indoor plumbing for a toilet. Instead they had an outhouse that they used during the day and a little porta-potty that they used during the night. That was always a fun and disgusting adventure. They also didn't have many doors on rooms inside the house. The porta-potty was placed at the bottom of the stairs that led from the main living room to the unfinished upstairs bedrooms. There was no privacy, other than a flimsy curtain that blocked off the area from the living room. However, it was also a high-traffic area for all members of the family. It was bad enough that I had to poop in a bucket during the middle of the night when I slept over, but I also had to do it as quickly as possible for fear that someone would come along and catch me with my pants down. Literally. Anyway, not sure how I got onto that subject.

One of the other kids who lived near Tim was a girl named Rosie, who I kind of liked, in a Grade-2 kind of way. Do I even need to say the roads all around this hippie village were unpaved? Of course they were. They were long, straight and perfect for gathering speed on a bike. Tim was a genius. Literally. He was a gifted student and did everything well academically. Not so much with the physical coordination, though. Geez. I still haven't even gotten into this story, which actually isn't very long at all. So Tim wiped out on his bike on this gravel road. I knew this because he wasn't at school one day, and Rosie told us of his grave injuries. She said that she'd heard a knock at the door, and when she'd opened it, she'd seen Tim standing there with his entire face covered in blood. What an image this created in my mind. However, it also triggered a need for some of this attention that was being rapidly directed toward my absent friend. "Oh, that happened to me, too," I proclaimed. The other kids' heads swivelled in my direction, thirsty for more tales of gore, and I created a highly original story on the spot. "One time I was riding my bike down a gravel road, and I was going really fast, and then my front tire hit a rock and I went over my handlebars and landed on my face on the road, and I was bleeding everywhere." Instead of basking in the attention and belated sympathy that I hoped this tale would generate, I saw doubt swim in the eyes of my classmates. Somehow they seemed to know intuitively that I was lying. There were no follow-up questions, no exclamations of horror, and no gentle hands of comfort laid on my shoulders. Rather, they all looked away, back to Rosie, and starting asking more questions about Tim.

The really ironic thing is that by the time I escaped my childhood in Salmo, I didn't need to make up fantastic but obviously false and plagiarized stories of biking horror. I had many legitimate examples to share. Two in particular stand out to me. Our bus stop in rural Erie, the literal ghost-town where I lived, was about 500 feet from our house. That doesn't sound far, but when you're a little kid, waiting unsupervised by the side of the highway for the school bus, it sure feels far from home. Anyway, the street leading from our house up to the bus stop was a long, gentle, straight slope. In other words, it made the perfect runway upon which to gain speed for spectacular bike tricks. One day, as I was virtually flying down this launching pad, I decided to impress my younger brothers by putting my feet up on my handlebars. Not satisfied with this daredevil display, I decided to up my own ante by subtracting my hands from the equation. I'm sure I had seen this somewhere in a movie or video or something, but I underestimated two vital aspects of the stunt. The first is the difficulty of controlling a speed wobble. We've all seen--and some may have experienced--a speed wobble. When travelling at a high speed, the slightest change in weight can have a huge impact on the balance of the vehicle, be it a skateboard, motorcycle, or in this case, BMX death trap. The speed wobble is just as it sounds, with the bike rocking rapidly from side to side as it hurtles forward. I guess I was going pretty fast, because as soon as I took my hands off, the speed wobble began bucking me like a rodeo bull. This is where the second aspect that I had underestimated rose to the forefront.

I had grossly overestimated my skill at steering a bike with my feet. Once I realized that my feet were going to fail me, I tried to remove them from the handlebars, but in the midst of panic I forgot to grab with my hands again, leaving me momentarily in the midst of a speed wobble, off balance, with no limbs attached to the handlebars at all. I say momentarily because this situation did not last long. Soon the bull finished its bucking, sending me launching like my professional wrestling heroes leaping from the top rope for a finishing elbow smash. Unfortunately in my case, the recipient was not a willing foe in spandex but the hard, unforgiving asphalt. The pain was intense, probably worse than anything I had ever experienced up to that point. My arm was gushing blood, and I ran as fast as I could to my house, screaming as if amputation was the only cure. Instead, my dad calmly cleaned the wound and told me he was going to put something on it called mercurochrome, which was some kind of iodine, I think. Needless to say, I wasn't too thrilled about the prospect of pouring medicine into my gaping wound, but my dad told me that it wouldn't sting at all. Reassured by his words, I consented to the treatment. But he'd lied.

A short time later that summer, I was swimming in the public pool. The scab on my elbow was gigantic and so thick that I couldn't even begin to pick it. This didn't stop me from jumping into a pool with all the other kids, of course, because nobody thought that was gross, apparently. Man, have things changed. Anyway, I had spent a long time in the pool, as we did every day of the summer in Salmo, when I felt something flapping and touching my arm. I looked down at my arm as I climbed up the ladder and was surprised to see my water-logged scab hanging down from a single point of attachment. At the time, I was fascinated to see the layers that had been peeled off by my accident, as the pores on my skin stood out in sharp relief to the surrounding area, like a permanent case of goosebumps. I simply detached the scab from its remaining anchor and, like the responsible kid that I was, quickly tossed it over the fence before anyone else could see it. Oh yeah, I knew it was gross, and I knew that everyone else would think it was gross, and I had to get rid of the evidence fast. I think I'm going to puke now.

Another great moment in BMX occurred when my brothers and I were determined to build the best jump possible out of the scrap lumber and garbage we had lying around our little redneck homestead. We began with a simple but effective double 2x4 and plywood special, which was able to produce some decent distance but almost no lift. As kids with brains like ours typically do, we gradually upped the risk, and the reward followed along, as greater ramp height inevitably led to greater jump height. However, as kids with brains like ours often do, we engaged in some simple miscalculations, concluding that if we increased the ramp height by six inches, we would increase the jump height by a similar amount. If this was true, what if we increased by 18 inches? All at once. With no test runs or quick physics calculations, I volunteered to be the hero, demonstrating the peak achievement of our ramp-building prowess. I returned to the bus stop 500 feet away and began pedaling as fast as I could. No fancy tricks this time, just pure speed. As I hit the ramp ... oh, did I mention that we increased the height of the ramp but not the length of the ramp? I'll leave it up to you math geniuses to figure it out, but the long story short is that the ramp was on a greater than 45-degree angle. As I hit the ramp, instead of flying on to glory, I flew over the handlebars. Well, that's not exactly accurate. I don't fully remember exactly what happened, but as far as I can piece together, I ended up upside down in the air, perhaps still astride my death machine. Gravity quickly won the argument, however, and I landed with full force on my bare head (we didn't need no stinking helmets!) on the pavement. Such a pain I had never experienced. Does that sound familiar?

I literally crawled from the road across our gravel driveway and tried to make it up the stairs. I think I passed out at one point, and I was crying so hard I couldn't even make sounds come out of my mouth--like one of those terrible dreams where you are screaming for help but no one can hear you. One of my brothers had run into the house ahead of me to get my mom, who came out the front door to see me half-dead on the front steps, unable to move any farther on my own. Somehow, she managed to get me up and inside the house, where I lay on the couch with an icepack--most likely some frozen peas--on my head. After I'd been lying there in incredible pain for what felt like a very short time, my mom announced that we would be leaving for piano lessons and that I needed to get ready. I couldn't believe what I was hearing. Are you serious? Piano lessons? I just about died out there. However, I think my mom was a bit desensitized to this kind of thing by this point and didn't really take me seriously. She feels terrible about it to this day and is probably a bit horrified that it is now recorded for the world to digest and judge, but I have never had hard feelings toward her for it. In the end, I made her aware of the seriousness of my injury when, while waiting patiently outside the piano teacher's studio, I began to feel more and more sick to my stomach. I didn't know at the time that this was a sign of a serious concussion. However, the nausea finally got to be too much. For some reason, instead of using my teacher's bathroom, I wandered out into the front yard, right in front of the big picture window that looked out from the studio. There, Mrs. Schreiner and my brother Spencer, seated together on the piano bench, had a front-row seat as I puked all over the lawn. The shame my mom felt when she came to pick us up, only to be told that I hadn't had my lesson that day because I was obviously too injured, was probably great, but like I said, being married to my dad, she'd seen worse. And with my brothers, the worst was yet to come.

SIX

I CAN DO THAT

CHILDHOOD IS FULL OF DELUSION. We think we're sneakier than we are, smarter than we are, bigger than we are, stronger than we are, and safer than we are. Most of these delusions have a healthy, insulating effect for us. Imagine how overwhelming it would be if children realized that they knew nothing, could do almost nothing, and were actually in near-constant danger. The shadow side of these delusions is that they are eventually revealed as such, and the world rarely teaches these lessons in gentle ways. We might get embarrassed by the superior strength of someone older, get the answers wrong that we were so sure of, get caught performing some act that we were forbidden to attempt, and in the case of safety, we might end up bruised and bleeding in the dirt. Or on the pavement. Or at the bottom of the pool. Or in countless other places where our confidence may wreak physical havoc, stripping delusion with merciless frankness. For example, after watching some movie as a young kid, I got the idea that gymnastic moves like flips and such were not actually as hard as people might think. All you really needed was the right set-up, I reasoned. After all, those kids on the TV can do backflips, and I'm just as cool as they are, because of course, coolness is all that is required to perform any athletic feat, as we all know.

Anyway, I took our small stepladder into the living room, along with several couch cushions and pillows, and made my preparations for glory. See, I wasn't totally reckless. I knew there was a slight chance of injury, so I readied my landing spot by layering some bedding on the floor at the foot of the ladder. It was only a four-step ladder, probably about three feet tall, but I was only about four-and-a-half feet tall myself. I reasoned that this would be more than enough space. So, I confidently climbed to the top of the ladder, not even really hesitating as I launched myself into the air and began a tightly-rolled front flip. I was not successful. At least I landed on my butt on the cushioning I had prepared. Unfortunately, I was spinning with quite a bit of force and the cushioning was (to me) surprisingly insubstantial. As my butt threatened to drill a hole in the living room floor, my top teeth sank deep into my tongue--because why not stick your tongue out when attempting risky stunts? The pain was so intense and so unexpected. The last place I thought I would be hurting following this adventure was my tongue. I panicked and ran, confused, to the bathroom to check the damage in the mirror and was both shocked and excited to see blood pooling on the surface of my tongue. While it hurt, I also thought it looked pretty cool. I also knew that I couldn't tell my mom what had happened because she would probably teach me some valuable lesson about not doing stuff like that.

SEVEN

A TERRIBLE CARPENTER

ALONG WITH A LACK of indoor bathroom amenities, Tim's house did not have a TV. This might have had some connection with Tim's academic success, but it definitely had a connection to his collection of hobbies. He built Lego, he read books, and he built models. Not model cars, but model *Star Wars* spaceships. He had several of these, and they were displayed on a shelf in his bedroom. Tim shared a bunk bed with his brother, and when I went to play at his house, the bunk bed became a place of adventure. I remember one time when I was on the top bunk and quickly climbing down, I reached my hand out and placed some of my weight on the shelf that housed his collection. Tim's dad was a carpenter, and as such, you might expect that a shelf in his home would be solidly constructed. If you made this assumption, you would be wrong. In fact, the shelf was not attached to the brackets that it sat on, something that I discovered the hard way.

As I placed my weight on the shelf, I was horrified to watch helplessly as it gave way, with some of the models simply sliding off onto the floor and some of them soaring majestically and tragically to the same destination. Unfortunately, not all of the models survived. I knew how important these models were to Tim, and I knew how hard they were to build, because I had given up in chaotic frustration more than once while trying to build my own models. For some reason, model glue never agreed with me, and model paint never seemed to dry quickly enough. I also was not a fan of following instructions closely. The idea of building a model is appealing, though, and a few years ago I got one for Christmas. I vowed that this time around, as an adult, I would be meticulous and thorough and follow all the steps in order. I did better than I ever had in my life, but in the end, the model ended up with no steering wheel and glue smeared all over its windshield, and is now proudly displayed under a pile of socks in a box in my bedroom.

Anyway, when I saw the models crashing in pieces on the floor, I immediately felt sick to my stomach. A combination of shame and anger washed over me, but mostly shame. Tim came rushing into the room to see what all the noise was about, and I began apologizing profusely. He was in shock but didn't get mad or anything. The same could not be said for his dad, the shoddy shelf-maker. He came and poked his head through the curtain that served as the bedroom door (did I mention hippies?), surveyed the damage, and asked what had happened. I explained with flushed cheeks the chain of events that had led to this disaster. In response, he shook his head with a look of disgust and said, "Ted! How could you do something so ..." he hesitated, and I held my breath. My mind finished his sentence ten different ways but none of them anticipated his actual word. "... stupid!?" While I had felt stupid many times in my life up to this point, this was the first time anyone, especially an adult, had ever uttered the word out loud to me. The shame I felt, tinged with anger, underwent a transformation, becoming anger tinged with shame. In the midst of my quivering stomach and reddened cheeks, I felt my heart harden against him, and I vowed to never like him again. And I didn't.

EIGHT

SON, I AM ALSO A WEIRDO

Our house in Salmo was really quite big, as it needed to be with such a large family. Having said that, even with all that space, we still had to share bedrooms most of the time. I always shared with my older brother, and in many ways the two of us could not have been more different. One thing we had in common, however, was our propensity to pee in weird places. Of course, in Spencer's defence, the only time he was guilty of this was when he was either fully or mostly asleep. I wish I had this same excuse, but nope, I can't blame my weird pee decisions on anything other than a combination of laziness, impulsivity, not being able to foresee the consequences, and developmental self-centredness. And weirdness. Of course, you can't discount my innate weirdness.

One of the many bedrooms I shared with Spencer was in a space between the living room and the family room on the main floor of the house. There was also a door in my room that led down to the largely unfinished basement. When I think of this arrangement now, I can't help but think that I must not have had much privacy in this room, since it was the only door down to the basement, meaning it must have been a main traffic artery in the house.

Anyway, I remember the door to the basement stairs had some weird patterns that appeared in the grain of the wood that created a perfectly monstrous face. What would a door leading to a staircase down to an unfinished basement be without a creepy monster face leering out at the kid in whose bedroom the door was located? There must be some sort of universal cosmic rule that doors to basements in kids' rooms need to have creepy faces in them. If so, my door followed that rule. Why am I talking so much about the door? I thought this story was about pee. The door was really creepy. I remember lying in bed just staring at the face. It had two big swirly eyes and a gaping mouth, stretched open in an anguished wail. I had many internal conversations regarding this door, reasoning that it was just a door, and it was just my imagination, with the retort usually along the lines of, "Yeah, but it kinda looks like Freddy Kreuger."

So, anyway, like I said, on the other side of this door was a wooden stairway with no railing leading down to our unfinished basement. The stairs were kind of hazardous, but somehow we all managed to survive, although my younger brother Ben did have a serious fall one time and had the biggest bump on his head that I had ever seen in my life. It looked like someone had put a hockey puck under the skin on his forehead, the way it was swelled up. I thought he was going to die, but he didn't. During the middle of the night when I would wake up, bladder bursting, I had a choice to make. I could either get out of bed and make my way through the house to the small bathroom, or I could approach the doorway to the threshold of hell, stand at the top of the stairs, and pee down the stairs into the basement. I often chose the latter. Seriously? How did I think that this was a good idea, or even remotely defensible? It's not like it was a construction site in the basement. It was unfinished, but we all did stuff down there all the time. Our TV was down there, some toys were down there, my dad's workbench was down there, and we all used the space on a regular basis. Somehow this was all put to the side during the middle of the night, with the only priorities being my need to 1. empty my bladder, and 2. avoid walking more than 10 steps. Oddly enough, no comment was ever even made about an odd smell in the basement. Having gotten away with it, there appeared to be no consequence, and so I continued to sporadically use this backup bathroom.

A few years later, when my bedroom had been relocated to the basement, I once again made some very questionable urine and laziness-based decisions. My room in the basement was a long distance from the nearest bathroom, to be fair. I reasoned that now that I was in the basement, it wouldn't make much sense to go to the top of the stairs and pee down the stairs, so I came up with an alternative plan. In my dad's basement workshop, and I use that term generously, there was a floor drain. Of course, being a kid, a dark hole in the floor must only lead to a deep, bottomless pit and would therefore be an ideal place to pee in an emergency, so I began to employ this new location from time to time. It finally caught up to me one day, however, when my dad asked if I had any idea why it smelled so much like pee over by his workbench. My stomach clenched, but I seamlessly lied that I had no idea why. He accepted my answer (but probably knew that I was lying) and went back to whatever he was doing. Probably because he didn't press the matter further, I felt very guilty. Later, I found my mom and confessed my weird habit to her. Rather than scold me, she told me that I should go and tell my dad the truth. I followed her direction and found my dad, then tearfully admitted my sin. I was shocked by his response. He told me that he was glad that I had told him the truth and that he understood where I was coming from--that when he was a kid, he had done virtually the exact same thing. Rarely have I loved my dad more than in that moment, when he accepted my weirdness and informed me that I had come by it honestly.

NINE
ANGER - 1, MR. T. - 0

WHEN I WAS A KID, my toys consisted mainly of nature. There was Erie Creek, which came straight from a glacier and trickled until it turned into the Salmo River. There was Erie Lake, a clean, crisp body of water that hosted many an impromptu swimming party, with kids fully clothed and exhausted from a day of (avoiding) work in the West Kootenay summer sun. There were unnamed mountains, countless trees, logging roads which served as launching pads for our BMX bikes, and even the occasional black bear, found sitting in the apple tree beside the driveway. Yet, despite this idyllic setting, a trip into the nearby city of Trail led to a chance for exposure to what would soon become an obsession. As we walked through the local Woolco department store, trying on Velcro-strapped Bullit shoes and thinking of the many uses of the zipper-pocket of the unaffordable Kangaroo-brand shoes, I happened to see an icon of the 1980s, Mr. T.

No, Mr. T, the bedazzled, Mohawk-sporting and heavily muscled bad boy from television's *A-Team* had not gotten lost and wound up in B.C.'s hinterland looking for some cheap running shoes; he appeared in the form of an action figure. It was an awesome spectacle, and I knew that I had to have it. I asked my mom if she could buy the action figure for me and was told that we couldn't afford it--a common reply in those days. I had known that this would be the answer before I'd asked, but this was different. This was Mr. T. This was the embodiment of the tough-guy persona that I craved, the tangible representation of society's fantasy of rebellious power. Plus, he was rad. I begged, I bargained, and finally I persuaded my parents to purchase the toy for my birthday, which was still some time away. Knowing that Mr. T awaited his unveiling, still freshly packaged and unblemished, made the days leading up to my birthday painfully slow in passing. Finally the day arrived, and I retired in fantastical aggressive bliss as I vicariously handed out attitude adjustments to a variety of toys that quickly appeared dimmed by the brilliance of Mr. T's gold-encrusted machismo. It was as good as I had hoped it would be and even better. Knowing that I had to work so hard to obtain this priceless prize made him all the more valuable to me. I played with him continuously and refused to share him with any of my brothers. Despite the great meaning of this possession, it was not the gaining of this blessing that sticks with me to this day; it was its loss.

Erie, where we lived, was technically a ghost-town, as far as communities are officially classified. There were a few families that lived within a two-block radius that formed the skeleton of what was once a boom-town, built upon the discovery of gold in the nearby creek. Since that boom, neighbouring settlements had overtaken Erie in prominence. The final nail in the town's coffin was the fire at the Erie hotel, upon which ground our log home now stood. Because of the remote location of our home, we actually had to drive into the nearby village of Salmo to get our mail. For some reason buried deep within me, this was always something I looked forward to.

One day, my mom was preparing to leave to go into Salmo to check the mail and run some other errands. I asked her if I could go. The answer was no. Not this time. I don't remember the reason, probably because I wasn't listening well enough at the time to have internalized it. All I know is that I desperately wanted to go with my mom. I yelled and screamed, but she calmly refused my skillful persuasion and walked out the front door and down the stairs, then outside where she opened the car door. I followed her, yelling, crying, and repeating what I believed to be a compelling argument: "But I want to go!" Somehow she was able to resist my logic and began to get into the family car. In a fit of rage, I raised Mr. T, omnipresent in my right hand, high above my head and hurled him to the gravel driveway at my feet. In horror, I watched as his pelvis disintegrated, the rubber band that held his muscular legs in place flying far from the heap of plastic wreckage. His legs were not only askew, they were broken. They were irreparably broken. What had been a fit of impotent rage immediately gave way to a blow of devastation greater than any unexpected punch to the stomach. I bent to pick up the pieces of my prized possession, and I immediately knew it could not be fixed. My tears burned from anger, frustration, and sorrow. I looked at my mother, who had paused in entering the vehicle. Whether she looked at me with pity or not, I can't remember. What I do remember, to this day, and without a hint of resentment, are the words she spoke. They were neither comforting nor elegant, neither harsh nor punitive. Instead, they were a simple statement of undeniable fact. "That's what happens when you lose your temper."

TEN
LET'S BURN IT DOWN

As a counsellor, I work with kids who are getting into trouble at home, at school, or with the police. I remember sitting with a client who had been referred for some reason, and his mom got onto the subject of starting fires. "He's been setting things on fire around the house. Can you even imagine doing that? He's been setting things on fire out behind the school, too. Can you even imagine doing that?" She recoiled, somewhat in disgust and somewhat in defeat, when I told her, "Well, I don't need to imagine it, because I can remember doing it." What she didn't know was that she was talking to one of the all-time pyromaniacs. I say all-time, but I'm sure there were worse--kids who literally burned the school down on purpose or set someone on fire--but the only thing that really stopped me from being that kid was some sheer dumb luck and ineptitude. Pyromania really runs in my family, as Leavitt family get-togethers often feature something being on fire. I don't just mean sitting around a campfire, either; I mean let's find (or someone bring) an old piece of furniture and throw it in the fire, stoke it with industrial fans so the flames are unbearably hot, and enjoy the incineration. We've burned couches and dressers and even an old TV that left a gigantic plume of black smoke that actually had my dad worried about getting caught for burning out of season on his property. Oh, and many of these things were set on fire after we had pushed them off an 80-foot boom lift that we keep on the property for just such occasions.

When I was a kid, I learned to play with matches. Of course, when we are kids we are supposed to learn NOT to play with matches, but where's the fun and adventure in that? One of the most enjoyable things I did with fire started with cutting cardboard boxes of various shapes and sizes into buildings with doors and windows, like those you might find on a movie set. An effective facade with no substance behind the walls. I would then use these buildings as a setting for my GI Joes or WWF wrestling action figures. I was industrious enough to take the time to sketch out the doors and windows and sometimes even color the exterior of the box-buildings to make them more realistic. However, this soon became boring to me, so I would set up my GI Joes in the windows of these buildings and shoot them with my BB gun. This was taking place downstairs in the basement, a perfect place to shoot guns. The novelty of this adventure wore off quickly as well, and I turned to the next level of entertainment, fire. I thought it would be neat if I set these buildings on fire and watched them burn to the ground, just like in real life. I was clever enough to take this stage of the plan outside, at least. At first, I would just burn the buildings. Then I moved on to burning the buildings with the GI Joes in the windows. It was always my unrealized fantasy to create a small street of cardboard buildings, just like an Old West town, and then link them all together with a small stream of gasoline, which I would light at one end of the town and watch as each building exploded into a ball of fire. Luckily, I could never quite get organized enough to pull this off. However, I did manage to incorporate gasoline into my adventures with fire soon enough, including one incident in which I narrowly avoided complete disaster.

It was a harmless setting for fire-starting, really. From time to time in the summer, my brothers and I and the other local hillbillies would dig underground forts to hang out in. These never fully materialized into the grand castles that we envisioned, but it was fun to dig and fun to imagine. Usually, rather than fully tunnel underground, we would just dig a really deep hole or two in the ground and put some plywood on top for a roof and call it an underground fort. It was on one of these tinder-dry planks of plywood that I decided to set myself a nice campfire. Also, it was in the midst of a hot, dry summer next to a hot, dry field of hot, dry grass. Long hot, dry grass. What could go wrong? So, I got my fire going, which doesn't really take much effort if you have the right amount of paper and dry wood, and I had lots of both. But, when you build a roaring fire out of paper, the initial burst of flame doesn't last long enough to be satisfying. So, as it began to die down, I got creative in trying to keep it going. It didn't seem to bother me that the roof of our underground fort was quickly becoming a part of my fire. Then inspiration struck me. Gasoline. I knew where my dad kept a gas can that was supposed to be used to refill the lawn-mower, but let's not kid ourselves, when was I ever really going to cut the lawn? Instead, I sprinted across the street, grabbed the can and a bucket, and made it back before the last embers of the fire had disappeared completely. I grabbed some more paper and sticks and dried grass and began to build the blaze back up. When it was going strong again, I figured that this was the perfect moment to add fuel to the fire. You know, once you've actually added fuel to a fire, that metaphor seems particularly apt.

Not fully understanding the nature of combustion, I decided to pour the gasoline from the bucket directly onto the fire. I envisioned a small explosion of flame that would quickly die out, but what actually happened was that the flames quickly began to travel up the spout of pouring fuel, towards the main bucket, which is where the explosion would most likely be taking place. In the bucket. That I was holding onto. Panicked and confused, I distinctly remember thinking to myself, "I didn't know that's what would happen. I didn't know that's how it worked." Instead of just dropping the bucket, my reflexes resulted in flinging the bucket high in the air over my head. I remember looking up at an arc of flame as it shot over top of me and fell to the earth. Somehow, I managed to escape without any damage to myself or the large field of long, dry grass right next to me. Of course, this adventure was going to stay on the down-low. I didn't want them locking up the gas can because they didn't trust me.

ELEVEN

GOOD THING NO ONE WAS PAYING ATTENTION

As I SAID BEFORE, I wasn't the only one in my family who had a fascination with destruction. Far from it. I think the chief instigator of this love affair was my dad. He loved watching the demolition derby and shooting glass pop bottles with guns up on mountain roads. One of the highlights of the year for me and a few of my brothers was when we got to burn all of the old, dead grass on the two acres of field that surrounded our house. I don't know why we needed to do that, but when presented with the opportunity to burn things with permission, do we bother with dumb questions? No, we just burn the stuff! When I was in Scouts, at the age of 11, we had a meeting up at the church. We were told that we were going to be working on lighting a fire. You might as well have told us that we had all won the lottery. You mean I could get a badge for something that I actually loved to do and that would otherwise be frowned upon? Maybe I didn't hate Scouts, after all. My enduring memories of Scouts are of having my fingernails inspected, a weekly humiliation (due to the omnipresent dirt underneath the edges) that demonstrated that shame was not enough to get me to remember to wash my hands. The Scoutmaster gave us simple instructions: Find someplace around the church property and light a fire using whatever we had at our disposal. There was no supervision, no instruction, just a dare.

My friend and I quickly climbed to the top of a tall mountain of rock behind the church, because what better place to find fire-making stuff than on top of a barren piece of granite? We had only considered how cool the fire would look on top of the rock cliff and left out the bit about how we would actually build the fire, equipped only with a box of matches. We scrounged for bits of dried sticks or leaves, and our frustration set in as the sun went below the horizon. I was not worried in the slightest about not getting my fire-starting badge, but I *was* worried about losing out on the chance to burn something. Then an idea struck me. A Boy Scout is wise in the use of his resources, the motto of the Scouts Canada. Resources, meaning things that I had access to. I looked down from our lofty position on top of the rock cliff and saw the church building below. I knew that inside, in one of the offices, was my dad, who was serving in a leadership position at the time. Inside his office were boxes and boxes of the junior pyromaniac's best friend, paper. I quickly made my way down off the rock in the dark, somehow managing not to die. I knocked on his office door and explained that I needed some paper from his office. He asked why, I'll grant him that. When I innocently explained the mission that I was on, he didn't bat an eye and said, "Go ahead." I couldn't believe that I had permission to not only burn stuff but to bend the rules while doing it on top of a dangerous cliff in the dark. Thank goodness it was my dad in that office and not my mom (or anyone else who didn't have ADHD). Triumphantly, I returned to my friend who was still waiting in our treacherous position at the top of the cliff. We gathered what little bits of nature we could find and scrunched the paper up into little balls, as if trying to convince ourselves that the success of this fire still depended on our know-how and not on the flammability of our materials. As we lit the first few paper balls, the flames spread in that satisfying and mesmerizing way that lights the internal fire of the pyromaniac. Once it was going, we lost all pretense of demonstrating skill and just began throwing whole sheets of paper on the pyre. What a glorious moment we enjoyed with our bright, blazing bonfire, glowing on top of a cliff of rock, overlooking the town of Trail. I never did get the fire-starting badge, but it didn't matter to me. I had my moment.

As a family, we used to rent movies under the series name of *Havoc* (*Havoc 6* was the first one we watched, not knowing that it was episode number six in the series), which featured two hours of race cars crashing and burning, monster-truck accidents, motorcycle-racing accidents, and best of all, rally-car crashes. We could not get enough of this action. We did have enough impulse control to stop ourselves from going out and smashing the family car with hammers (though that would erode over time), but I needed an outlet for my destructive and aggressive tendencies. I made the repetitively impulsive decision to sacrifice my own toy cars and GI Joes. If the phrase 'repetitively impulsive' seems to be an oxymoron, then you don't know much about ADHD. Repetitively impulsive decisions are ones that we regret almost immediately after making them, yet we continue to make the same decision when presented with the next opportunity. Now, I didn't just light these cars on fire, because that would be too simple. Instead, I first smashed them with a hammer (or a rock if I couldn't find the hammer, which adaptation became known as a "Salmo Job"). I wanted to make them look like they had been in a terrible accident, completely mangled beyond repair. Only then did I light the match and watch as the little plastic seats, dashboards, steering wheels, and wheels slowly melted away, leaving only a hollow metal shell, just like in real life. Of course, the GI Joes were too big to fit into little Hot Wheels cars; instead, they were cut or smashed and then lit on fire. I was endlessly fascinated by this process. In fact, after I got my first camera, several of my first blurry pictures were of a shirtless plastic man in army fatigues, melting in hot flames. Also featured in that first album were pictures of a horse from way too close, a hamster stuck in a jar, a giant triple-decker sandwich, and the flag of the Soviet Union that I had hanging on my bedroom wall. I was an eclectic weirdo, I'll say that. Of course, my fascination with fire was not always quite as innocent as burning my own toys, but I'll get to that later.

TWELVE

MY CAREER IN LANDSCAPING

I THINK it's probably true that farmers traditionally had lots of kids because they made for cheap labour. A big family meant a big, low-cost workforce. I grew up for the first half of my childhood in rural British Columbia, in a log house with a couple of acres, a couple of horses, a vegetable garden, and a gigantic yard. I was the second of seven kids, six boys and one girl. You would think that such a labour force and such a setting would be a perfect match, but then you wouldn't be factoring in the ADHD that defines our family tree. My parents tried countless strategies to motivate us into doing chores, but none of them worked for very long. I remember one time when I was in my teens, my mom gathered all of us kids together to teach us about her new system to ensure that dirty laundry was delivered to the laundry room and clean laundry was returned to our drawers and closets. She hadn't gone very far in her sales pitch when my older brother, Spencer, interrupted her, saying, "Mom, what's the point? Nothing you try is going to work." I felt bad for my mom, seeing her get shot down like that, but at the same time, I knew he was exactly right. Nothing would work, and nothing did work for very long. This is something I talk about a lot with people who are trying to come up with an ADHD-proof system. There is no such thing. If people believe they can find a way to remove the inconvenience of the ADHD brain, then they will be continually disappointed. There is no such thing. There is a series of things that work for a little while and then stop working. Giving up on the idea of a thing to rule them all (yes, *LOTR* reference), is actually quite freeing. Clinging to the idea of a thing is discouraging.

Anyway, one thing I remember about doing chores was that any chore that I was *not* asked to do was immediately preferable to any chore I *was* asked to do. If I was supposed to be weeding the garden, I wanted to cut the lawn. We had a really big front lawn and only a small push mower to cover the whole thing. To my young ADHD brain, you may as well have asked me to bail out a lake with a teaspoon. However, I also knew that I had better do it. I remember one time when I thought it would be neat (though really it was just a way to make something very boring a bit less boring) if I mowed a design into the lawn. I mentioned it to my dad one time, and he discouraged me from exploring my creativity in this way.

However, despite his negative outlook, I decided one day during the summer to put my plan into action. The grass had grown long (no big surprise there, as we weren't always right on top of things), and I figured it would be cool if I could "shave" my name into the lawn. Of course, being as creative as I was, it wasn't enough for me to just shave "Ted" into the long grass. Instead, I cut the long grass and intended to leave certain parts uncut, creating a relief-style grass portrait of our surname, Leavitt. This was quite the project, but I set out, determined to do this to impress my dad when he got home from work. What I didn't anticipate, of course, was the amount of gas that was in the lawnmower when I started my task (not enough to finish it) and the lack of a handy backup supply (I had probably used it all to set things on fire). So, after I had mowed most of the giant lawn, leaving only a L-E-A-V remaining, the lawnmower decided to quit. I searched for more gas, but there was none. This meant that instead of my dad coming home to see my glorious grass sculpture paying homage to our heritage, he came home to a half-cut lawn with some sections strangely left long. When he questioned me and I explained how my perfect plan had gone wrong, he said, "Yeah. that's why we don't do stuff like that." He may as well have called me an idiot for how I felt. I don't think he said it in a nasty way. It was probably just tinged with some exasperation for having to explain this to me, but it felt like a stinging rebuke. Like he was saying, "Ted, everyone knows that's why we don't do things like that. How come you don't know that?"

Anyway, lawn-sculpting adventures aside, if I was supposed to be cutting the lawn, I wanted to be feeding the horses. If I was supposed to be feeding the horses, I wanted to be pushing a wheelbarrow full of rocks. I have to admit that last chore sounds a bit like something you would see prisoners doing in an old-time movie. But no matter how undesirable the chore was, it was better than what I was currently doing. The funny thing is, no matter how many times this played out, and no matter how many times my dad pointed it out to us, each and every time I was convinced that if I could just trade with one of my brothers, then things would finally be okay. Just as funny is the fact that they were equally slow to learn this lesson, and so I almost always had a willing trading partner.

THIRTEEN

LET'S BE DANGEROUS

LIVING in the West Kootenays was a perfect fit for us crazy kids (and our crazy dad), and this was never more evident than in the summer, when we were free to roam the wilderness unattended, with only the stretched limits of our own recklessness to provide any loose restraint. When I say wilderness, I am not speaking metaphorically. It was not unheard of to see a bear in the apple tree beside our driveway or on the road behind the lake, or a cougar having a nap on our lawn during the early morning hours. There were mountains and rivers and lakes and streams, wild animals, and of course, weird neighbours. In a way, it was the perfect zoo for a family full of ADHD boys. Our main pastime was exploration. I remember one day some of my brothers and I decided it would be a good idea to ride our bikes up across the highway, park them on the side of the logging road, and wander into the forest. Our destination was what we called "the mountain." It was a rock face, jutting out from between the trees, probably 300 feet tall. We had never actually gone there, just looked at it.

So, on this day, as we made our way to our destination, we decided to do what all good explorers do: mark our territory. No, I don't mean peeing everywhere, though I imagine there was a fair bit of that going on as well. What I mean is that we looked at the big, bare rock face as something of a canvas and determined that we should leave our mark by laying out several large rocks in the shape of an "L" so that everyone who drove by on the highway below would see our letter and know that the Leavitts ruled this part of the country. Did I mention that this was not what modern parents would consider safe in any way? Three or four little boys, under the age of 10, scurrying around on a bald rock face, arranging boulders. What could go wrong? Luckily, nothing did. We were industrious when we had a task we were interested in and made a very thorough search of the area for rocks that would fit our purpose. Some time later, feeling hot, sweaty, and tired, we headed back home, down the mountain to our waiting bikes, back across the highway, and then turned to admire our work. While we escaped with our health intact, what we noticed was that our masterful L was actually backwards on the rock face. Our moment of triumph quickly turned into a moment of sheepishness.

When I wasn't creating nature-themed artistic interpretations of dyslexia on mountains, I spent a lot of time on my bike. Our neighbours were loggers and had all sorts of heavy equipment at their disposal. Everything from bulldozers to skid steers to graders to front-end loaders. Their dad, much to our delight, used his equipment to build us an awesome BMX track in the dirt across the road from our house. It had everything from little jumps to big jumps and banked corners and flat stuff. Do you like my BMX vocabulary? I don't know what that stuff is all called, and I can't be bothered to look it up right now. Anyway, I focus on the banked corners because a banked corner is only a banked corner if you use it to go around the corner. If instead of turning with the angle of the corner you come from a different angle with great speed, a banked corner just turns into a fantastically large and steep jump. Now, one thing you might have noticed about me so far is that I was not one to think particularly deeply about consequences and was very driven by doing something even bigger, badder, or more dangerous than the last time, upping the ante, so to speak. So, naturally the progression with the banked corner went like this: 1. race around the corner, 2. jump off the back of the corner and land in the grass field on the other side, and 3. jump off the back of the corner and land in the trees. Yes, that was the ultimate challenge for me. I would race into the corner, but instead of turning, I would make a straight beeline for the back edge and launch myself off the top. My landing place was literally in the branches of some nearby trees. I remember they were birch trees, and the branches were very small and fragile. I went crashing through them onto the ground with great sound and fury and enthusiasm. I'm not sure how I avoided serious injury, but I do remember the thrill of literally crashing through a tree and coming out the other side.

This approach was also used when I stayed over at my friend Dan's house. He had a large rope swing that was attached high up to a large tree branch. When I say rope swing, I don't mean like a swing-set swing. I mean the kind of rope swing you see on funny fail videos where unsuspecting people underestimate the amount of strength it takes to hold onto a rope while they launch themselves out over the lake and instead find out just how much dirt they can eat in the process. This rope swing did not extend out over a peaceful body of water. Instead, it just brought you back to earth, if you held on. So we held on, at first. I remember one day in particular. We were playing outside, and it began to rain heavily. Something about being outside and soaking wet and cold seemed to empower our craziness, like standing in a puddle while grabbing the electric fence, not that I ever did that. On purpose. Anyway, somehow I got the idea that it would be fun to not only swing out on this giant swing, but to let go. Not by accident, but on purpose. I would take a running start, hold onto the rope as tightly as I could as it swung me up off the ground, and when I was almost at the peak, I would let go and land, crashing through the trees and bushes onto the wet and muddy ground. I remember distinctly thinking, "I feel like Rambo."

While our options were more limited in the winter due to the extremely cold and snowy conditions, we still tried our hardest to blur the boundary between "great idea" and "walking disaster." For example, skiing is a fun activity. Skiing through bushes and trees outside the groomed runs is dangerous but also fun. Flying at breakneck speed down the most difficult and dangerous run on the hill, losing sight of the biggest jump on the hill and flying off that jump only to realize with certain dread what pain awaits upon landing is also fun, but it's going to be disastrous. In my case, disaster meant crashing down, feet first, so hard that my chin was driven with full force into my knees, knocking me momentarily unconscious. When I opened my eyes to try to regain my bearings, this was complicated by the fact that everything I saw was a bright shade of neon green. There was no contrast between snow and trees and sky, just neon green everywhere. When that moment of panic passed, after considering that this might just be my new normal, the next phase of fallout began. Literally. I felt something rattling in my mouth and spit out half of one of my molars. The other half came out later while I was recuperating and drinking hot chocolate in the lodge. We never had the nicest stuff, but we didn't let that stop us from having a good time on the slopes.

In the Kootenays, we got a lot of snow. Now that I live in the lower mainland of B.C., six inches seems like a lot of snow, but when I was a kid in Salmo, I remember walking past the swing set in our backyard and having it only come up to my mid-shins. In the summer, the swing set was taller than my head, so that ought to tell you how much snow we got. Our log house had a lower, sloped roof ledge, with the main roof on the very top of the house. The snow would pile up several feet high, and then gravity would take over, leading the snow to slide off onto the ground below. It became commonplace to hear the scrape and thump as tons of snow pounded down, piling up in front of the large windows in the living room. I remember at least one year where the snow was piled higher than the windows themselves, making it impossible to see outside. We also had a car that sat idle over the winter one year. By mid-winter it was barely visible under the snow, between what had fallen and what had been thrown over top of it by the routine passes of snowplows through the neighbourhood. Now why am I focusing so much on the amount of snow we got? I want some context when I tell you my story about diving off the shed headfirst into the snow.

Amongst the many risky activities that I have engaged in thus far in the story, many could have gone horribly wrong, leading to serious injuries or worse. However, even someone who would think it is an okay idea to pour a bucket of gasoline onto a live fire would think that it was a bad idea to dive headfirst off a shed unless there was enough snow to cushion the fall. This propensity to make questionable decisions leads to a tendency to over-explain things, to make my line of reasoning perfectly clear. This is something that can be very useful when teaching someone something but can also be really annoying for someone who might just want the condensed version once in awhile. So, we had this shed on our property that seemed really old to me. I have no idea how old it actually was or what purpose it originally served. I do know that when the time came to tear the shed down, it was accomplished by hooking a chain from the corner of the shed to the back of the van and simply driving away until the whole structure toppled over. There were lots of these kinds of buildings on the property, some of which were decades-old remnants of the once-thriving mining village of Erie. I don't know if this shed was one of those or if it was more recent, but anyway, that's probably enough context.

One winter when we had even more snow than usual, we decided it would be a good idea to use a ladder to climb to the roof of the shed, about one story high, and jump into the many feet of snow that lay on the ground below us. What could go wrong? Nothing, really. This seemed like one actually foolproof plan. Of course, I couldn't be content with just jumping feet first, so I progressed to cannonballs and backflips and front-flips and so on. The move that really stands out for me, though, was when I decided that it would be a good idea to dive headfirst into the snow. I had seen many cartoons and comics that depicted rich folks like Scrooge McDuck (I almost said rich people, but then I thought that he's not technically a person, but I suppose he's just technically not a human, which doesn't necessarily mean he isn't a person, unless of course you have a definition of person that requires humanity, in which case I have played it safe by including Scrooge McDuck in a category under the heading of "folks," though some might think that still seems a bit too peopley for their tastes, but you can't please everyone) swimming in their gigantic bank vaults full of cash and coins. Of course, this would be impossible, and if a person (human or otherwise) were to try to dive into a vat of coins, it would really hurt and do a lot of damage. However, there were also some highly influential Dr. Seuss books that led me to think that diving into things other than water was a good idea.

Armed with this evidence, it seemed natural to move from front flips to swan dives off the shed. I assumed proper diving position, as I had been taught in my summer swimming lessons, and leaped off the edge of the roof, aimed headfirst for the snow, and awaited the applause of the small crowd of brothers gathered to watch. There may have been applause, but I couldn't hear it, because I was buried upside down in the snow up to my waist, my arms pinned by my sides. Turns out that when you hit the snow with your arms in perfect diving position, the snow doesn't move out of the way as water does. Instead, your arms get split apart, and your graceful swan dive becomes a head-first missile into the snow. I wasn't hurt, but I was trapped. It was dark, cold, quiet, and my arms were stuck at my sides. This led to instant panic and visions of suffocating to death in the backyard with no one able to hear my muffled screams. This may have been amplified by the fact that when I was quite a bit younger, a playmate of mine actually did suffocate to death when the sand tunnel that we regularly played in together collapsed on her when I wasn't there. That was not funny. So, here I was imagining a snowy and breathless grave for myself, and I decided that I wasn't going to go out quite so easily. I channeled my rage and desperation and used the extra energy to wiggle my arms free enough to bend at the elbows. From there, I was able to quickly dig my hands out in front of me, giving me the ability to push down, like doing a handstand push-up, freeing me from certain death. Well, it felt like certain death, but it probably wasn't, although people do die from being buried in avalanches, and I guess in a small way, this was a similar predicament. Yet another case of not fully considering the consequences of a brilliant plan.

FOURTEEN

REMEMBER THAT WEIRD KID WITH THE TAMBOURINE?

GRADE 7 at Salmo Elementary was one of the best years of my entire childhood. I was popular, my teacher liked me, I had a major growth spurt so I didn't feel like a little kid anymore, and--as the oldest kids in school--we felt like we ran the place. The best part of the year for me, though, was being a part of the cover band that my teacher put together. This wasn't the standard school band, with kids squeaking out animal calls from brass instruments or clanging cymbals. This was a rock band. My teacher, Mr. Yule, was an aspiring rock star, himself, and incredibly talented with multiple instruments. I'm not sure if he saw potential in us or if this was just something he was planning on doing anyway, but he gathered a group of us and formed a band, which I had the (mis)fortune of naming The Travelling Mildewies. My aforementioned friend Tim's parents were big fans of Roy Orbison and his ensemble band, the Travelling Wilburies. Tim had mentioned this to me on one occasion, and the name had stuck in my head. I really have no idea why I changed the second part to something mold-based, but it's an even bigger mystery why the rest of the band and Mr. Yule would agree to it. I remember that even though I was happy that they had gone with it, I still felt embarrassment as I saw what I felt were confused looks in their eyes. How did they not think this was a good name? Was it a good name? Did I pick a good name, or did I just make myself look like a weirdo?

I was initially one of the rhythm guitar players, but I was not a big fan of the guitar. It was difficult, it made my fingers sore, and most importantly, there wasn't much glory attached to acoustic rhythm guitar for a 12-year-old kid in the late 1980s. What I coveted was the position of drummer. I knew that I had good rhythm, but Mr. Yule had assigned Nathan T., the most popular kid in school, to that position of glory. However, I was able to pull off a coup later in the year, as my friends and I were allowed to hang out in the music room at lunch instead of wandering the playground getting into trouble. Once I got in there, I went straight to the drum set and taught myself how to play a basic rhythm. We then wrote an even more basic song and announced to Mr. Yule that we wanted to play it for our class during our next music block. Once he saw me pounding out the drums, he quickly made the change in the band, moving Nathan to guitar and me to the back of the band, where I felt front and centre. This was one of very few victories I had over Nathan throughout the course of our friendship. It also helped push me into a position that would lead to one of the more embarrassing moments of my elementary school life.

Later in the year, we had a special visitor to our tiny school. Her name was Charlotte Diamond, and she was a famous Canadian children's songster. She must have been making the rounds to all of the Podunk schools in the area, because I have a hard time imagining someone as renowned as she was making a trip to Salmo just for us. Anyway, at one point in her concert, she asked for a volunteer, and of course, dozens of hands shot up. I was going to say hundreds of hands, but I don't think there were that many kids at Salmo Elementary. The real moment of truth came when Ms. Diamond said that her volunteer needed to be someone who had good rhythm. Kids of all grades turned to look at me. As the drummer in the rock band, this was one of the things I was most known for. At that point, I was no longer volunteering for the job, I was being nominated by other kids. What a moment of pride for me. I was being recognized for something I could do well in front of all my peers. Ms. Diamond, slave to her fans, went with the crowd and invited me up onto the stage area, where she handed me a tambourine. All I had to do, she said, was keep a simple beat on the tambourine while she played the song. I imagine the song was about a tambourine. Nope. I just googled it. She has no songs about tambourines. Not sure where I got that idea. Maybe it was because the tambourine felt, to me anyway, like the central focus of this particular song. Probably because I made it that way.

Ms. Diamond did not realize that she had chosen an attention-seeking class clown to accompany her, but I think this quickly became apparent as she started performing the song. Rather than simply tap the tambourine against the heel of my hand, as most people would do, I decided that the best approach was the unhinged hillbilly approach. I not only smacked that tambourine like it had stolen something, I paired it with some vigorous backwoods floor stomping, like my dad's country singing idol, Stompin' Tom Connors. Ms. Diamond was no stranger to kids and relating to an audience, so as the kids at the school broke out in howls of laughter, she raised her eyebrows at me in an encouraging way. Oh man, I could not get any higher. The kids loved me, and Charlotte Diamond thought I was super cool. However, this was not a well-thought-out plan, and after the initial burst of laughter, the audience's reaction fizzled out. Rather than change my approach, though, I doggedly continued to stomp my foot and pound the tambourine. The looks from the audience changed from laughing admiration to confused awkwardness. I looked directly at Mr. Yule, who smiled an embarrassed smile. Looking back, everyone was giving me permission to stop the act, but I just couldn't do it. I felt trapped by my own behaviour and continued stomping away, like in that scene from the first *Nanny McPhee* movie where the kids were magically being forced to help out in the kitchen and could only watch helplessly as their initial fascination spiralled into terror. Kind of like the terror I experienced when I watched the second *Nanny McPhee* movie, which never should have been made. It was horrible. Anyway, as for the tambourine debacle, to my credit, it was one of the few times in my life that I didn't quit, continuing this increasingly humiliating display right to the end of the song. The feelings I had returning to my seat were the polar opposite of those I'd experienced when I'd been triumphantly selected by the crowd and made my way to the stage. Once again, I felt like I had taken something good and poisoned it.

FIFTEEN
MAN, YOU'VE GOT A BIG MOUTH

As a kid, I was usually bigger and stronger than my peers, especially in elementary school. It was not uncommon throughout my life to engage in play-fighting and wrestling with my friends and brothers only to be shocked as my partners began crying, choking, or getting blindly angry. When I was in Grade 7, my best friend Tim van Wijk had said something that I didn't like, but I don't think we were even fighting or arguing at the time. Whatever the trigger, I wound up and punched Tim in the stomach. As I mentioned before, Tim was a cognitive genius, but physical gifts such as strength and coordination always eluded him. I underestimated how hard I had hit him, and I underestimated how hurt he was by the blow, but my heart was stabbed when I saw his eyes welling up with tears. It dawned on me that I had hurt my friend. Just as this horrible realization hit me, I was dealt a stomach punch myself. Not a literal one, but an emotional one as the girl I'd had a crush on since I'd laid eyes on her in kindergarten went out of her way to reach out to Tim, comfort him, and then turn to me and spit out, "You're such a jerk!" I felt less than two inches tall. I tried to apologize to Tim, but he was still in quite a bit of pain and wasn't ready to hear it. I wish I could say this was such a painful lesson that I learned to be more careful, but then you wouldn't be reading this book. Funnily enough, another painful experience was built around this same girl, but for different reasons. In fact, you'll read about her more than once in this book.

As I mentioned, I'd only had eyes for this one girl since the first time I saw her. All these years later, I can't tell you what it was, but I just knew that my one goal in life was for this girl to like me. Unfortunately, there was an obstacle in the way, my frenemy Nathan T. Nathan was bigger, stronger, faster, more popular, had a sweet mullet back when mullets were sweet, and in the back of my heart, I knew that Nathan was the one she wanted. Somehow, I was able to keep this delusion at bay for a long time, but finally in Grade 6, it began to unravel. I was talking with one of this girl's friends, who was telling me about a conversation with some girls from another school. Apparently, these other girls had been talking trash, and the girl of my dreams had proudly announced that her 'boyfriend' could beat up anyone from their school. The word 'boyfriend' cut like a knife, to quote Brian Adams. I knew whom she was referring to, but I asked anyway. Her friend said that she was talking about Nathan, of course. I said that I didn't know they were going out, and she said that they weren't, but that she really liked Nathan. I pretended to be excited by this juicy tidbit of Grade 6 gossip, but in reality, I was dying inside. Then, a fateful thing. Her friend told me that Nathan wasn't supposed to know (because that's how things work when you're 11 years old) and that I wasn't allowed to tell anyone. I readily agreed to this; after all, why would I want my romantic rival to know that he had won? However, not long after this clandestine conversation, I found myself with Nathan and a few other boys. For some inexplicable reason, I felt the pressure of my secret build within me, and before I knew it, I had blurted the whole thing out to Nathan. As soon as I had done it, I felt doubly sick because it made it all seem real, and I had betrayed her confidence. Somehow, this eventually got back to her, and she had some choice words for me, because what a terrible thing it is for the object of your affection to know that this is the case. But this wasn't the last time that Nathan and Jennifer, yes that was her name, combined with an impulsive decision to create a painful situation that played a central role in a devastating experience in my life. But I'll get back to that later.

SIXTEEN

YOU DON'T KNOW YOUR OWN STRENGTH

In our computer lab at Salmo Elementary, the computers were a bit anachronistic, if you know what I mean, and if you don't, what I mean is this: the rest of the place was a dumpy little country school in the hills in the late 1980s, but the computers had giant, full-colour screens and amazing graphics. Not only that, but they could talk! I can't remember the brand of the machines, but there was a program into which you could type anything you wanted, hit the button, and listen as the computer spat out swear words, rude jokes, or long strings of nonsense syllables like kolokoiokoloklokokogorotoyofodoy-orogodoyoyoyoyooooo. The computer lab was definitely the desired destination for kids with crazy ideas and a distaste for boring old schoolwork. Because it was so desirable, though, the lab could only be used after students had finished all their boring old school work. Since I was often lost in dreamland, or forgetting what I was supposed to be doing, I was usually one of the last kids in the class to earn this privilege, meaning that all of the computers were often gone by the time I got there, and I would just have to sit back and watch someone else as they cajoled their computer into robotically saying, "I have to poop in my poopy pants!" just as the teacher walked by.

Occasionally, I was sufficiently on top of things to avoid being one of the last, and one particular time, I was actually able to secure one of the prized machines. It was my friend, Garnet, who had lost out this time, forced to watch over my shoulder.

I'm not sure why--I probably just had to go to the bathroom or something--but for some reason, I had to step away from my computer for a few minutes. When I came back to the room, Garnet was sitting in my chair at my computer, stealing my hard-won opportunity. I'd like to think that I asked him to move, but I probably just told him to get out of my seat. Garnet did not agree with my assessment of the seat's ownership and refused to move. I then reasoned with him in the way that only big kids can, grabbing him by the back of the neck and squeezing hard, trying to lift him out of the seat. At this point, though I was being aggressive, I was still thinking of it as playful aggression between friends. However, this is easy to confuse when you're the one doing the squeezing. Something about the squeeze--and who knows what else--really flipped a switch in Garnet that day. Instead of obediently moving out of my chair, he jumped up, spun around, and punched me hard in the face. Not once but twice. I was stunned. I had never been hit before, and it stung, but the sting came not from the blow but from the surprise. I had no idea that he would ever react that way, that he was so upset, or that I had hurt him enough to warrant this response. I didn't tell on him; I didn't say anything to him, and he never apologized. He just sat back down in the chair to continue playing on the computer, and I quietly took a seat behind him to watch him have all the fun.

This same scenario played itself out again, almost identically, one other time, only that incident featured my younger brother Mike, who was well-known for punching people in the face, even from a young age. When we caught the bus to school, living in Erie, it was a bus that carried all of the kids into town for school, regardless of their age or grade. This meant that impressionable and anxious little kids in kindergarten were sentenced to ride along with foul-mouthed and aggressive teenagers in Grade 12, listening as they bragged about their latest drunken escapades. One of the worst kids in town, and definitely the worst to sit by, was a kid named Jason Campbell. He was nasty and seemed to enjoy being that way. In my mind, he is a blond version of Scut Farkus from *A Christmas Story*: a sneering, jeering punk who delighted in the power he obtained torturing smaller humans (and probably kittens and puppies, too). One day, Mike was unlucky enough to be cornered on the school bus by Jason Campbell, stuck against the window side of the seat, while Stephen blocked his access to the aisle and escape. I suppose it was ironic that the sign above Mike's head described how to operate the emergency exit of the bus, because as Stephen leaned in to Mike, breathing out the most vile threats he could come up with, "I'm gonna kill you. I'm gonna smash your face in" (no one said he was a genius), Mike came up with his own emergency exit that was based mainly on punching Jason Campbell in the face as hard as he could and as fast as he could. The explosion caught his assailant so completely off-guard that he actually didn't retaliate. He probably spent the rest of the ride wondering if he would ever be safe again. Anyway, Mike used this same response on me one time, although the setting was a couch in the foyer of our church. Other than that, the situation was almost identical to the incident with Garnet in the computer lab. Mike took my seat and refused to move, and I grabbed him by the neck. He not only leaped up to punch me twice in the face, he actually climbed up and wrapped his legs around my waist as he did so, like a true savage. Once again stunned not so much by the blow as by the response itself, I wandered off and stood behind a portable room divider, wondering what the heck had just happened.

SEVENTEEN

JUST LOCK IT AWAY

In Dostoyevsky's incredibly long and uneventful novel *Crime and Punishment*, which I read just to be able to brag to no one who cares that I actually finished the dang thing and to pretend that I'm really quite bohemian and cultured when, in fact, I like lighting things on fire and watching demolition derbies, the protagonist, Raskolnikov, who is also the antagonist because he murdered someone and then lost his mind until he confessed all (so now you know what happens and you don't have to read the whole thing), says, "Man grows used to everything, the scoundrel." Raskolnikov utters this zinger after surveying the terrible conditions that his fellow poor people live in, and in some ways, this is very true. I've been known to say to people that guilt is not an effective motivator for me, since I've been feeling guilty since I was four. It'll take a bit more than that to move me from my stubborn hideaway. Not even the rank smell of rot was always enough to get me to take action. When I was staying in the bedroom that I mentioned before, where the haunted doorway was a conduit to both hell and a makeshift urinal, I was sick with the stomach flu. Now, I wasn't known to be a high-maintenance sick person, I just puked and slept as expected, unlike Spencer whose penchant for puking in the worst possible places was legendary. For example, I remember Spencer lying on the couch in our family room as a young boy, sick with the stomach flu. My mom thoughtfully placed an empty ice cream bucket on the floor near his head, telling him that if he needed to puke (though she never would have used that word), that all he needed to do was roll over and the bucket would be right there. I'm not sure if Spencer misheard her or didn't hear her at all, because the next time he needed to puke, he rolled over, but in the opposite direction, puking not into the waiting bucket but into the space between the couch cushions. Another time, when we were riding on the gigantic ferry between Nova Scotia and Newfoundland, Spencer got sea-sick. There were several decks of cars and passengers on this ferry, almost all of which featured windows or ledges with a sheer drop straight down to the ocean below. The only exception to this was the top deck, which was tiered. Of course, this is where Spencer's sea-sickness became overwhelming, and like most who feel overcome in this way, he raced to the edge of the boat, hoping to discharge his breakfast into the waves below. Unfortunately, as I said, this was the one deck that was actually tiered, so instead of his vomit harmlessly becoming fish food, it splashed onto the deck below, luckily missing any fellow passengers.

Anyway, Spencer was not a great puker, but I didn't really have any issues in this area. As I have previously established, however, I did have a bit of an issue making what I felt were arduous and inconvenient trips to the bathroom. This not only applied to urinating, unfortunately, and this particular bout of flu left me lying in my bed, half asleep and completely drained of energy. I had reached the stage of puking where there was nothing really left to produce but the most disgusting bile and acidic nastiness that the human body can manufacture. It was this concoction that I retched into a small bowl next to my bed, because I was simply too weak and tired to make it to the bathroom in time. See? I did it like I was supposed to. Then I got weird. For some reason, I pushed the bowl under my bed. I don't know why. Obviously, the bowl had been placed there for that reason, but maybe it wasn't. I think it was a small plastic bowl, and I can't imagine that my mom would have given me such a small receptacle for puke (or 'throw-up', as she would have called it). So maybe I wasn't supposed to be puking in that bowl after all. For whatever reason, it ended up pushed under my bed, out of sight. But not out of smell. And that bowl stayed there, untouched and undiscovered, for a long time. Like, a really long time. Long enough that by the time I rediscovered it, the puke had either evaporated or hardened into a crusty yuck, clinging to the edges of the bowl. So then I took it to the kitchen and scrubbed the bowl. No I didn't. I pushed it further under the bed. Why would I do that? Was it so hard to just go wash out the bowl? Surely not, but nonetheless, the bowl stayed under that bed for a long time before anything responsible was ever done about it. I don't even remember the outcome, but I have a vague memory of just throwing it in the garbage eventually.

This ability to compartmentalize, or just decide to put something out of your mind, even though you know it's there and eventually it's going to show up again, is both a blessing and a curse with the ADHD brain. I guess it's a form of denial, but it sounds fancier to say compartmentalize. It allows us to persevere in the face of what our brain is telling us is inevitable defeat. It allows us to forget previous failures and look forward to the next adventure with seemingly delusional optimism. It also prevents us from taking small preventative actions or even small restorative ones because we can put the issue out of our minds so effectively. When I was older, in my early 20s, my wife made a delicious apple dumpling dessert, and we ate more than half of the pan together. The rest of it, we left on the counter in the kitchen for later. Unfortunately, some water was spilled in the kitchen that day, with a good amount of it ending up in the dumpling pan, ruining the dessert. Rather than immediately trying to fix the situation or throwing the dessert in the garbage, we just left it sitting there. For a few days. Then it started to look and smell funny, so we threw it in the garbage. No we didn't. We put the plastic cover on the pan and snapped it down tight so we didn't have to smell it. After quite a few days of walking past this pan, with a gnawing feeling that eventually I would have to deal with it, I decided to take some action. Unfortunately, long before I had made this decision, some household flies had made a similar decision and taken up residence in the decaying dessert. This happened before I had so cleverly solved the problem by putting a lid on it. This meant that when I finally pulled the lid off, I was met by not only the vilest of smells and sights, but also a host of freshly hatched maggots and flies, with the latter happily swarming into my face. It was this final assault on dignity that finally prompted me to take action, and I washed out the pan. In the garden. With the hose. On the 'jet' setting. From 15 feet away. This could easily have been prevented, of course, but that's just not how I roll.

Just like the time I had a bowl of tuna salad in my car, originally taken for the hour-long drive to Vancouver where I worked, but abandoned in favor of much tastier fast food from a nearby mall. The tuna salad was moved from the front seat of honor to the back seat of neglect and eventually the floor of forgetfulness. There it stayed for days. Okay, maybe weeks. After all, it had a lid on it, so I was mercifully shielded from the sight and smell, and it was buried under a pile of clutter. My wife has, more than once, described the interior of my cars as having the appearance of a homeless camp. Eventually, the strength of fermentation could not be held back by mere plastic, and the smell began to permeate my car. So, I then took immediate action and cleaned the whole thing out. Nope. I just compartmentalized and got used to it, like a scoundrel. Eventually, I couldn't take it any longer. In the parking garage at the mall near where I worked, I decided to investigate the situation fully and found that the liquified nastiness had actually seeped out onto the floor mat, where the bowl lay upside down. I looked around the nearly empty garage, searching for a dumpster in which I could deposit my unwelcome package, but of course, there was none to be found. Despite the fact that I had been hosting this disgusting colony of bacteria for a few weeks, I determined that I couldn't bear one more second of it in my life and impulsively decided that the best solution was to remove the bowl and the floor mat together, place them on the ground in the garage, and then drive away from the scene of the crime as fast as possible. So I did. This tendency to procrastinate and compartmentalize is far beyond a conscious choice, though that may seem difficult to believe. Often it seems as if I am watching someone else make the choice while feeling powerless to intervene, even though I am aware of the inevitable outcome. I realize that makes me sound like a really crazy person, watching myself make decisions, but I think most people with ADHD will be able to relate.

EIGHTEEN
OH MAN, SO STUPID

In the late 1980s, my dad decided to take our family of nine, including my 6-month-old baby brother, on a two-month trip, driving from one end of Canada to the other, stopping at many locales and interesting sites along the way. One of these was the Jellystone Park Camp Resort. As the name indicates, the campgrounds are based on the Yogi Bear cartoons, and my siblings and I were thrilled with the idea that Yogi himself would be making an appearance as part of the evening program. Did I mention that I was 11 years old at the time? It seems hard to believe now that at that age I would still be so enraptured by the promised appearance of a teenage kid in a Yogi Bear costume, but my naiveté was part and parcel of my ADHD. As the evening progressed, I found myself impatient with the antics of the human performers and watched the side-stage area, hoping for a glimpse of the mischievous snatcher of picnic-baskets. Throughout this time, I fantasized what I would say to Yogi if I got the chance to meet him. Again, let me emphasize that I was an intelligent 11-year-old who was excited to make an impression on a stuffed animal.

Finally, the moment arrived at the climax of the evening program, and Yogi made his long-anticipated entrance, to the delight of the campers. I remember that his costume was somewhat disappointing, but despite this brush with conscious awareness, the potential fame that awaited me following my interaction with the famous character was too intoxicating to be slowed down by a low-budget attempt at recreating the glory of Yogi Bear. I had decided upon my winning verbiage during the program, and as Yogi waded into the crowd to dole out high-fives and silent hellos, I forged my way, trembling with anticipation, through the sea of children, most of them not as tall as my chest. I reached out my hand to the famous Yogi Bear and said, brimming with pride, "Hey, it's the Yogster ..." All I got was a silent response from an emotionally neutral stuffed Yogi head, but within that silent response, the seeds of intense shame were sown and instantly fertilized. I felt a wave of embarrassment wash over me that far outweighed (in retrospect) the offence that had created it. Reality became stark to me as I realized that this was not Yogi Bear but a minimum-wage camp employee. He was not impressed with my handy 80s lingo, but most likely amazed at my immaturity. How could I have been so swept up in the Yogi hysteria? I chastised myself harshly and repeatedly, and I do not remember anything else from the evening.

NINETEEN

DUMB IN LOVE

As I have previously mentioned, throughout my elementary school years, there was only one girl who was the object of my affection, though my feelings remained unexpressed except for in typically awkward ways. For example, in Grade 2 our teacher decided that it would be a good idea to create a newsletter to send home to keep parents up to speed on goings on in the class. She also decided that it would be a good idea if each kid in the class drew a small self-portrait in a little frame. These framed portraits would then surround the outer edge of the newsletter. When it came to my turn, not only did I draw a wonderful self-portrait, I also decided to add to the portrait of my love. I'm not sure what I was planning, but it went horribly wrong, and for the rest of the year, the class newsletter included a picture of Jennifer with a beard. It really makes me laugh out loud as I write this, but at the time, I was not laughing. It was embarrassing. It made me seem like either a really bad kid, vandalizing an innocent girl's drawing, or a really dumb kid who just did dumb things. And really, why wouldn't the teacher find a way to fix the mistake? Why make me and Jennifer live with it for the rest of the year? Another awkward time was in Grade 6, when I got a valentine from Jennifer on Valentine's Day, because that's when people give out valentines, but for some reason it felt like I needed to include that detail in the sentence, as if you might not know when or for what reason she had given me a valentine. Anyway, I wrote in big letters on the valentine, "My Favourite Valentine" and made the mistake of leaving it lying on the top of my desk for someone else to see. Someone who practiced the same amount of self-restraint as I did, who proceeded to tell Jennifer. She said nothing, but I felt like crawling into a little hole and hiding--because what could be worse than the girl I was in love with knowing about it?

This reminds me of another thing that happened around the same time. Remember when I said that Jennifer was the only one for me? Well, that wasn't strictly true. There was also a girl at church, quite a few years older than I was, with whom I was quite entranced. One evening, our family went up to the church for a family dance, which is a weird idea in some ways, for a whole family to go to a dance together. I guess it's weird if the reason for going to the dance was to check out girls, which of course it was. Almost immediately after I'd arrived at the dance, this girl, out of nowhere, came running up to me and grabbed my hand. I was about 11 years old, and she was probably 14 or 15. Keep in mind that I had fantasized many times about a moment such as this, so what did I do when the moment became a reality? I freaked out. She pulled my hand towards her, trying to draw me out onto the dance floor. I pulled back, saying I didn't want to go. She laughed and pulled harder, and I resisted even stronger. She gave it one last try, and instead of just saying that I didn't want to, I wrenched my hand out of her grasp and yelled that I didn't want to, and sprinted away sobbing. Ouch. I'm sure she thought she had just made contact with a weirdo, and I was sure she had, too. I ran to another part of the gym and tried to explain to myself just what the heck that was all about. To this day, I'm not totally sure.

Anyway, back to Jennifer. As I mentioned before, through the years, I had always dreamed that someday she would think of me as I had thought of her, but as we grew, it became apparent to me that this was not going to work out in my favor due to the presence of Nathan T. This brings us to one of the worst moments of my entire childhood. You might think I'm exaggerating, but I'm serious. I've always told this as a funny story and even wrote about it in a song, but each time I've sat down to write about it for this book, a giant block has appeared--an invisible hand, restraining me from going down this particular memory lane. I suppose the event was much more harmful to me than I realized. It was the Christmas dance in Grade 7. We had spent a lot of time together so far that year, me and Nathan, Jennifer, Rosie, Jessica, Heather, Garnet, and Tim, as members of Mr. Yule's school rock band. On top of that, we spent a lot of time outside of class together, working on special projects and hanging out, so we had really gotten to know each other fairly well. Or so I thought. Earlier in the year had come the fateful day when I'd heard Jennifer refer to Nathan as her boyfriend, but even then, my ability to compartmen-talize served me well. I was able to almost willfully forget what I knew about Jennifer's feelings for Nathan and maintain the hope that I still had a shot. Weird, for a second there I felt like I was writing or even reading some cheesy middle-school romance novel, and then I remembered that this was real and it was my life. Again, with the denial.

Anyway, in Grade 7 we started having class dances, which is really one of the weirdest things, if you really think about it. During the regular course of our school existence, for the most part, the boys were separate from the girls. Of course, there was flirting and awkwardness, but mainly we kept our physical distance. Then, because it was some holiday like Halloween or Christmas, we brought chips to school, turned off the lights in the classroom, moved the desks to the edge, and stood facing each other with boys' hands on girls' waists and girls' hands on boys' shoulders, doing the Grade 7 shuffle: step to the left with the left, tap to the left with the right. Step to the right with the right, tap to the right with the left. We did this for a three-minute interval, accompanied by Poison or some other awesome hair band, then parted ways, as if it hadn't happened. But since this was the Christmas dance, it was actually held in the gym. I remember it very well. I was known as a bit of a crazy dancer, which I know is hard to believe, given all of the restraint I have demonstrated up to this point in the story. But it wasn't a frenzy of funky dancing that led to my pain in this instance--it was one slow dance, the last one of the day.

Of course, Jennifer was slow-dancing with Nathan, and I knew I had to put a stop to it. I couldn't just overtly approach them and elbow him out of the way, of course, though I would have loved to be that bold. Instead, I came up with the genius plan of making them feel uncomfortable enough that they would naturally separate from each other. I grabbed some mistletoe that was being used as a decoration and began harassing the other couples that dotted the darkened gym floor. I couldn't make a beeline straight for the happy couple, because that would have been too obvious, so I started on the periphery and ran from couple to couple, holding the mistletoe over their heads, causing them to squeal with mock horror and pull away from each other, running in some cases. Finally, I approached Nathan and Jennifer and held the mistletoe aloft, ready to plunge a knife into their obvious comfort with each other. To my absolute horror, instead of the squeal-and-run response, I watched as Nathan leaned down and Jennifer leaned in, eyes closed, and they kissed each other. This wasn't just a peck, either, like some other kids out on the playground whose kissing seemed like they were being asked to put their lips onto the backside of a horse. This was a real kiss. Like a Hollywood romantic kiss. I was speechless. I felt like someone had punched me in the stomach and the head and many other painful places. Of course, I couldn't let on that this was the single most devastating moment in my life up to that point; after all, I was the class clown. I had put them up to it. How could I be upset? After all, I knew that they liked each other and that Jennifer had already made her choice (not that I was ever even in the running).

I forced a laugh and quickly made my way to the gym door. I

burst through it, out of the darkness and into the light. Of course, it felt like the opposite. I had descended from my moment of triumph to ultimate failure in an instant. Perhaps the worst feeling of all was not the disappointment of having seen with my own eyes that my chances with Jennifer were gone forever but that I was instrumental in my own downfall. I sat down heavily on a wooden bench in the hallway, all by myself, and stared numbly at the opposite wall while I heard the 80s rock ballad streaming muffled through the wall behind me. I cursed myself for the mistletoe idea. I blamed myself, reasoning that if I hadn't given them the opportunity, they never would have kissed. Of course, this wasn't true, but it sure felt true. It felt like my impulsiveness had once again done me in. As I write this story now, I feel faint pangs of the emotion that I felt on that day, but mostly I feel sad that she couldn't see what a great kid I was, that it was actually her who missed out. That's not sour grapes; it's just growth on my part.

TWENTY
SEEMED LIKE A GOOD IDEA

In Erie, there was everything that an active, imaginative and impulsive kid in the 80s could want. As I have mentioned, nature was our playground, and we spent entire days outside exploring the world. Erie was also a ghost town, and there were remnants of its former existence everywhere. On the far side of our driveway was a broken-down concrete structure that I was told used to be a bakery before the Erie Hotel had burned to the ground, taking the bakery with it. There were ancient barns and a chicken coop and several old trucks that appeared to be from the WWII era, broken down and rusting in the grass field opposite our house. I spent a lot of time sitting behind the wheel of these trucks, pretending to be racing after bad guys or away from good guys, depending on my orientation of the moment. After we had lived there for several years, we decided to convert the empty fields and bakery area into a horse pasture, so my dad asked his friend who had a bulldozer to come by and clean the place up. When you have tons of concrete to get rid of and nowhere to put it, the best solution seems to be to bury it, so that's what they did. This involved digging massive holes and moving literally tons of earth around in the field. We were in absolute heaven to be witnesses to this kind of stuff. Also cool was what was unearthed during this excavation project.

As we boys went digging through the dirt piles and climbing in the deep holes, we began to come across fully intact glass bottles, many of which had glass stoppers still in place. The bottles were empty, but they likely used to hold alcohol that was served and sold at the Erie Hotel prior to the fire. The coolest find, however, belonged to me. When I first dug it out of the ground, I couldn't even tell what it was, so of course I assumed--as most kids do when they dig something out of the ground--that I had found some sort of dinosaur bone. Soon, however, it became apparent, as I scraped away the years of dirt and mud, that what I had was actually a vintage fire hose nozzle, clearly left behind from the great hotel fire. When I think back on this find now, I grit my teeth with regret, wishing I'd known what I had and that I had taken better care of it. Why do I feel that way? Because when we moved from Salmo to the lower Mainland in 1989, the nozzle was lost in the move. I assumed it was the movers who'd stolen it, but it is probably just as likely that I'd left it somewhere and it hadn't even got packed in the first place. It may sound like hyperbole, but it really is one of the great regrets of my life that I wasn't able to hang on to that piece of history.

Anyway, we made great recreational use of everything Erie had to offer, and this included the train tracks that ran through the village, not more than 50 feet from our front door, because of course they did. Why not have a completely unguarded and unprotected railroad crossing running through a remote village within less than a stone's throw of the houses in the neighbourhood? And, of course, in keeping with the close supervision that is attendant in all of these stories, we were free to wander up and down these railroad tracks for miles in either direction. It was the quickest way to walk to the lake, that's for sure. It is a miracle that no one was ever hurt by the train. Especially when you consider one of our favourite pastimes with the train was to lay pennies on the rails. When the train would pass over them, they were flattened into shiny copper ovals, not even recognizable as coins.

Of course, if you've learned anything about me by now, you will know that we weren't long content to just put simple pennies on the tracks; we needed to take things to the next level. This is where things get foggy with the collective memory of my brothers and me. I asked them for input on this story before I began writing it because I don't want this book to be full of lies. There is a diversion of opinion and memory, so I will tell the story with the caveat that my brain may have recreated history to some degree. Having said that, I do have some definite corroborating evidence.

Anyway, our neighbour Rick, who was several years older than we were and lived up the road (I think it was his dad who'd built the BMX track for us), had access to building materials and stuff that we either didn't have or couldn't use. My memory is that someone suggested that we get some of my dad's .22 bullets and put them on the track, and of course, no one thought this might be a bad idea. Part of me thinks that couldn't have been the case. Did we really have access to bullets? I know we were unsupervised, but to that degree? My brothers don't remember this at all, but I do. I wonder if maybe Rick's dad had some sort of construction materials that were explosive, like little blasting caps or something. In my mind it was a bullet. Whatever it was, we laid it on the track and stood back, though not very far back, to watch the event unfold. As the train passed over our item, I remember a loud and surprising bang, then looking down at my leg and seeing something metallic implanted just under the skin at the bottom of my right thigh. There wasn't a lot of blood, and I don't remember pain, but then no one really remembers pain, do they? I remember digging whatever it was out of my leg and feeling like I couldn't complain to my mom about the wound, as I was apt to do, for fear that she would be upset about whatever we had done to cause it in the first place. To this day, I still have a scar in that part of my leg, in the same shape as the original wound. If this story is remotely accurate to the way I remember it, then it was probably the single most reckless moment of my childhood, and that's saying something.

TWENTY-ONE

REMEMBER THOSE REALLY DUMB KIDS?

WHEN LIVING in a ghost town like Erie, you have limited options when you want to hit the town. The first step in hitting the town in Salmo is to leave town. My dad worked about a half hour away in the city of Trail. I just looked up how long the drive actually was, because when I was a kid, it felt like hours. I remember riding in our old brown van, staring up at the little dots on the ceiling until my eyes started playing tricks on me and the dots appeared to be in 3D, like those pictures that were all the rage in the early 90s--the ones that seemed to just be abstract until something went weird in your eyes and then a 3D image would appear, to the endless frustration of those beside you who couldn't quite get the trick to work. My eyes used to do that in the van on the seemingly never-ending drive to Trail. Magic Eye. That's what those pictures are called. Now that I think of it, those Magic Eye pictures are a perfect metaphor for what math was like for me, not just as a kid, but even now. It's like the answer, or even the right equation, is just on the tip of my conscious awareness, but I can't quite get it into focus enough to see what it is.

Anyway, driving to Trail. You know how your body gets conditioned into a routine with simple things because you just always do certain things at certain times? I went through a time as a kid where my brain was unfortunately conditioned to really need to pee about halfway between Erie and Trail. There was no stopping the Leavitt bus, however, once it was on its way, so this led to countless times pulling into the parking lot of the church or the mall where my dad's office was, with me literally bouncing up and down on the seat like a pogo ball. Remember those? That was another trend from the early 90s. What was the attraction? A more difficult version of the pogo stick? Anyway, I would just be bouncing away, staring at my 3D ceiling, and grabbing my crotch. It actually makes me laugh out loud to picture this in my mind right now. I wonder what my mom thought, looking back in the rear view mirror, especially since I wasn't the only one who was stuck in this routine. Once we got through the little towns of Fruitvale and Montrose, we came around a corner and began the descent into Trail, which stretched out in front of us like a sprawling metropolis. At least that's what it felt like to some hillbillies from Erie. It's funny to look back on now, that the kids from Trail used to make fun of us kids from Salmo and Erie for being country kids, but even today, 30 years later, Trail has fewer than 8000 residents.

We typically made the trek to Trail for one of three reasons. We were going to the mall to do some shopping at Woolco, going to church, or visiting my dad's office upstairs in the mall, where he worked for West Kootenay Power. I have no idea why we would want to go to my dad's office or what he did there. We only ever went with him after hours, so we had free reign of the place, but it's not like there was a ton of excitement to be had in an accounting office after dark. I do remember the computer room, which was essentially a large section of the second floor full of large humming computer servers. Of course, this was the 1980s, and I had no idea what I was really seeing. It just seemed high-tech, and memories of it are tied to the *Superman* movie featuring Richard Pryor, where the lady gets sucked into the giant computer in the cave and then becomes some creepy robot lady. That one gave me some nightmares for a while. Anyway, when we weren't racing around my dad's office, lighting fires behind the church, or shopping for shoes and tank tops at Woolco, we might occasionally have found ourselves enjoying the treat of a lifetime: a trip to McDonald's.

The main feature in Trail was, and probably still is, the Cominco Smelter. I just love the word smelter. It so perfectly fits what a smelter does. It smells. I have no idea what a smelter does. Okay, now I do, because I looked it up. Apparently, it uses heat to extract metal from ore, which I think is rock. The thing I just read says that one of the other elements that is usually attached to the metal is sulphur, which explains why when we crested the hill leading down into Trail the first thing I noticed was the smell of farts. But not just normal farts. It was the smell of farts mixed with the heavenly aroma of McDonald's, because right smack in the middle of the Waneta Mall complex was the only McDonald's for miles. For our large family of hillbillies from Erie, McDonald's was the ultimate in fine dining, and it was a rare occasion when we got to eat there. One of those times really stands out in my mind, though thankfully today the only scars that remain from the incident are in my memory. It was a dark evening, so it must have been in the winter time, and we had just finished our meal as a family, when my brother Mike and I decided that we needed to go pee before we began our trek home. Makes me wonder why we never did that before we left for Trail in the first place, which would have saved us all that time bouncing on the bench seats in the van and contemplating the social impact of walking into church late, having peed our pants on the way there. That was some mental torture.

Anyway, we headed off to the bathroom together, and as we were leaving, Mike somehow managed to get his fingers shut in the door. Not on the side of the door where the handle is but on the side where the hinges are. This was a thick, solid, heavy door, so I can only imagine the physics (because I never took physics) that resulted in

Mike's fingers being crushed so badly. I heard him screaming and wondered what the heck was happening. He was stuck, panicking as he felt the pain stab through him, and it took me a second to figure out what was going on. I rushed to open the door and stop the pain, freeing his fingers from the trap successfully. His screams and howls had attracted the attention of a few McDonald's employees, who came rushing to see what had happened. Never a dull shift at the Trail McDonald's, I'm sure. I was feeling heroic as I stood there holding the door open and explaining to the staff what had happened. This feeling of pride and heroism (and compassion for Mike) rapidly disappeared as I felt my own bewildering but intense pain suddenly begin in my fingers. I looked to see what was happening and was shocked to discover that despite rescuing Mike from his predicament only a few minutes earlier, I had now found myself in the exact same situation, with the giant, heavy door of death crushing my fingers on the edge right next to the hinges. There was no playing it cool, however, no way to hide my mistake, as the pain quickly overrode any embarrassment, and I began to scream and howl in exactly the same way Mike had, leading to the same response from the staff, who must have thought this was some sort of prank or a field trip of special kids who clearly needed more supervision. I can assure you it was definitely not the former, though the latter wouldn't be far off. The staff were great, though--there was only a minimal amount of chuckling as they led us both back into the kitchen, which felt like I was being shown the inside of an Egyptian pyramid, so great was the wonder and mystery. I was finally getting to see where all the magic happened. They gave each of us a cup full of ice chips, and--using their highly advanced first-aid training--told us to stick our fingers in the ice. Once the pain had started to subside, and the miracle of the McDonald's kitchen had worn down, that old familiar feeling returned with a vengeance: embarrassment. As bad as the pain in my fingers was, the pain of doing something so dumb was far greater. I noticed the smiles and snickers of the staff, and I felt the embarrassment of my dad as we were brought out of the kitchen, with all of the customers' eyes cast in our direction. I felt a bit like I was being led out onto the circus floor, the dazzling Leavitt Moron Show, for all to see. In actual fact, most of them probably didn't notice us at all, but it was burned into my brain very deeply that once again, I had blown it.

TWENTY-TWO

HE'S SO NICE AND ALSO A JERK

My Grade 7 year at Salmo Elementary School was a year of great highs and profound lows. I discovered music for the first time, real popularity, great embarrassment, and of course, girls. Well, actually I discovered girls in kindergarten. It was also the first year that I was involved in any kind of athletic endeavour. I was tall for my age, as were a few of my friends, and so when the school formed a basketball team and we played against other elementary schools, we dominated. When you have three kids who are almost 6 feet tall in Grade 7 and the hoops are only 8 feet tall, it is a recipe for disaster for the other teams. Anyway, I tried all sports that year as they came up on the calendar, too naïve to realize that most people aren't good at everything. The sport that was probably the worst match for me physically and mentally was cross-country running. This didn't stop me from joining the team, of course--any excuse to get out of school or do anything extracurricular was something I would gladly sign up for, even if it meant limping along, drenched in sweat, wanting to puke, while struggling to breathe. Wow, when I say it that way, it really says a lot about my feelings toward school at the time. Of course, as a big, lumbering kid, I was hardly nimble enough or blessed with enough endurance to make my mark as a cross-country runner. I remember one particular race, however--one that has stuck with me for a variety of reasons.

It was an overcast, wet day, and when the race began I started plodding along, quickly making my move towards my usual spot at the back of the pack. After completing a few laps of the route, I was running (and I acknowledge the very generous use of that term) alongside my good friend Garnet, when we came to a 90-degree turn in the track that was covered with fallen and decomposing leaves. This made for some slippery conditions, but of course, at the pace we were moving, it was not much of a hazard. However, one young runner from another school, in his determined effort to place well, went hurtling past us as we entered the turn. His feet planted on the wet leaves, and his momentum caused him to lose his footing. As the leaves skated out from under him, he crashed to the ground, injuring his hands, shoulder, head, and pride. Garnet and I, we were nice guys. I had won the citizenship award almost every year in my class throughout elementary school. Of course, the one year I didn't win it, I didn't take it well; perhaps this was a sign of things to come. Anyway, on this particular occasion, Garnet and I stopped running, which was not a difficult thing to do since we were hardly blazing along, and helped our fallen comrade to his feet. Because of the seriousness of his injuries and the distance from the starting line and all of the adults, we felt that it would be important to stay with him and help him back to safety. We recognized that we had no hope of doing well in the race, anyway, so it was not a big sacrifice for us to essentially drop out. Thus, we supported our fellow runner physically and emotionally as we carried his weight and his spirits back to his coach.

At that point we continued on with the race, although our chances of anything remotely resembling a respectable time were long gone. Garnet and I took the opportunity to have a good conversation about who knows what, probably astrophysics and life goals, but possibly girls. We walked and we jogged, and somewhere along the line, we realized that we were the last two people who would be finishing the race. In a show of solidarity, and in a decision consistent with our noble actions from earlier in the race, we decided upon a pact that we would cross the finish line in last place together. We decided that that would be the fairest thing to do. I don't remember who suggested this idea, but I have a bad feeling it was me. Why do I say bad feeling? I say that because of what I did next. After we had agreed upon this finishing strategy, our conversation moved to other subjects. We began jogging as we reached the halfway point of the final lap, and it was here that my insecure, emotionally immature nature emerged, rather horrifically in my view. While jogging along step for step with Garnet, I decided that I did not want to come last. Of course, I didn't let Garnet know this. Unless, of course, you consider my suddenly sprinting away from him towards the finish line without any warning a form of explanation. I was bigger and stronger than Garnet, and this allowed me to push harder at the end and finish in a glorious second-to-last place, leaving the ignominy of last overall to my good friend. I remember the look of betrayal on his face as we made eye contact following his finish. I could hardly look at him, I felt so ashamed.

TWENTY-THREE

YOU DON'T BELONG HERE

My Grade 7 year, as I may have mentioned but I don't remember mentioning (but I must have mentioned), was the best year of my entire school career. Now, I'm not sure if I should say why, because I might have said it already, and then you'd be reading it again for no reason. Although, I suppose it's possible that you are like me and might need to read things more than once in order for them to really sink in. It's also possible that you don't care why it was such a great year, and you just want me to get on with the story. Anyway, I seem to remember spending a lot of time in Grade 7 outside the classroom. Of course we did regular classwork. I know this because I remember having to do a book report on a novel that I read and really liked, but when it came time to do a one-paragraph summary of the novel, I had no idea where to start. So, I borrowed my older brother Spencer's book report from the previous year. I had no premeditated intention to cheat; I just needed a hint on how to go about condensing a novel into a paragraph. Spencer had got 100 percent on his book report the previous year, so I figured it would be a good template. I have no idea where I found this report or why it was still kicking around our house.

Anyway, I began by copying his first sentence, and before I knew it, I had plagiarized the entire thing. Of course, I was innocent enough to think that I could now hand this work in to the same teacher as he had, and no one would think anything of it. So I did. It felt good to hand in my homework, finished on time (though worked on at the last minute, of course). It was a few days later that Mr. Yule called me over to his desk during class. I walked over and was surprised to see that he had also kept a copy of my brother's report from the year before. "As I was reading your report," he said, "I realized that it looked very familiar to me, but I couldn't figure it out. Then I remembered where I had seen it before." This is when he dramatically pulled a copy of Spencer's report out of his desk drawer. He said that my version was identical to Spencer's, although he conceded that my grammar and spelling were much better, and that because I had basically cheated, he had no choice but to give me only half marks. The reality, of course, is that he did have a choice. He could have given me nothing. He was well within his teacher's rights to give me a zero for cheating, but instead he gave me 50 percent. I think on some level he recognized my naïveté and believed that I hadn't really realized what I was doing.

As I said, I spent a lot of time outside the classroom working on special projects, practicing for the band, and clumsily flirting with the girls. Toward the end of the year, I found myself in the small town of Nelson (that felt like a giant city to us Salmo kids) for some sort of brain Olympics. We had to build bridges out of popsicle sticks and other similar brain events, but in great irony, I had no idea that this event was for the smart kids. I really thought I was there because my friends were there. I hung out with Tim and followed his lead and wandered around wondering what was going on. This was the disparity between my view of myself and others' view of me. My teacher clearly saw that I was capable of representing the class at an event like this, but I had no idea what was even happening and thought I was there because I was likeable. The damage to my identity had been repeatedly inflicted so long previous to this that even the successes of this year and the recognition of those whose job it was to recognize were not enough to shake loose the belief that I was not smart.

TWENTY-FOUR

TRY TO FOLLOW ALONG THIS TIME

JUST AS I was reaching the height of my popularity in Salmo, my parents dropped a life-changing bombshell on us. We were moving. We had lived in the Kootenays since I was four years old. It was really the only home that I had solid memories of. I had never once even thought of living somewhere else. Needless to say, I was crushed. We were leaving our hillbilly homestead, our mountains, rivers, lakes, and bike jumps for the suburbs of Langley, B.C. I didn't know anything about where I was going or what to expect; I only knew that my friends would be left behind, probably never to be seen again. Complicating matters was the fact that the real estate market in Langley was slightly different from the one in Salmo. We sold our large house and property and bought a much smaller house with no property, while paying almost 300 percent more. I didn't have to be a math genius to know that things were going to be tight. In addition, our first week in the new town, our house was not quite ready to move in. This meant that our family of nine was forced to live in two adjacent motel rooms just off the bypass in downtown Langley. We did our back-to-school shopping at Value Village, and I combed through the cast-offs of other people trying desperately to create an ensemble that would allow my social standing to pick up right where it had left off in Salmo. Of course, this was 1989, and without the internet to connect me to the bigger world out there, I was culturally at least a couple of years behind. I had no idea what TV shows people were talking about, what music they were listening to, and certainly not what clothes they were wearing.

One nearly humiliating event occurred not long into my Grade 8 year as I was walking from one class to another with a girl who actually happened to be one of the cool kids. I'm not sure how I happened to be in that position, but I do know that I was really nervous to be in her company. As with most of the cool and popular kids at that time, and in that particular part of Langley, this girl was obsessed with clothes. Not just with what they looked like, but with what brand name they were, where they were bought, and how much they cost. "I got this shirt from Le Chateau and these jeans from Guess and these shoes from blah blah blah." Of course, I pretended to know the significance of all of these brands and stores, even though I had never heard of any of them. Now, I should mention that Value Village has had an image makeover in the years since I was the new kid in town, as it is now considered somewhat chic (can I even use that word without sounding like I'm pretending?) to get a good deal and to wear throwback-style clothing. Back in 1989, however, Value Village had not yet come into its own and was very much considered the place where the poor people and losers shopped. I was able to pick up on this subtle distinction when kids at school used Value Village as an insult while they were going about their daily duties of picking on the less fortunate. Even though I kind of liked the clothes I had picked out.... Funny, I almost said that I 'rather' liked them. This is because I'm currently watching a lot of *Sherlock* on Netflix, and my brain has the tendency to get so absorbed in fiction that it can sometimes lose the line between fantasy and reality.

I liked the clothes that I had picked out (a plain white turtleneck and some vertically striped pants that I don't think even had pockets), but I also knew that I had to keep their origin a secret for fear of sliding even further down the food chain in the jungle that was Fort Langley Junior Secondary School. So, while I was walking with this girl and she was inventorying her wardrobe and social status to me, she looked at me, pointed at my clothes, and said, "Value Village, right?" I tell you, my heart must have literally stopped. Even as I write the story all these years later, I can feel the tightness in my chest as I realized that my secret was out. I began to stammer out a reply, about to naively admit that she was right, not fully comprehending the damage that my honesty would do, when she laughed in a carefree way and said, "I'm just joking, of course!" And then we continued on our way. I wanted to be sick. It was a close call that allowed me to see my place in the hierarchy without having to feel the pain in full. You might be wondering what this story has to do with ADHD. Nothing, really; I'm just trying to set the scene for what a fish out of water I was at this point in my life. Whatever need I had for attention and whatever insecurities I had hidden up to this point were being dragged out into what felt like the world's hottest spotlight. I felt like I was drinking from the firehose (which is a great scene in the Weird Al classic "UHF," by the way) when it came to trying to keep up with what was cool and what wasn't and desperately trying to learn the boundaries of normal before accidentally falling off the edge into the bottomless abyss of lame.

One of the cool kids, and I have to smile as I write this, was in Grade 10. I won't name him, because I don't want him to get mad at me. He was in Grade 10, but he had a full mustache. And long, beautiful blond hair. I mean beautiful in the sense that it was flowing with a slight curl, and bangs that fell down into his eyes. And a blonde mustache. Are you serious? This was one of the cool kids? He had Salmo written all over him! I was standing behind him one time in the lineup for the drinking fountain. The fountain was located in the main lobby of the school, and there were always a million things going on there between classes. I was absentmindedly staring at the back of this guy's head and probably inadvertently eavesdropping at the same time, but I was really just zoned out. All of a sudden, this kid turned on me and snarled, "Did you hear me say that?" I was shocked out of my trance and replied, "Say what?" This was not convincing enough for him, so he turned fully to face me and barked, "If you tell anyone, I'll kill you." I assured him that I had no intention of telling anyone anything because I hadn't actually heard anything he had said, which was true. This seemed to work, and he stalked off with his friend. It took me a few minutes to figure out what had just happened.

Somewhere in the back of my mind, my brain became aware that I had overheard him give his locker combination to his friend. I must have appeared to be listening in, and he'd assumed that I was going to use this information for evil. This incident is such an interesting combination of the mysterious workings of the ADHD brain. On the one hand, the chaos of the busy hallway had spread my focus so thin I was not aware of how obviously I had honed in on one particular piece of the noise. But at the same time, even though I had honed in on that one piece of the noise, I was spread so thin that I didn't even get the information in real time. Also, my brain was able to go back in time and process what had just happened, guided by the unconscious sense that I had heard something that I wasn't supposed to hear. My brain was then able to connect the dots and figure out what that piece of information was, though it couldn't remember the information specifically. And of course, in the moment, this was all a mystery, and my conscious experience consisted of wondering what the heck he was talking about. You don't realize how many times I had to resist the urge to speak in the voice of Sherlock Holmes as I was writing that paragraph. So many times. Of course, as wonderful and interesting and mysterious as my brain is, it would also be nice to have been aware in the moment and therefore retain the ability to eavesdrop without detection. Sometimes the thrill of being different seems much smaller than the relief of being normal.

TWENTY-FIVE

ALL BRAWN AND NO BRAINS

As you have no doubt gathered from several of the stories so far, I was definitely drawn to aggressiveness as a kid. If something could be smashed, crushed, burned, or otherwise destroyed, I was first in line to wreak havoc. Of course, I wouldn't have been able to wait in a line if that was required, and if you think about it, what a funny picture that would be, waiting in line to wreak havoc--but now that I say that, I remember a rugby fundraiser at my junior high school where people could pay to have ten swings with a sledgehammer on an older beater car, and people were literally waiting in line to wreak havoc. I also remember being very unsatisfied with the amount of damage that guys were able to do with a sledgehammer, and the rugby coach, Mr. Smith, must have felt the same, because when it was his turn, he broke the rules by rolling up the driver's side window and destroying it with a flailing blow, sending bits of glass showering over the assembled students, much to their delight rather than horror.

These were really my people, in a way. Mr. Smith was an odd cat. He had a bit of a nervous tick where he would squint and bare his teeth. I say it that way intentionally, because it wasn't exactly a smile, but it wasn't threatening, either. Anyway, he was mostly pretty chill, although I remember a specific time in Grade 9 social studies with one girl, who was a repeat offender for the terrible crime of talking in class. I guess Mr. Smith was having a bad day, or he'd just had enough, but instead of sending her out or even just giving her a detention, he calmly walked over to her desk, picked up her binder, opened the outside door (the class was located in a portable, so the doors opened directly to the outside rather than into the hallway), walked out to the top of the short staircase and energetically flung her binder away, towards the athletic field, leaving a beautiful rainbow of loose-leaf paper cascading down all around him. He then loudly invited the girl to follow her binder and not come back. At the time, I'm sure there was a part of me that found this entertaining. After all, I was a kid whose default setting was "destroy." However, I do remember feeling a stab of sympathy for her as she was already a kid who was excluded and ostracized, and I could tell, even at that young age, that her home life was probably not the greatest. Anyway, not sure how I got onto that subject. Oh yes, destruction and havoc.

My favourite pastime as a kid was wrestling my dad. There is a family photo of me and some of my brothers attacking my dad in the living room, and you can see the look of pure joy on my face. Nothing could be better, as far as I was concerned. So, naturally, when I was exposed to the growing, soon-to-be exploding 'sport' of professional wrestling, I was instantly hooked. The massive muscles, the colorful stretchy pants, the mullets and mustaches, the bad guys, and of course, the smashing, kicking, slamming, and punching were like the nectar of the gods for someone wired like me. And wouldn't you know it, my dad liked it, too. I became obsessed with professional wrestling, begging for my parents to buy me magazines and merchandise and even attend an event in Spokane, Washington, two hours away. The less sensitive adults in my life loved to point out that wrestling was fake, but I refused to believe it. I mean, even as a 12-year-old otherwise intelligent kid, I was convinced that Ricky 'The Dragon' Steamboat really did have his esophagus crushed over the steel railing from a flying elbow delivered by Randy 'Macho Man'

Savage. I remember the first time I began to consider that this might not all be real when Macho Man and Hulk Hogan, former allies, were tangled in a love triangle featuring Macho Man's 'wife,' the Lovely Elizabeth. Elizabeth was caught in the crossfire during a match and was crushed by a 250-pound muscle man, necessitating her removal from ringside via stretcher. Her husband, the Macho Man, didn't seem concerned with her injuries and continued to wrestle while Hogan, the 'Real American,' was so preoccupied that he left Macho Man behind to go and tend to the fallen Elizabeth in the locker room. The cameras found Hogan weeping beside Elizabeth's stretcher, praying that she would be okay, while the Macho Man was nowhere in sight. It was at this precise moment, where Hulk Hogan, the ultimate champion, stood crying beside a stretcher, that the thought first crossed my mind that this didn't seem to be genuine. Again, though, I was able to compartmentalize that growing awareness and put it out of my mind, allowing myself to fully embrace the engineered image of Macho Man as the bad guy.

Even as my awareness of wrestling's 'fakeness' grew, it did nothing to dampen my burning desire to be a professional wrestler once I reached physical maturity. As soon as I had the opportunity, I began lifting weights in my home. We had a rickety little bench and those old-fashioned plastic weights filled with cement or sand or something. I read muscle magazines and practiced posing in front of the mirror, and when I began junior high school in Grade 8, I was quick to sign up for the wrestling team. I knew that there would be no funky costumes or angry speeches delivered into the camera and that there would be no punching or kicking. I knew by this point that these guys were mostly just actors, but it still didn't dim my idea that professional wrestling was my true destiny. The wrestling coach, Mr. Leung, was also my science teacher, and I imagine he was happy at the prospect that a kid my size (5'10" and 140 pounds in Grade 8) was signing up for the team. Little did he know how much his patience would be tested by my inability to internalize his coaching. I should say that I have no negative memories of Mr. Leung at all. I remember him as very patient and relaxed. I recently ran into him again, 25 years after we first met, as he attended a seminar I was presenting on helping kids with ADHD. All these years later, Mr. Leung is still trying to help kids, now as a principal of an elementary school.

The thing about me as a wrestler is that I had some natural gifts. My aforementioned aggression was definitely one. I was naturally strong, even before weightlifting became part of my life, and I was big. In wrestling, athletes are separated into categories based on weight and age. There weren't that many kids my age who were my weight, other than kids who were really overweight. I was pretty much made of muscle at that point (though I didn't have defined abs, which of course is the sole defining characteristic of someone who is in great shape), so wrestling chubby kids was very easy for me. Also, I was the only one my age in my weight class on our wrestling team, so when it came time to practice the techniques that were being taught, I always had the advantage of outweighing my opponent, which made things much easier for me. I remember wrestling a kid who was two years older than I was, and the eventual provincial champion in the 120-pound weight class, but because I outweighed him by more than 40 pounds, I beat him easily. We would spend our entire practice learning various attacking and defending techniques and then be given an opportunity to implement what we had learned. Very typical of the ADHD brain, my wrestling learning consisted of grasping the basic takedown moves and then making up the rest as I went. This is how I have learned to play most games and sports, and it's also the way I read self-help books. Read a few chapters in and then say, "yeah yeah, I got it."

Anyway, because of my size and strength, I could get away with this until I ran into someone who was of equal proportions who had actually learned some skills, at which point I would be pummelled into defeat. Following my mediocre first season of wrestling, I was approached by the wrestling coach and asked if I wanted to attend the B.C. school sports summer camp for wrestling. I was honored to be asked to attend, thinking that it was an indication of my prowess, but then I found out that someone else had been asked first and had not been able to go, so I had been the backup choice. While this stung my ego a bit, there was no way I was going to tell anyone that I was the backup. I was able to compartmentalize the disappointment and tell myself a different story so that I could feel proud of the accomplishment. I spent a week on the campus of BCIT learning from high-level coaches and surrounded by high-level wrestlers and athletes. At the end of the camp, there was a small tournament. I remember flailing around and out-muscling an opponent just as one of the coaches stopped by my mat to observe. I was thinking he'd be impressed by my victory; however, he stood and stared with his head cocked to one side, then said, "You definitely have one of the most unorthodox styles I have ever seen." Despite his attempt at subtle reframing, his message was clear to me: "What the heck are you doing? That's not what we taught you." Again, I found a way to reframe the sting into a backhanded compliment, making an effort to interpret it as praise for my creativity and ingenuity.

Armed with no new wrestling ability but 20 more pounds of muscle and bone, I signed up for the wrestling team again the next year. It went exactly the same way as before, with very little, if any, absorption of coaching and technique but plenty of kids pushed to the mat. Until my final match, that is. There was this one First Nations kid who was the same size and strength as I was, but he had learned how to wrestle along the way somewhere. He also had an aggressive streak that made me look like Ghandi. In the gold-medal match of the Fraser Valley Championship, I was overmatched, and I knew it. My last wrestling memory is of holding my opponent off with a neck bridge as he methodically worked to destabilize me and throw me off balance with my shoulders inching ever closer to the mat. I remember peeking over at Mr. Leung, who was kneeling at the side of the mat, along with a few other guys from the team. He was repeatedly shouting instructions for me to escape my predicament, but I had literally no idea what he was talking about. I had a vague sense that it was something we had practiced and that it was something I should have known how to do--and even in the heat of this moment, I took time to introspect on what a dummy I was and how disappointed Mr. Leung must have been with me as a learner, let alone as a wrestler. Following that defeat, I quit the wrestling team, reasoning that it was too much effort for too little payback.

TWENTY-SIX

WHO'S THE WEIRD KID?

It SEEMS, as I read through these stories, that there is a bit of a theme developing. Not the theme of seemingly always doing just the wrong thing at the wrong time or the theme of not fully thinking of consequences before acting, though those are both strong themes, as well. Another theme seems to be the undying attraction to girls who were just unattainable. Once I left Salmo for the big city of Langley, this was even more pronounced as I was now exposed to high school girls, and that was a different thing altogether. One particular girl caught my eye, of course, and I locked onto her with the tenacity of a Pit Bull but the assertiveness of a field mouse. Of course, I found her attractive, but she was also a year older than I was and two grades above me, because apparently she was so smart she had skipped a grade. Sure, totally in my league, right? Anyway, needless to say, our paths didn't cross much, but toward the end of the first year of junior high school, an opportunity presented itself, and I leaped at the chance to impress. When I heard that we would be having sports day, I was super excited and a bit confused. I was confused that high school kids would be participating in water balloon tosses and three-legged races and egg-in-spoon relays, since this was what sports day was to me, a remnant of my glory days in elementary school. This was 1990, though, and I guess the kids weren't yet too cool to play crazy games in the name of school spirit. I was excited about sports day for at least two reasons: 1. Any reason to not be in class doing schoolwork was a positive thing in my life, and 2. The object of my obsession, er, affection was actually assigned to be on my team. Of course, so were 35 other kids, but they were just background noise to me. Then my chance appeared.

In the gym, a race was set up that required us, when our number was called, to race to the centre of the gym, sit on a balloon until it popped, and then race back to where our team was waiting. A fantastic idea began to grow in my mind, and since I didn't vocalize it to anyone, nobody had the opportunity to tell me that it was actually a terrible idea, doomed to fail spectacularly. Here was my chance to show this girl, and really the whole student body, exactly what kind of guy I was. Which I did. Unfortunately. As my number was called, I sprinted like a cat to the centre of the gym, with my teammates cheering me on. I grabbed the first balloon I saw, but instead of just sitting down on it like everyone else, I upped the ante by jumping as high as I could in the air, placing the balloon under my butt, and landing with a loud crash straight onto the floor with no cushioning below. I had popped the balloon, yes, and I had also popped the bubble of popularity, the one that had kept me from being one of the cool kids. Except I hadn't. There was no cushion when I landed, because for some reason that must only be explained by quantum physics, I had completely missed the balloon. I still held it in my adrenaline-shaken hand, completely intact. Not only had I looked like a complete weirdo, I'd lost the race. When I sheepishly sat down on the balloon, I didn't hear the pop, but I half-heartedly sprinted back to my waiting group where I remember this girl making eye contact with me for the first time all year. Instead of a look of longing and admiration, however, it was a look that very clearly said, "Who's the weird kid?"

TWENTY-SEVEN
I HAVE NO IDEA WHAT'S GOING ON

AFTER TWO HARD and frustrating years of wrestling in high school, I decided that it wasn't worth the effort. I remember distinctly thinking that working so hard in practice that I thought I was going to puke was not paying off enough to justify the effort, so I quit. I didn't quit so that I could start something else; I just knew that I'd had enough. Little did I know that the sport I would take up next would require more effort than I had ever expended in my life. Rugby. This was a sport that appealed to my natural recklessness and aggression. Plus, sometimes we played in the mud, so that was also great. My friend Keith had already played a couple of years of rugby, and I'd heard that he was a good player, so when he mentioned that rugby was starting up, I naturally followed along. Keith was the first friend I had who actually had other friends, and I considered him to be one of the cool kids. He had grown up mostly in Langley and gone to elementary school there, so he knew people; whereas I knew hardly anyone. Anyway, rugby is a game that has many rules, and many of them are subtle and difficult to interpret, leaving referees and players in a constant grey zone. This is, in one way, a good fit for the ADHD brain, but I remember after we were about 75 percent of the way through our season, in which we were gloriously undefeated and steamrolling other teams, I was called offside in a match. I wasn't sure what I had done wrong, so I bravely pulled Keith aside and admitted that I had no idea what offside really was and asked if he could explain it to me so that I wouldn't get called for it again. In one of the great moments of my life, Keith sheepishly admitted that he didn't really know, either, and that he just kind of ran around and hit people. This was a great comfort to me that even after two years of playing, he was still confused. It was almost as if not being the only one who was lost was more important than actually not being lost. Now that I say that, or at least write it, I think there is a lot of truth to that.

One of the advantages of playing rugby was that it exposed me to some of the more popular and well-liked guys in school, but not really the cool guys who I didn't like. I got to go to their houses, laugh and joke with them, and they started to get to know me, not just as the quiet weird kid in the Value Village clothes. One thing that we did for fun, being that we were a group of rowdy, aggressive, teenage boys (with more than a healthy sprinkling of ADHD across the group) was to box on the trampoline. No, I'm not talking about two guys wearing gloves, trying to punch each other in the head while jumping on the trampoline. I'm talking about FOUR guys trying to punch each other in the head while jumping on the trampoline. There were no teams, no alliances, and not really any rules. Just four crazy rugby guys punching whomever they could wherever they could. I may have drop-kicked one friend right off the trampoline, but my memory is a bit fuzzy. This might be because of one time when my friend Josh nailed me so hard I saw stars. I was sneaking up behind him, at least I thought I was, but in reality, how do you sneak up behind someone on a trampoline? Wouldn't every step I took behind him be an obvious tip-off that I was coming? Of course it would, but I wasn't thinking that far ahead. I was only focused on my plan. Does this sound familiar? Anyway, just as I got to within striking range, Josh spun around and hit me with a spinning back-fist, right in the side of the head. I wobbled and went down, but not completely out. These were the kinds of things we did for fun when we didn't have rugby practice. Another little side note: while we were inflicting mild concussions on each other, we were blasting music from a stereo in the backyard. The soundtrack to my near-miss with unconsciousness? *Simon and Garfunkel's Greatest Hits.* Because what goes better together than hippie songs about peace and love, sung with delicate harmonies and acoustic guitars, and trying to knock your friends out cold for fun? Nothing goes better together.

TWENTY-EIGHT

BECAUSE OF COURSE I DID

ONE TIME our family went out to this place called Castle Fun Park for our family night activity. This outing involved activities such as mini-golf, arcade games, and this awesome game where you got to hit a punching bag as hard as you could and then it would tell you how tough you were. Needless to say, this is what I spent quite a few of my tokens on. The other main attraction for me was the batting cage. I was never able to play organized sports when I was a young kid. With seven kids on a shoestring budget and a dad who worked a lot, it just wasn't an option. I always thought that maybe I could have been a decent baseball player but never got the chance to play outside of P.E. class, until my teacher described me one year with the following glowing praise: "Ted is not the most gifted athlete, but he does try hard." This was a blow to my self-image, I assure you, and I am forever grateful that Mr. Schimpf found it vital for me to know this in writing.

Anyway, the batting cages at Castle Fun Park came in a variety of speeds, either baseball or softball. I loved it. I found that I was able to make good contact with the ball and even hit a few towering home runs. The release of aggression from the combination of repeatedly smashing a punching bag and repeatedly smashing a ball with a bat, however, did not reduce my pent-up aggression but seemed to have some sort of igniting effect on it. So much so that by the time we got home from the activity and were making our way into the house, I spotted, with my eagle eye, a small plastic baseball bat lying in the carport. It was not one of those giant red toy ones; it was a smaller, thinner, bright-yellow version, and it was just asking for it.

So, in a frenzy of aggression, I grabbed the bat and smashed it down as hard as I could on the driveway in front of me. Rather than being able to enjoy my hulk moment, I was sent reeling backwards with a sudden sharp pain in my face. I had smashed the bat so hard that it broke in two pieces, sending the larger head of the bat hurtling back up towards me, where it smashed me in the mouth, splitting my upper lip in two. Not my lip itself, but the little place between the lip and the nose, which I'm sure has a proper name, but I don't know what it is. What I do know is that I have a permanent scar in that location from my adventures in driveway baseball. By the way, that area is called the philtrum, or infranasal depression. I like the word philtrum, and I like the fact that it is spelled like the name Phil, because when I think of someone named Phil, I think of someone who has a mustache, and the philtrum is the mustache part of the face. Thank you, science, for making sense.

TWENTY-NINE
I FOUGHT THE LAW

THE INTERNET IS useful for a lot of things. If you like weird stuff, there are lots of weird people talking about weird stuff and taking pictures of weird stuff and probably even writing fanfiction about weird stuff. If you want to watch live streaming video of weirdos taking pictures of other weirdos writing fanfiction, I'm sure you could find it somewhere. Also, it's useful for finding information. I know I'm not saying anything revolutionary when I say that not enough people use the internet in a way that improves their lives, but what I'm really saying is that back when I was in high school, the internet would have been kinda useful for when you heard something that sounded true but you weren't sure. Back then, you basically had two choices: Believe it or don't. You thought I was going to say believe it or not? Maybe? But that wouldn't have been grammatically correct, because if I separated it into two sentences they would be "I believe it" or "I don't believe it." I wouldn't say "I not believe it" unless I was a caveman. This grammar lesson is a courtesy. No need to thank me.

Anyway, this is a really awkward introduction to a very eventful evening for me, my friend Greg, and two of my younger brothers. It was an election year in B.C., though I can't remember exactly what year it was--but that's probably for the best, once I get finished with this story. Someone told me at school that if you vandalize an election sign before the election, then it's a felony, but if you do it after the election, then it's only a misdemeanour. Let's say for a moment that this was true. What is missing from that statement is that either way it is a crime. The kind that if you are caught, you might have a criminal record. In my mind, and in the minds of my friend and brothers, misdemeanour basically meant that someone would be mad at you and that that would be the end of it. Of course, we didn't want to risk any serious jail time, so we dutifully waited until after the winner had been announced on election night and then began our own campaign. Of destruction. Imagine that I said that in the voice of a movie trailer narrator. Oh, did I mention that the information we were told was not actually accurate--that the seriousness of the charge really just depends on the seriousness of the crime? Yeah, like I said, Snopes.com is useful for cleaning up cobwebs of baloney, which is a strange picture, cobwebs made from baloney. I have always liked baloney, by the way. It doesn't get the respect it deserves, especially considering that it may not even be meat yet manages to really taste like meat. That's not easy. Just ask tofu.

On this election night, we decided that our main vehicle of destruction would be ... you guessed it, fire. After all, the pyromaniac tendencies nurtured as a young boy weren't easily quelled just because I had been transplanted to the suburbs. Also, the election took place in the fall, which meant that firecrackers and fireworks were being illegally sold out of many high school lockers and the backs of cars. Fire and explosives and election signs, oh my. I think the first sign we tackled was a large wooden billboard mounted on a metal frame. This wasn't the kind of sign you'd see in someone's front yard. It was displayed in a field, just past the sidewalk, facing the street. Naturally, we decided that this was no place for a sign so glorious, and when no cars were nearby, we moved the sign out into the middle of the street, blocking most of two lanes. Then we hid in the bushes to watch the inconvenience unfold. It was disappointing.

Most people just drove around the billboard, but one guy actually stopped his car in the middle of the street and--with an annoyed look on his face--dragged the sign off to the side of the road. This was a mild payoff for us, but I'm not sure what we were really expecting. Did we actually think someone would come crashing through the sign at full speed, like in a movie? We decided that we needed to take it a step further, so we approached a newspaper box. You know those wooden boxes where the paperboy has the papers dropped off for him to deliver the next day? Well, this newspaper box still had a few papers in the bottom, and it was made of wood and we had fire, so it didn't take long for us to come up with a daring plan. This time, instead of an innocuous billboard, we dragged the newspaper box out into the middle of the street, set the papers and box on fire, and then ran and hid in the bushes to watch. This plan had a much better outcome. It was similar, with a driver pulling to a stop in the middle of the road, only this time he got out and stood there looking mildly panicked. This was before the days of cell phones, so he couldn't exactly call 911. I don't remember everything that happened, except that the situation filled us with great joy, and we took off running and laughing until we came to our next stop, a community mailbox.

We thought it would be a good idea to light off a few bottle rockets and drop them into the mail slot. Who knows what damage was done, but it felt very satisfying. Then we turned around and saw a simple plastic sign endorsing a candidate, planted on someone's front lawn. I volunteered to light the sign on fire, imagining that because it was plastic, it would just melt and drip onto the grass. Instead, it lit up like a flamethrower. I don't know what they put into that plastic, but once that sign caught fire, the flames were shooting up into the sky high enough to reflect in the second-floor window. This was almost more than we could have ever hoped for, and we celebrated by running for our lives, as we knew that it would only be a matter of time before someone came running out of the house to investigate.

We set off on a path of destruction, lighting fires and blowing things up all across North Langley that night. I'm not sure where our parents thought we were or what they thought we were doing, but it seems a bit odd that we were able to go out and wreak this kind of havoc completely unchecked. Well, unchecked until we arrived at a local elementary school with designs to light a large wooden real estate billboard on fire. We had completely exhausted our supply of firecrackers and all but one lighter. It seemed that as our night went on and our supplies dwindled, the need to up the ante had only heightened. Thus, whereas at the beginning of the night just moving the sign onto the road was fun, by the end of the night we were ready to torch the city. It just so happened that as I flicked the lighter to try to light the sign on fire, a pickup truck pulled into the parking lot and began racing towards us. My quicker-thinking friend and brothers took off running into the darkened field, but I just stood there frozen, not knowing what to do.

An older man got out of the truck and approached me calmly, asking what we were up to. Since he had seen me lighting the sign on fire, and I knew that he had, I knew there was no point in denying it. I just needed to come up with a realistic story as to why. The best I could come up with: we were cold and thought that maybe if we lit a small fire to warm our hands that no harm would come of it. As soon as the words were out of my mouth, I knew that my awesome story would not be convincing anybody. The man then informed me that he was the fire chief. I pretended like this incredible information had no impact on me other than to increase my admiration for the man. He then said that there had been a number of suspicious fires reported all through the neighbourhoods of Langley that night and that he wondered if I knew anything about it. I asked him where those fires were located, and he proceeded to describe the precise location of each fire that we had set throughout the evening. Then came the time for my boldest lie of the night. "That's weird that you say there were fires in those places," I said to him, "because we walked that exact same route tonight, and we didn't see any of those fires." I felt I was doing a good job of being believable, and now it was the fire chief's turn to look at me with a stunned expression. Of course, what had stunned him was my audacity in saying something so ridiculous and expecting him to believe it.

Despite my quick thinking in answering his questions, I wasn't quick enough on my feet to give him a false name, address, and phone number when he asked for them. He then said that he would be calling my parents within a few days to ask them some more questions. He managed to get the same information out of Greg, which led to both of us keeping vigil beside our home phones for the next few days. In the end, he never did call, and my parents never found out. I'd like to say that this close call was the end of our forays into the wild, but that would be another audacious lie.

THIRTY

UNRIGHTEOUS INDIGNATION

EARLY ONE MORNING, after spending the night at Greg's house, my dad phoned and told me to come home right away. This was not the panicked or concerned dad voice. This was the barely-withheld murderous-rage dad voice. I had no idea why I was urgently needed at home, but my mind filled with possibilities as I made my way back. Maybe I was finally busted for something, maybe we were moving again, maybe a million different things. I was not, however, prepared for the answer.

When I got home, he informed me that my brother Mike and his friend Marc had stolen the family car the night before and gone on a joy ride around Walnut Grove until they finally crashed it into a hydro-electric kiosk on someone's front lawn. Did I mention that my dad was in upper management at the hydro-electric company at the time? I'm sure that helped him deal with the 3 a.m. phone call in a very calm way. My dad informed me that because of Mike's decision-making deficit, all of us kids were permanently banned from all sleepovers. He had reasoned that his kids could simply not be trusted at sleepovers, and so the best strategy was to remove the temptation altogether for all of us. I was livid. How dare he remove my sleepover privileges for something that someone else had done! How could he hold me responsible for the actions of my brother? This was completely unfair! However, his decision was binding and final, and I sulked in my room for quite a while, fuming at the terrible treatment I was receiving.

Of course, the irony of this situation is that, in fact, the night before I wasn't simply hanging out with Greg, eating popcorn and discussing life goals. Instead, we were cruising around in his car, trying to find fights to watch or to get involved in, and when that had failed, we'd ended the evening by donating several eggs to a few different houses and cars in his neighbourhood. This was actually a fairly mild sleepover for Greg and me, and my dad was absolutely correct in his strategy. So funny, though, the ability to compartmentalize was once again apparent as I genuinely did feel I was being treated unfairly and that I hadn't done anything to deserve my dad's distrust. I was angry at Mike for blowing it for the rest of us but also shocked at the level he had gone to. On a side note, years later, Mike told me that this was actually not the first time he had done this; it was just the first time he was caught.

THIRTY-ONE

OOH, YOU'RE GONNA GET IT NOW

ONE OF THE paradoxes that I embody is that despite my aggressive nature, love of all things painful and destructive, willingness to take risks, and (historically) imposing physical stature, I have never been in a fight in my life. I don't know if it's because people were intimidated by me or because I'm just such a gentle and likeable guy that people had no reason to fight me, but I have made it this far in life without having to go at it with anyone. Of course, as I mentioned earlier, I was punched in the face by my friend Garnet and by my brother Mike, but I don't really count those as fights, because the shots were unexpected, didn't do any damage, and were not reciprocated. Using this definition, it is safe to say that I haven't been in a fight, even though I have punched a few people in the face. What a great opening line for a cover letter, by the way. Imagine applying for a job and that was your introduction to your future employer. "I've never been in a fight, even though I've punched a few people in the face. Please hire me to interact with your customers." The first time I punched someone was in Grade 10, in the middle of a rugby game. Now, rugby is a vicious, brutal sport, and I felt completely justified in punching my opponent in the service of a victory. The sport is so great that I was able to disguise my punch as part of my tackle, and I didn't even receive a penalty on the play. At the time, however, I didn't intentionally disguise it because I was going off of potentially faulty information that it was legal to punch in rugby. I now know that it wasn't, but I didn't stop to question things like that back then.

As I mentioned, when I was 13, our move from Salmo to Langley resulted in a precipitous plummet from near the top of the social ladder to near the bottom. I tried desperately to fit in with the new breed of cool kids, but for a number of reasons beyond my control, this was not going to happen. When I was in Grade 10, I began dating an older girl, against the strongly stated wishes of my parents. While they might not have approved of her or my choices at the time, and while I look back on the relationship with some questions of my own, it did lead to a turning point in my life. This girl was into alternative music, alternative fashion, and was, in essence, a hipster before hipsters were hipsters. That's kind of like the uber-hipster. Anyway, she taught me to do what you like and just be yourself. The complication with this approach to life is that sometimes being yourself alienates you from the crowd, and if you want to be part of that crowd, you have a choice to make. I remember distinctly making this choice one day in Grade 10. I was listening to an arrogant, fashion-conscious, exclusive dude put down people around him, laughing at their appearance and relative poverty, and the thought struck me, "I really don't like this guy. Why do I want him to like me?" I realized that if I ever did break through the glass ceiling and become acceptable to people like him, I wouldn't even want to hang out with them, anyway, because they made me sick to my stomach. It was at that point that I decided that I would just be myself, and if I needed to change myself to be accepted by people, then those weren't the kind of people I wanted to be accepted by, anyway. Thus began a change in philosophy from trying to learn and perfect the Running Man and the funky chicken and memorizing lyrics from top 40 songs to skateboarding, shopping at thrift stores for vintage clothes, and listening to punk and heavy metal music. It was during this same year that I met my before-mentioned best friend Keith, who was going through a similar transition, and together we formed a two-man band called "Who Farted in My Cereal." Our main band activities included terrible jam sessions, writing no songs, and making lots of jokes about being rock stars, while gaining a small level of notoriety as weirdos. Wouldn't you know it, this change in attitude actually led to my having more friends than before, but they were actually people I wanted to be around.

Just as I was beginning to gain some momentum socially, my parents announced we were moving again, this time to the city of Nanaimo on Vancouver Island. This was another stomach punch, since I couldn't believe I would have to start all over again. This time, however, things went a bit smoother as I was equipped with my new attitude. Consistent with my school experience from all grades, my friends came from disparate places. Most of the time, the only thing my friends had in common was me--a reflection of the variety of interests that I had and the chameleon ability I had to fit in wherever I wanted to. Of course, one of the first kids who befriended me was another kid on the social fringe. He was actually good to me, so I felt bad when a few months later I accidentally hit him in the face with an elbow while demonstrating my incredible martial arts skills before our chemistry class. We were having the conversation because my brother Mike was friends with this guy's younger brother, and we had recently all met at a park near our house to have boxing fights while wearing only karate sparring gloves. Because that's what we did for fun. Punched each other in the head. Anyway, this kid was the B.C. karate champion in his age group, a couple of years younger than I was. I was the big kid, though, so, of course, they wanted me to fight him. The fight started off with a shock as he leapt forward and began hammering me with punches in the back of the head. I won't go into great detail describing what happened next, but in the end, he was lying on his back, semi-conscious, mumbling something about not being able to see. It was a moment of glory, for sure. When I was talking about it with his older brother, he dutifully pointed out the difference in our ages, leading me to demonstrate my aforementioned skills, accidentally smashing his nose. I felt really bad about it, but class was just about to start, and I didn't really even get a chance to apologize. I don't remember even speaking to him again after that event. Ugh.

One day at lunch time, I was standing with my oddball mishmash of friends, talking in a small group in the atrium front hallway part of the school, when out of nowhere this kid comes running and jumps into the middle of us and starts body-checking each of us, yelling, "Moshpit!" while his friends looked on and laughed. While this is something that I could see myself doing, the thing is that we didn't even know this kid, and he was kind of known for this sort of obnoxious stuff. So, as the lunch supervisor came over and grabbed him by the arm to haul him off to the office, I took the opportunity to feel completely justified in quickly punching him in the face as he walked past. It wasn't a hard punch or he probably would have gone down like the karate champ in the park, but he reacted by screaming at me that I was dead. I was curious how this little string bean felt so confident in screaming these threats at me and laughed it off, aided by the pats on the back and chuckles of my friends who were happy that I had done what all of them had had the impulse control to not do. Later that day I heard a rumour that the kid I had punched had a dad who was a member of the Hell's Angels. These kinds of rumours tend to grow like weeds with high school kids, with little actual proof or evidence required. However, his cockiness in assuring me that I was a dead man, juxtaposed with his actual physical ability, seemed to give some legitimacy to the story. I'll tell you, for the next few days, I was pretty nervous, looking over my shoulder for some big burly biker to come and shoot me or hit me with a pipe or something. In the end, the whole thing blew over, and I escaped with nothing but a good story.

THIRTY-TWO

DRAWS IN NOTEBOOK

AND IMAGINES BEING A ROCK STAR

MATH and I were never very good friends. My brain is good at lots of things, but math was never really one of them. I got lots of A's in elementary school, but my perpetual grade in math was a B. Once I got to high school, however, B's were a distant memory. I remember my math teachers' names. Mr. Beall, Mr. Leung, Mr., Johnston, ... actually I don't remember my Grade 11 math teacher's name. However, I remember that he looked like he'd rather be anywhere than in math class, which was something we had in common. My working memory and attention problems wreaked havoc with my ability to learn math. When the operations were fairly straightforward, I could figure them out in my head, with my mental math skills being pretty decent. However, when it became multi-step math, with formulas to remember and rules to follow, I quickly became lost. It would basically go like this: *Step one* - got it. *Step two* - got it. *Step three* - wait, you lost me. *Step four* - I still don't understand step three, and I have no idea what step four is. *Step five* - (draws in notebook and imagines being a rock star). I remember there was this kid who sat at the front of the class who looked like a major stoner. He hung out in the smoke pit, rocked a mullet long after they were in style, and wore tight jeans and a leather jacket. I'm not sure I ever heard him utter a single word during all the time he was in my class. He got 98 percent in the course. Naturally, it did wonders for my self-esteem that I couldn't grasp even the simplest concepts and this kid was killing it with seemingly no effort.

Two things stand out to me from my Math 11 class: 1. I spent a lot time reading *Street and Smith's Pro Basketball Preview* magazine and wondering about this player named Shaquille O'Neal, who was apparently quite good, and 2. The best moment of the year was sponsored by Twisted Sister. In our school, during the breaks between classes, they played music through the PA system. It was actually a good idea and a bit ahead of its time, and I remember one rough day in particular, when I had math during the last period before lunch. If you could get graded for clock watching and calculating the number of minutes left in class, I would have got an A for sure, and as the minute hand moved into the magical place, the bell rang and the sweet, sweet sounds of Twister Sister filled the hallway: "We're not gonna take it!" Not sure that's the best anthem to inspire high school students, but man, the sun was shining, math class was over, I felt like kicking something out of sheer joy and excitement, and I wasn't gonna take it anymore! Then, of course, I had math the next day and nothing was different. Because of my chronic problems with math, my dad, who was an accountant and naturally good at the subject, decided to help me in Math 11 and spent time each day with me, going over my homework. He would impatiently explain concepts repeatedly, and I would frustratedly and defiantly eventually learn them. His go-to line was, "What do you mean you don't understand? I just explained it to you." I don't blame him. Not in the least. When something comes naturally to you, it's hard to understand how others can't just see what you can see. It's why great athletes don't always make great coaches and why I don't understand why procrastinating is so hard for some people. I'm just a natural at it.

Anyway, during the time that my dad was helping me with my math, I was actually doing quite well, and for my interim report card,

I had 83 percent in math. This was the best I had ever done in math in my life, and I was feeling great about it. My parents must have also been feeling great, too, believing I had turned the corner and was finally able to take the reins. So, the homework help faded out. Of course, I was only one of seven kids in school, and everyone except the oldest struggled with something or other, so there was only so much help to go around. Then the unit we were working on changed, and I was back to having no idea what was going on around me, not asking for help, and not progressing. By the time my actual report card came out at the end of the term, I was down to 35 percent in the class. That is a serious drop. Do the math: think of how bad I would have to do in order to go from 83 to 35 percent. One time I remember getting a test handed to me. I thought I knew what I was doing and began the first of 20 questions. I quickly got stumped, not knowing what step to do next. So, I skipped to the next question, where the same thing happened. I continued this sequence of getting stumped then skipping to the next question until I realized I had skipped all the way to the last question and didn't know how to do any of them. I had got stumped on every single one. As the panic and self-loathing set in, I went back to the beginning, desperate to wipe the fog off the window and see if I couldn't salvage something from this shipwreck. In the end, I got 1/20 on the test, 5 percent. The one mark was actually made of two half-marks from two different questions I had taken a run at. I was no stranger to bombing math tests or schoolwork, generally speaking, but this was a particularly crushing blow, to not know a single answer on the entire test. It was only amplified when the stoner up front, with a frozen, humorless mask for a face, quietly accepted his mark of 100 percent without even a hint of satisfaction. What is interesting, however, is that just as in previous years, as I approached the final exam, we figured out what I would need to get on the provincial final in order to pass the class. I don't know how we figured it out, because I'm not sure I was capable of that at the time. However, we determined that I would need to get 78 percent on the final to get 50 percent for the year and be finished with math forever, as Math 12 was not a requirement to graduate in B.C. I busted my butt and brain studying and learning math for the next few days leading up to the exam, and wouldn't you know it, I passed Math 11 and ran from the classroom knowing I was never gonna take it, anymore!

THIRTY-THREE

THE WORLD'S LONGEST BACKSTORY

Up to this point in my life, I was really only interested in sports that involved smashing, strength, and violence in some degree. I remember when I moved halfway through my kindergarten year, my first day on the playground, I sized up the kids around me, saw one who was about the same size as I was, and did what I did at home with my dad and brothers. I tackled him without warning and began to wrestle. Of course, given that he was a complete stranger to me and I gave him no warning, I'm sure the message that this was fun was lost somewhere in the delivery of headlocks and body-slams. This hard-wired tendency to be aggressive led me into sports like wrestling, rugby, and punching stuff. When I was first introduced to basketball in Grade 7, my experience was a bit skewed because I was very tall for my age. When you are in elementary school, the hoops are only at eight feet high. I was close to six feet, as were two of my classmates, one of whom was actually super athletic. This meant that when other schools played us, they actually had to contend with Nathan dunking on them. Not a typical concern for rural Grade 7 basketball in the Kootenays. After that, I lost interest in basketball because I thought it was a wimpy sport where you weren't allowed to be physical at all, and if you couldn't smash, I was out. I remember actually saying this out loud when asked if I was going to join the basketball team in Grade 8. However, in Grade 10, I began playing basketball up at the church with my friends and some of the men from our congregation. There I discovered that basketball, especially church basketball, had the potential to be very aggressive and physical. This led me to reconsider my previous position and to fully embrace a sport that I would never actually become very good at. As I mentioned, just as I was finally starting to make some friends at school in Langley, my parents informed us that we were moving to Nanaimo on Vancouver Island. The locals also called it Nanaim-hole, and in a very ironic and fitting turn of events, there was a strip mall downtown with a marquee out in front that said "The Heart of Nanaimo" right above the sign for a liquor store.

I was not happy to move to Nanaimo for a variety of reasons, not the least of which was leaving my highly successful rugby team. The school I was moving to was brand new that year: Dover Bay Secondary. In a rare and--to me--weird turn of events, it was decided that it would be unfair to students who were going into the last year of high school to have to switch schools and leave their friends for that year, and as such, Dover Bay had no Grade 12s in its first year of existence. At Grade 11, we were the oldest kids in the school. There were certainly advantages to this arrangement for those of us in Grade 11, but one area where it was a major drawback was sports. With teams made up entirely of Grade 11s and no Grade 12s, we were definitely outmanned in almost every athletic contest. In fact, some kids, knowing how bad it would be, refused to sign up for sports teams because they didn't want to get destroyed and humiliated. As for me, I had already invested several years of my life in getting destroyed and humiliated, often at my own hand, so this did not present a barrier. One teacher in particular, finding out that I'd had experience playing rugby, was very excited to tell me that because I was basically the only kid in school who knew anything about rugby, I would be looked at as a leader and someone to build a team around. After hearing this, I panicked, thinking, "I *still* don't even know what offside means; how on earth am I supposed to be the leader?" The pressure got to me quickly, and within a week, before we had even had one practice, I told the teacher that I wouldn't be playing rugby, after all. The look on his face was a mixture of disappointment and genuine confusion. It was hard for him to understand why a big, strong kid would turn down the opportunity to take on such a role. For me, as soon as I told him, I felt instant relief. Later in the year, when I walked with some friends in the freezing cold to watch the rugby team play against another school, I stood there in sub-zero temperatures, so cold that my lips wouldn't work anymore, and congratulated myself for making the decision that would spare me having to wear short shorts in that kind of weather.

Along with the anxiety of being a leader while feeling incompetent, one of the main reasons that I quit rugby was to focus on basketball. Possessing the knowledge and permission to be a bit of a bruiser in the sport, I had embraced it with enthusiasm. Unfortunately, hardly anyone else in the school did the same. The minimum number of basketball players on a team is five, because that's how many are required to be on the court. Our team had six, including a burned-out rocker, a burned-out skater, a burned-out surfer (see the theme here), a notorious streetfighter, and a future alcoholic. And me. For three of us, it was our first experience playing organized basketball. Think of this: a team where half of the players had never played basketball before. In Grade 11. The writing was on the wall so visibly that the basketball coach himself quit before the season even started. He suggested that a former student of his volunteer to coach the team, so we were now taking instruction from someone who was not much older than we were and almost eight inches shorter, who regaled us with stories of his glorious high school basketball career. Mostly, we just ran lines in practice. I literally don't remember one thing from my basketball practices with that coach (whose name I can't remember), other than one obviously untrue story about how he'd won a jump ball against a player a foot taller than him, just by being in the right position. That and sprinting until I thought I was going to puke.

As the season began, we really had no idea what we were up against. We were blissfully unaware of the tragedy that was about to unfold. Our record that year was 1-21. Our lone win came in the 21st game of the season. We had a few close calls during the year, losing by a few points here and there, including one particularly memorable game in which I had fouled out, along with another player, leaving us with only four players on the court. The team played short-handed for almost two full quarters and actually mounted an epic comeback, only to fall short at the finish line. I was somewhat prone to fouling, to no one's surprise, though I started the season playing rather gingerly. I was afraid to get called for a foul, so I would often play matador defense, allowing my opponent to get past me and push me out of the way for rebounds. After a few games, my coach pulled me aside and told me that it was okay to get called for a foul if the foul was necessary. Armed with this permission, I proceeded to foul out of the next three games in a row, leading to another conversation with the coach, who told me, "Okay, maybe not quite so much with the fouling." There were three times that season when we lost by more than 80 points. Those were not fun games. I remember one game in particular where I seemed to just run from end to end, watching us turn the ball over, watching them score, and then watching the same scenario repeat itself continuously. I remember distinctly thinking at one point, "Hey, this is just like running lines in practice. No wonder he gets us to run so much."

In our lone win that season, a stubby little man with a full red beard and a purple bandana headband (I kid you not, he looked like a cross between a hobbit, Larry the Cable Guy, and the lead singer of Suicidal Tendencies, who I listened to a lot, by the way, as a sign of how hardcore I was) kept smashing me in the back under the hoop. That little aside in the middle of that sentence was actually pretty long, and by the time I went back to my main sentence, I couldn't even remember what I was talking about. I had to go back and check.

You probably did, too. Anyway, he kept smashing me, but we were actually winning, so I was maintaining self-control and playing my best. At one point, very late in the game, with about a minute to go, he lowered his shoulder and drove it into my lower back for the last time. I looked up at the scoreboard, saw that the victory was assured, then put my elbow in his chest and my right foot behind his, pushing my elbow backwards and bringing my foot forwards in a move that actually has a name, but I don't know what it is. I want to call it sweeping the leg, but I think that's just from *Karate Kid*, when the evil sensei instructs one of his students to injure Daniel to prevent him from going further in the All Valley tournament. I remember watching that as a kid and thinking, how would it hurt someone to elbow the back of their knee when it was already bent? and also being very annoyed with Daniel for being such a crying baby. What an annoying hero for a movie. I wanted Johnny to win. Well, I do now, anyway--back then the movie just inspired me to want to learn karate, which I pursued by draping a blanket over the top of a doorway and launching flying kicks at it for an afternoon, after which time my love affair with karate was over. Anyway, how the heck did I get here? I took this little bearded munchkin hillbilly to the ground with a hard (and dirty) play, which resulted in my final foul and being ejected from the game. But because we'd won, I didn't care at all, and it totally felt worth it.

As you can see, even though I had transitioned from wrestling to rugby to basketball, the undercurrent of aggression was still very much alive and well. Following a year at Dover Bay, my parents informed us that we were moving back to Langley. While this was incredibly good news for me, it wasn't good news for everyone in the family. My youngest brother had just finished kindergarten and would have to start all over again. My oldest brother had just graduated from high school, after having to start at a new school for his Grade 12 year, and would be left behind all alone in town because he had enrolled in college. For me, it meant a reunion with my best friend Keith and a return to civilization. Even though Nanaimo was only a two-hour ferry ride from Vancouver, it felt like a million miles away, and I couldn't wait to get back. I remember knocking on Keith's door that first day back in Langley. He answered it looking pretty much the same, except much more like a skater, and he had this nasty orange hair, the kind you have when the dye-job just didn't quite work out the way the bottle said it would. It was great to be back, and we picked up where we'd left off, except for some reason neither of us played rugby that year. The coaches asked for us, and our rugby peers wondered why not, but I think they eventually just dismissed us as a couple of skater dudes who were too burned out to do anything productive. In reality, we weren't burned out at all; we just looked like it.

Anyway, back at Walnut Grove Secondary, I decided to join the basketball team. Unlike Dover Bay, however, where anyone who wanted to play was welcomed with open arms, Walnut Grove would be having tryouts. I remember being really nervous about having to try out, and so I played extra hard and worked extra hard to make sure I got on the team. I was told later that I had virtually no chance of being cut, but I'd had no idea of that at the time. I guess that's kind of typical of me and probably a lot of people with ADHD. We alternate between thinking we're better than we are and thinking we're worse than we are. Rarely are we accurate in perceiving ourselves. Anyway, there was this kid who was trying out for the team, and I found him obnoxious. Walnut Grove was definitely a part of Langley that had more well-off families than other areas, but I never felt like one of the preppy rich kids because there were so many kids in my family, so the money my dad made was spread very thin. This kid, however, looked and acted like a rich kid. Looking back on it now with my grown-up perspective, I can see that he was insecure and desperately wanted people to like him, and it was probably very hard for him to try out for the team and face the prospect of failure, because he actually wasn't very athletic or skilled at all. That's my adult perspective. My teenage perspective was that he was obnoxious. So, of course, being the aggressive kid that I was, whenever I had the chance to foul this kid, I took full advantage of it. I remember one particularly regrettable incident in which he was trying to either post me up or box me out (if you don't know what that is, both of them require one player slamming their butt up against the other player to try to move him out of the position that you want on the floor) and kept ramming his healthy-sized butt into me. When no one was looking, I hit him with a knee in the butt to try to get him off me. However, either I aimed poorly or he was insecure for no reason, if you know what I mean, because he crumpled to the floor, literally crying in pain. I was shocked. I didn't think I had hit him that hard (story of my life), but my knee had actually landed a deadly blow right in his junk. I still don't know how that was possible, considering his back was to me, but I remember people looking at me like, "What did you do?" and because I was genuinely confused about what had happened, I guess that look passed for innocence, because nobody ever asked me about it.

I just realized that this never-ending description of my high school athletic career is all just backstory to my main story. I think that might have to be some sort of backstory record. I think people with ADHD tend to get lost in the backstory sometimes. Well, actually, I know that we do. We know how it all relates to the main story, but the listener--or reader, in this case--will often get confused and/or annoyed that we can't just get to the point. So why do we do this? I think it has something to do with being habitually misunderstood. If you look through many of the stories I've told so far, there seems to be a recurring theme of people misreading me or my intentions. I think we are misread so often, and usually not in a positive way, that it becomes very important to fully explain ourselves--so that the listener can get the full technicolor picture. I think technicolor is probably a really old-fashioned way of saying vivid picture. I guess the modern equivalent would be the full 4K picture.

Anyway, I made the team, and we went about losing basketball games. Even though we were better than the Dover Bay team that I played on, that wasn't saying much. We continued to get beaten and beaten up, losing big but occasionally winning. I came off the bench for the most part as we had a full complement of semi-skilled players, all of us roughly the same size. Early on in the season, our coach nicknamed me Ted Shred during one of our practices. Or just Shred for short. At first, I loved this nickname, as I thought it embodied my aggressive style, but then I heard that it was also the name of some dude on the Top 40 radio station who was a traffic reporter on a bike or something. That diluted my love of the nickname, but I was still okay with it. It was the first and only nickname I've ever been given in my life, and namesake notwithstanding, it was a pretty good fit for my approach to sports. I remember in one game, I fouled out in three minutes. In another, we played against Brookswood, another Langley school. Interestingly, even though Walnut Grove was seen universally as the snob school, that's how we saw Brookswood. I wouldn't say they were our crosstown rivals, because that would give the impression that we were somehow competitive with them, which we weren't. They had a couple of guys on their team who were skilled and stood at least 6 foot 6 or taller. I realize that currently that's kind of a minimum requirement for a successful basketball team, but in 1994 in Langley, that was unique, and they were killing teams. We knew we weren't making the playoffs that year with as many losses as we'd had, but in one of our final league games, we hosted the Brookswood team, and we were psyched up for the contest. I think it was David looking forward to getting some cheap shots in on Goliath before inevitably being pounded into the ground, which is how it actually played out. They beat us badly, but not without wondering what crazy pills we had taken before the game. I remember one play in particular in which one of our team members committed a really hard foul against one of their big guys, sending him sprawling to the floor. Our bench celebrated the foul like it was a spectacular play, and our player was treated to some high-fives from those of us on the floor at the time. I remember making eye contact with the Brookswood player as he was being helped to his feet and seeing the genuine confusion on his face as he wondered what we were so excited about, considering the score was lopsided in their favor. I suppose he had never had the experience of being the underdog who had a chance to damage the champion, so he couldn't possibly relate to the exhilaration that comes with that chance.

On my particular team, aggression was not just tolerated, it was celebrated, and thus, to be named Ted Shred, and to stand out for that reason, was a real badge of honor for me. I knew I wouldn't be leading the team in scoring any time soon, although that did happen one time--and it was great, but that's another story--so I focused on playing my role the best I could. Toward the end of our season, we played an exhibition game against a club team from Bellingham, Washington. They probably weren't that good ... I just had to delete something because it would have given the story away, but just take my word for it that they weren't that good. Anyway, it was a tough, physical, low-scoring game, as you might expect, given our track-record, and it came down to the final seconds. Their team had been fouled and had a player going to the free-throw line for a single free-throw that might tie the game. I was sitting on the bench, where I had been parked most of the game. At this point, our coach called out, "Shred!" I was shocked that he was calling me into the game. He told me to go out there and do one job only: grab the rebound and/or stop their guy from getting the rebound. I guess that's kind of like two jobs, but they're tied together, so it's really like one job. Plus, it sounds better if the person says, "I have a job for you" than if they say, "I have possibly two jobs for you, but if you do one of them it might be good enough, because the two jobs are kind of tied together."

Anyway, if their player missed and we could get the rebound or stop them, we would secure the victory. My teammates slapped me on the back and encouraged me, as seemingly this was the job for which I had been preparing for through this incredibly long back story. I checked into the game and took my place along the lane. I had the inside position and every advantage to succeed in this crucial assignment. Well, every advantage except one. I couldn't pay attention to save my life. I remember that I was looking at all of the players, our bench, our coach, and the shooter, but I wasn't paying attention when he actually shot the ball. Predictably, he missed the shot, and the rebound came to my area. However, because I wasn't paying attention, the guy I was supposed to prevent from getting the ball squeaked around me and grabbed it. This isn't the worst part. It gets worse. Because it can always get worse. Not only did he grab the ball, he then went straight up with it and scored the game-winning basket right in front of me. I was too shocked to even foul him. I remember that none of my teammates said anything to me afterward, and I remember the pleading look of disbelief in my coach's eyes as he saw me afterward from the sideline. His eyes sent the message, "Really? You had one job to do. There was no way you could mess that up, but you did. How is that even possible?" He didn't need to say it, verbally or nonverbally, because I was already saying it to myself. It's experiences like these that add up over the course of an ADHD lifetime to create the sense of inevitable doom and disaster that seemingly always lurk in the background. When people wonder why I can't just enjoy a success or an opportunity for success, it is because they don't know that for my brain, every opportunity for success is a reminder of a humiliating defeat.

THIRTY-FOUR

IT MUST HAVE BEEN A FLUKE

My high school basketball experience, fun and painful as it was, was also indirectly linked to a brief glimpse into the world of normal people doing normal things. One of my most enduring memories of high school is walking to my Biology 12 class and my brainiac friend Justin asking me if I had studied. "Studied for what?" I asked, because I had no idea what he was talking about. "The unit test," was his answer. I still didn't know what he was talking about--clearly the answer was no. This was my standard answer in high school for any situation that questioned my readiness for tests, assignments, projects, or learning in general. Biology in particular was a struggle in both Grades 11 and 12. I remember in Grade 12, my in-class activities alternated among falling asleep while attempting to take notes, convincing Justin to lend me his pencil so I could throw it across the classroom, and pushing Justin's books onto the floor. What a great friend I was, in retrospect. Justin was one of the first friends I made when I moved to Langley in Grade 8, and he endured the changes in personality that I underwent in high school, from shy wannabe to shy weirdo to shy non-conformist. Our paths diverged in many ways, but he was always nice to me. I wish I could say the same thing for myself.

Anyway, because of a tournament located four hours away in Kelowna, we would be missing a couple of days of school (yessss!) including another biology unit test. Normally this wouldn't have crossed my mind as a thing, but for some reason it was on my radar this time. Remember that kid who tried to make the team but I sabotaged his tryout by accidentally kneeing him in the junk? That sentence does not make me sound like a quality person. Thank goodness we don't hold people prisoner for their worst moments. Well, I guess we kind of do, actually. Both personally and culturally. People can become known as their worst moment or their best moment, which is why we are surprised when people who are famous for doing good stuff then turn around and do bad stuff or vice versa. Anyway, this kid, though he wasn't on the team, still wanted to ingratiate himself with several team members, so when one of my teammates approached him about telling us what was on the exam, he was more than happy to help us out. The reason he knew was because he had taken the test the day before. As basketball players who were going to miss the in-class exam, we were going to have to take the test on our own in the counselling office a day early. This kid had already taken it, so he was able to tell us exactly what to study.

Keep in mind that I had never studied for something in my life, other than the scrambled cramming I had done for my final exams every year, the only thing that had kept me advancing from grade to grade. So what made me study this time? I think that perhaps it was the excitement that came from doing something wrong and the chance of getting in trouble. What a weird way to motivate someone to study and try hard in school. It's not like this kid told me the answers--he just told me what to study. So I studied and came to school the next day and wrote the exam in an office all by myself in the counselling centre. I got 84 percent. You should have seen my teacher's face as he handed the test back to me. His eyes lingered on me with something between a smirk and an expressionless mask. It's weird how much information we can get from eye contact without words being exchanged. It was as if he was saying, "I don't know how you pulled this off, but there's no way you got this mark without cheating." In a way, I guess it was sort of cheating, but not really. Imagine if the teacher had just said in class, "Make sure you study this and that because it's going to be on the test." We wouldn't look at that as cheating. Am I really trying to justify my actions 24 years later? It appears I am. What really stands out from this event, however, is the feeling I had when I got my test back. I felt surprised. Genuinely surprised. I was probably as surprised as my teacher. I remember very distinctly the thought, "This must be what it's like for other students. They study, they learn, they do well." You might think that this experience of cause and effect was enough to turn my school experience around, leading me to see the value of hard work and preparation, revealing that my brain was capable of learning if I could just do the work. If you think that's what happened, then you, like me, must not have been paying attention, because it was an isolated blip on the radar of underachievement that defined my school career.

THIRTY-FIVE

WHAT'S A HOI POLLOI?

PROACTIVE PREPARATION HAS NEVER BEEN my strong suit, except when it came to coming up with cover stories, excuses, or hiding my tracks in other ways. But in responsible, prosocial arenas, my main objective was more accurately described as trying to make chicken salad out of chicken poop in 60 seconds or less. Whether it was last-minute cramming in university, last-minute cleaning of my room, last-chance handing something in before it was too late, or last-chance withdrawing from a course in university before it would count against my GPA, I came to specialize in this kind of breakneck-speed, razor's-edge approach to getting things done. For example, in my Grade 11 English class, we had an assignment where we had to present a poem to the teacher in a creative way. That's pretty broad criteria for someone like me and simultaneously presented an opportunity to get really creative and explore all sorts of ideas and procrastinate on following through on any of them until it was too late to gather the resources to do any of them well. This is what I did, of course. It wasn't until the night before that I quickly rifled through one of my mom's old books from university and found a poem that I didn't hate, something about innocent childhood or something like that, and started thinking of a creative way to present this to my teacher. My final product consisted of a recording of me reading the poem in a very dramatic, over-the-top voice, with dramatic over-the-top orchestral music playing in the background, creating a ridiculous (and, I thought, pretty funny) juxtaposition between the tone of the presentation and the actual content. I scrambled to finish it and handed it in the next day.

My room in Nanaimo actually had a green light bulb. It was the only light in the room, my ceiling fixture, and I convinced my parents that it would be okay for the light in my room to be dark green. When I think back on things like that, I really do appreciate my parents' willingness to let me be weird, because that kind of weird was nothing like either of them. Well, maybe my dad, but in a different way. My dad was weird in that he liked songs like "Dead Skunk in the Middle of the Road" and wearing a bathrobe over a ski jacket on Christmas morning and stuff like that. He was unique and quirky. I made people think I was on drugs. I brought up the light bulb because my memory of recording this assignment was that I was in the dark, in my room, scrambling to be creative, but it wasn't really dark, it was dark green, the color of my light bulb. Anyway, after I'd spent a few days doodling in my journal during my English class, the teacher handed back the graded assignments. He gave me an A. I was shocked. Then at the top of my assignment I noticed a comment that he had written. It said, "When are you going to stop slumming with the hoi polloi?" I had no idea what this phrase meant, so I asked my mom that day when I got home. She was also shocked as she explained to me that it meant that he thought I was really under-achieving in my class, as hoi polloi meant something like commoners or peasants. He was essentially asking me why I was content to be normal like everyone else when I clearly had such potential. His other comments were something along the lines of, "Who else could take such a boring poem and make something so meaningful out of it?" I was sitting there thinking, "Oh man, do I have this guy fooled. He thinks I was looking for deep meaning, but I was just trying to be funny." I guess this was the second thing that stood out to him as earlier in the semester I had correctly guessed that lupicide meant to kill a wolf (only because I remembered that loup-garou was French for werewolf, and I knew that French was a language with Latin roots and that the words that ended in -cide referred to killing and were probably also Latin and made the leap that lup- and loup probably came from the same place). When I correctly answered the question, I remember him looking at me in complete shock, mouth hanging open. He was probably doubly surprised that someone had guessed his pet stumper and that it was *me*, the kid who looked like he probably had a green light bulb in his bedroom.

Another instance in which this particular teacher, whose name I can't quite remember, saw my potential was during a creative writing assignment. I wrote a short story about a paranoid deer hunter who felt that he needed to justify his killing of the deer by concocting a scenario in which the deer were after him and he was only defending himself. It was intentionally ridiculous to highlight how ridiculous his position was, telling stories of deer perched in the trees with rifles at the ready. We had to peer-edit these compositions, and I remember getting mine back from a girl in the class who was not known for her ... brilliance. She had made a few well-intentioned suggestions, but the one comment that stood out the most to me was scrawled in the margin, "How could a deer hold a gun?" I was shocked that the point of the story had missed her so completely. I took the story to my teacher, now knowing that he was a fan and a sympathizer, and pointed out her comment. I asked him if I really needed to change the story just because she couldn't grasp it. He tried to hide his smile in a very professional way and gave me some diplomatic direction about how to make it easier to understand.

That's it, I'm looking up his name. I think it's Mr. Mitchell. That would be weird if I could suddenly remember his name. My old year-book is downstairs right now, I think, but I don't feel like going to look. It's weird how it's such a simple thing, to just go down the stairs and look, and I even really want to know the answer, but the thought of doing it feels like gearing up for some blood-letting. Okay, I forced myself to do it. The book was actually there, and Mr. Mitchell was the principal of the school, as it turns out. The guy who most looks like my memory of the English teacher was named Mr. Anderson. That name doesn't sound remotely familiar to me, but his face looks the same. It's weird how my brain associated the school with the principal's name, even though I had exactly zero interaction with him during the year that I was there. Brains are cool and weird. That sounds like the name of another book that is waiting to be written. One thing at a time.

Thanks to Mr. Anderson's glowing opinion of my language genius, my mom signed me up for Advanced Placement English for Grade 12. This is a funny thing to me. When it comes to my kids' course planning, we discuss it quite a bit and help them decide what would be best, but I feel like I just showed up to find out what classes my mom had picked. That might be partly true, but I also took weight training as an elective, and I'm not sure my mom would have picked that for me. My class lineup in Grade 12 was quite funny: English AP, history, biology, P.E., weight training, Business Ed 10, Art 11, and French 12. It's a funny mix, especially when I examine each class individually. Apart from the typical academic classes, which I barely passed, and the remedial classes, which I barely passed, and the P.E. classes, which I solidly underachieved in while having a great time, there is this lone ranger, English AP. The way the course was laid out was that we sped through the regular English 12 curriculum in the first part of the year and wrote the final exam in January. I got 84 percent on the exam and then dropped the AP portion of the class. Whether I was naturally skilled in the area or not, at that age I simply had no interest in analyzing existential poetry.

I had pulled off many close calls throughout my English class doing things at the last minute and flying by the seat of my pants. I remember one assignment in which we had to create our own myths, using mythical language. About 10 minutes before the class, I came up with the legend of the Tormalapstas, which was a word I'd just made up on the spot. I also made up several other words, including nouns and verbs, and wrote a paragraph of complete and utter gibberish. I got a score of 8/10 (two marks taken off for lateness) and the comment, "Interesting mythical language." Once again, I couldn't believe that I had got away with what I believed to be complete laziness. But my teacher, Mr. Kirsh, saw something in me, like Mr. Anderson before, and rewarded my creativity, if not my work ethic. I repaid him by zoning out in class, staring at the girl across the room from me, continuing to be disorganized and late, and pulling out a miracle mark on the final exam. Then I dropped the course and got myself a spare block, which would have been very handy for getting caught up on all of the courses that I was behind in, but was in fact used for playing with the photocopier in the library. Seriously, for the next six months, during my spare block, I went to the library and mastered the art of photocopying my face and hands.

I discovered that as the little light bar moved across the screen, that was what was being copied, so if I moved the picture (or my face) with the bar, I could create monstrously distorted pictures, such as a picture that started on one side of my face and then rolled over to the other side, or a picture of my hand with really elongated fingers. Words cannot do these pictures justice. I look back on this time and wonder, how did I get away with it? How did the librarian look the other way for so long? How did no one hold me accountable for wasting so much time? When I wasn't creating photocopy art, the only actual schoolwork I did during my spare block was for my art class. Well, technically it wasn't really for the class, but it was art. A lot of it was quite abstract, using words and weird faces, and more than one person suspected that I was a drug user because of the combination of strange and unfiltered stream-of-consciousness content that came from my pencil, pen, and paintbrush. But this creativity was not drug-induced at all. One of the gifts that I had cultivated and developed over the course of my high school life, since deciding that being cool was, in fact, lame, was the ability to almost completely disinhibit my creativity. I wrote stream-of-consciousness stories and poems and drew stream-of-consciousness pictures and said stream-of-consciousness things and wore stream-of-consciousness clothes. It was quite liberating, and I had a great but small group of friends who liked and encouraged this part of my personality. It might have led to a few embarrassing moments, but those were drops in the ocean of the unintentional self-deprecation that was my life. Just because it was uninhibited doesn't mean that I was mindful, and there were more than a few occasions where I left people scratching their heads or avoiding me altogether.

As for my art class, in fact, I didn't do much art in my class at all. I did last-minute, rushed versions of the basic stuff, but there were some things that I just didn't even do at all. It reached a point where, late in the school year, with graduation hanging in the balance, my teacher approached me to tell me that I was not in good shape, grade-wise, and was in danger of not passing the class. Despite my haphazard, disorganized, scattered, and unmotivated journey through school, I had never failed a class. This was really bad timing, as failing this class would mean not graduating from high school. However, my teacher made me a very reasonable offer. She said that she really loved an abstract watercolor painting I had done earlier in the year and that if I would be willing to paint another copy of it and give it to her to hang in the classroom forever after, she would pass me. I immediately agreed and tried my best to copy the original. Even though I thought the second wasn't as good as the first, she was satisfied and kept up her end of the deal. It's weird to think that this was how I managed to graduate.

School had been full of stories and events, only very few of which have been relayed in this book. Some were among the best and worst experiences of my life. I do remember the day I graduated--after I had crossed the stage and was walking through the courtyard at the back of the school, making my way back inside to hand in my gown, a huge smile crossed my face, completely of its own volition, as I realized that I was really actually finished. No more school, no more books, no more teachers' dirty looks. No more late assignments, no more forgetting, no more embarrassment, no more being told that I was underachieving and wasting my potential, no more tests, no more projects, no more deadlines, no more desks, no more classrooms, no more confusion. You might be thinking as you read this, "Wait, didn't he go to university and then to graduate school?" And if you are thinking that, you are correct, but as I was walking across the courtyard that day, you couldn't have picked a fantasy more removed from my reality than voluntarily going back to school. And that's saying something, because my post-graduation life plan was to work and save money, travel to Australia and live on a beach for a year, then come back and move to Seattle with Keith, where we would begin our careers as legends of punk rock and own a skatepark, where we would also live. This is why, when I work with teenagers who are stressed out that they haven't figured out what they want to do with their lives by the time they are 15, I tell them it's not that big a deal.

THIRTY-SIX

HE WAS RIGHT ABOUT ME

NOT LONG BEFORE I graduated from high school, I finally got my driver's licence. You might be wondering what took me so long. After all, someone with my decision-making skills, zest for risk, and general irresponsibility was surely made to drive a 2000-pound death machine through the streets at high speeds, right? Well, that's what I originally thought, too. I turned 16 when we lived in Nanaimo, and like most kids who turn 16, I immediately went out and took my learner's test and got my little slip of paper saying that I was obviously responsible enough to trust with the health and safety of all other drivers, pedestrians and stray pets. I don't remember studying, but of course I must have, because I wouldn't have been able to recognize street signs without looking them up first. Ironically, having been a licensed driver for almost 30 years now, I know what a yield sign and a stop sign look like, but that's about it. And if I do recognize a sign and know what it means, I certainly wouldn't know what to call it. I wonder if that sets me apart from other drivers or if that's normal. It would be scary if it's normal. How do we all not die on the roads? Anyway, I remember the first time I actually drove. Legally. When we lived in Salmo in the 80s, things were a bit more ... liberal, like riding around in the back of a pickup truck or being pulled behind the van on a toboggan or crazy carpet during the winter, or this one time when my dad went big and borrowed the hood of a car to use as a sled so that he could pull up to five kids at a time, and then one of the girls ended up smashing her face on the sharp edge of the hood, resulting in a cut on her nose that somehow, listening to my dad's explanation, was obviously her fault. There was this gravel pit relatively near our house, and I remember my dad letting us occasionally practice driving the car over there, but it probably just meant steering, because the car was a stick shift, and there's no way I could have done that at a young age. When I finally learned to drive with a standard transmission in my early 20s, it was a nerve-wracking gong show, so I don't imagine I had quite mastered it before I was 13.

My first time driving, my dad needed to run to his office to pick up something that he had forgotten (ADHD for the win!) and asked if I wanted to drive there and back with him. It was late in the evening and the roads were likely to not be very busy, especially since this was Nanaimo. I said sure. Now, you have to realize, I had never even driven on our street, let alone navigated traffic lights and lane changes, but this was a classic example of my dad's lifelong philosophy of "It's fine." There were some linguistic variations to this: "It will be fine." "It was fine." "You're fine." While these might seem like reassuring statements--and he was often correct--they also, at times, could have been translated as "Your feelings are invalid. Stop that feeling." In this case, he was wrong. My fears were valid, because I had no idea what I was doing.

I nervously made my way across town, and just as we were getting mercifully close to his office, I came to a four-way stop. In many ways, now that I think of it, this situation was such a perfect metaphor for the ADHD brain, with several thought and behaviour options all arriving at the same time and my brain needing to decide whose turn it was without really understanding the rules. My study of the driver's manual must have been fairly mediocre for this portion of the repertoire, because when I pulled up to the stop sign, I had absolutely no idea what to do. To make matters worse, two other cars had pulled up at around the same time. Seriously? What are the chances that late at night in rural Nanaimo (as if there is an urban part of Nanaimo), on an isolated road outside of town, three cars would all arrive at the same four-way stop at the same time? I asked my dad what I should do, anxiety quickly rising up through my throat and chest. His advice was simple, "Just go." Go? How could I just go? There were other cars there. What if they decided to go at the same time? How did he know it was my turn? What if it wasn't my turn and I went and they were mad at me? What if I crashed and killed everyone? I asked him some of these questions frantically, and he responded with, "Just go!" because sometimes when you repeat the same instruction but with shouting it really clarifies the message. Instead of clarifying things for me in this case, however, it raised my panic to the level that I, the ultra-aggressive, big, muscular, 16-year-old kid, began crying. I was paralyzed. I start-stopped a few times, faking out the other drivers, who probably just thought it was another drunk driver out on the town, before I finally and impulsively just put my foot on the gas and drove out into the abyss. None of the aforementioned tragedies or disasters occurred, but I was really mad at my dad and told him there was no way I was driving home. Not only did I not drive home, but I didn't drive again for over a year.

It wasn't until I was getting close to my tenuous graduation that I realized how pathetic I was for still not having my driver's license. After all, most of the other kids my age had their licenses, and a few of them even had their own cars, including Keith, who had this sweet Volkswagen Beetle that had been lowered and totally suited our collective persona. I decided that it wasn't right that I was approaching my 18th birthday and still didn't have my driver's license, so I began in earnest to practice driving with my mom and dad. I don't really remember those driving lessons, and I don't think I had very many, as indicated by my first driver's road test. Back then, the test was devised that certain infractions were awarded specific amounts of demerits, up to a total of 35. Awarded doesn't quite seem like the right word for a penalty. As long as you had fewer than 36 demerits and hadn't committed any of the cardinal sins that would result in an automatic fail (speeding, running red lights, etc.) then you were free to put the rest of the public at risk forever after. Unfortunately, my lack of preparation showed itself as I garnered 77 demerits and at least one automatic fail (waiting in the middle of the intersection to turn left while really slow people used the crosswalk--you know, something that *all* drivers do *all* the time). Apparently, shoulder-checking was not my forte, but my take on the situation was that the tester was so busy writing down my mistakes that he missed half the times that I did, in fact, shoulder-check. Anyway, he was not nice about it and recommended that I get some driving lessons. I did not do this. Instead I came back about a month later and tried again, this time scoring 35 demerits, right on the nose. This meant that I was literally the most dangerous and neglectful licensed driver that I could possibly be. What a sense of achievement. You might look at this as a terrible score, which the tester did, telling me that while he technically had to pass me, he would *strongly* encourage some driving lessons. However, I looked at it as a great achievement, cutting my demerits down by almost 55 percent. I thanked him for his time and suggestion, got my picture taken, and raced home, almost getting in an accident on the way. But, it was fine.

Did you know that people with ADHD pay higher premiums for life insurance? Did you know that if you are diagnosed after the age of 18, your risk of dying prematurely from accidental death is four times higher than the boring old regular population? Did you know that teens with ADHD are four times more likely to have accidents while driving and are four times more likely to be at fault? Did you know that teens with ADHD are six times more likely to have their licenses suspended for dangerous driving? None of these facts probably surprise you, but I'm happy to say that I defy these statistics. Actually, now that I think of it, I don't really. I was going to say that I haven't had an accident in over 20 years, and I haven't had a speeding ticket in around the same amount of time, but then I remembered that the statistics related to teens with ADHD. The reality is that between getting my license at almost 18 years old and the time I hit 20, I had already been in four accidents, with many close calls, like this one time when I ended up speeding the wrong way down a one-way street in downtown Vancouver at night. Luckily it was so late that there were hardly any cars on the road at the time, so no one died.

My first accident came when I was driving myself and my friend Len home from work in Vancouver (more on that job later). I was rocking out to my Nirvana tape, singing along to the super chill song "Something in the Way," when in the ultimate irony, I rear-ended a woman's BMW that had stopped abruptly in front of me. Of course it was her fault, somehow. I'm not sure how it happened, but it was stop-and-go traffic, and we had been stopped for a while. I was getting impatient, even though Kurt Cobain was keeping me company. I still remember when I found out that he had died. I was in Grade 12 and someone came by my locker and said, "Did you hear that Kurt Cobain is dead?" I don't remember who it was, but I remember that they had a smile on their face because they knew that Keith and I lived and died for Nirvana, and they knew that this would be crushing news, which it was. I felt sick in my stomach, thinking that there would never be another album released. Kind of weird that that was my main concern. Not for the person whose suffering was so great that he saw only one way out but that I would miss out on whatever creative genius lay still untapped in his mind. We had gone to the last concert on Nirvana's last tour to promote *In Utero*, and in retrospect, you could kind of see it coming. While they sounded so awesome at the concert, he looked downright forlorn on the stage. Kurt Cobain had extremely low energy, and at one point between songs, when he was talking, someone yelled out, "Cheer up, Kurt!" to which he replied, "What do you want me to say? Do you wanna rock?" This last line was delivered dripping with sarcasm and irony, and when it resulted in a loud and raucous cheer from the crowd, he just rolled his eyes, shook his head, and started his next song.

Anyway, this hot day in the summer of 1994, his voice was groaning away as the lady in front of me finally started to accelerate. Relieved that I was about to be in motion, I gave my car some gas as well. Then she slammed on her brakes for some reason. Just as I was accelerating. I swear I was paying attention. This was in the days before smart phones, so I wasn't distracted by that, but I slammed on my brakes as soon as I could, and it was 99 percent effective. The problem was, after I had come to a stop I took my foot off the brake for half a second, at which time the car lurched forward and tapped her bumper. I said all of the colorful words I could think of, put the car in park, and got out to survey the damage. The amazing thing is, there was none. In reality, I had barely grazed her car. There was literally not a scratch or a scuff or anything. She was angry, of course, that I had dared to drive on the same street as her flashy BMW with my decidedly non-flashy Dodge Aires. The Aires was the unofficial Leavitt family vehicle, as this was the third one we had owned in three years. Believe it or not, we once fit the entire family into the little car on our way to church because that's how you do things when the law doesn't apply to you because "it's fine." Anyway, she just shook her head and muttered at me in Chinese and got back in her car. I felt lucky to have escaped so easily, but this was only round one with me and the Aires. The next round was much worse.

My first job after high school was basically my first job ever, and it was the best of times and the worst of times. I will talk more about that later, but I mention it now because when I first started there--a warehouse job where I would theoretically be working hard, doing physical labour all day--I was told by my friend's mom, who got me the job, that I would be in the best shape of my life. I looked forward to this, because I was already in really good shape, having played some form of sport almost every day up to that point. Instead, what happened was I spent the vast majority of my money on food, McDonald's, specifically. After working there for some time, I weighed more than I ever had, and it wasn't muscle. However, I attempted to balance it out by going to the gym religiously. I'll talk more about that later, too. You have no idea how many side trails I have resisted the urge to follow in the last three minutes writing this paragraph. I can feel the tug-of-war between my brain's natural state and my Adderall heating up. So far, the Adderall is winning. I just keep telling myself that I will be able to talk about the other later--that it's not now or never--and that if I wait to talk about it, it will fit into the story better. My brain is looking at me with a combination of a smirk and a scowl. I distracted it by checking my Facebook messages.

Back to what I was talking about. Eating lots of food, getting fat, and going to the gym. I signed up for a membership at a gym in downtown Langley called Fitness Unlimited. It was probably about a 15-minute drive, which is funny, because if I had to drive that far now, I wouldn't go. Back then, it was the only real option, so I willingly made the effort. Of course, because of my excellent driving skills, this set the stage for one of the more traumatic things that has happened in my life. So far. There were two ways to get to the gym. One of them involved staying on the main, well-lit and traffic-light-controlled roads, also known as the worst way. The second was driving down a winding dark road with few houses and very little traffic and not one traffic light, also known as the best way. These stupid Facebook notifications keep popping up now, because it's open in one of the 38 tabs that are always open on my computer, so I closed the tab, which sometimes feels like sending one of my children off to war, the parting is filled with such angst. It's like my brain really believes that I will never find that page again and miss out on something life-changing as a result. Anyway, I liked to drive fast down this dark and winding road on my way to the gym, usually singing as loudly as I could to some high-tempo grunge, punk or heavy metal music. This night in particular, I think it was The Offspring. Since it was not only dark and isolated but also raining and slippery that night, I decided it would be a good time to see if I could beat my record for how fast I could fly through this shortcut. Tunes cranked and wipers flying, I sped faster and faster, checking the little digital clock to see my time.

Then I came around a corner and into a relatively straight stretch, leading to more acceleration. As I came to the end of this stretch, the road leaned to the left, and I began to turn. However, a mailbox on the right side of the road seemed to charge straight for me. I panicked and thought I was going to hit it, so I cranked my wheel to the left. At high speed. On a wet road. This little lesson in overcorrection led me to the opposite side of the road, onto the shoulder. Again, the panic led to another overcorrection, and I found myself on the opposite shoulder, where this debacle had begun. Because I'm a big fan of repetition, I figured one more overcorrection ought to do the trick, and I ended up heading for the other side again. By this time, I had figured out what I was doing wrong, so instead of steering like a mad man, I just braced myself as my car went off the road, into the ditch.

When I say it like that, it sounds so simple, but in fact, there was so much more to it. The ditch was probably at least five or six feet deep with at least three feet of water along the bottom of it. As my car hit the muddy water, which sprayed and slapped against my windshield, the car began to rotate on its horizontal axis, and two distinct thoughts occurred in my brain. The first was how similar this was to when Luke Skywalker crashed his X-wing fighter on Dagobah in *The Empire Strikes Back*. It was like I was in the movie. The other thought was, "Dad is going to be so mad." I've often reflected on this over the years. As my life flashed before my eyes, my defining thought in that moment was about letting my dad down. Even though the word my brain used was 'mad,' I knew that it was more than that, deeper than that. It's like when you're having a dream and you're talking to someone, and even though they don't look anything like the person in real life, your brain knows who they are. The word was mad, but the feeling was disappointment. It was always curious to me that this would be my thought in that moment, because my dad was not really an angry guy. He wasn't known for losing his temper, nor was he prone to guilt-tripping or saying things like, "I'm disappointed in you, Son." So where had this thought come from? I realized years later that my dad was the standard by which I judged myself. This was not because he had set himself up as the standard in any way. The fact was that my dad was a rockstar. He was gifted with intelligence, humor, leadership ability, communication skills, and athletic ability. Everywhere he went, he was a leader and was admired and recognized for his unique talents and gifts. And he was my dad. I don't think anyone needs to tell a young boy that he's supposed to turn out like his dad in order for him to feel it. I realized this when my own son, Luke, at the age of 3, leaned up against the kitchen counter and attempted to cross his ankles in a spot-on imitation of my own standing position. I realized that because I was his dad, he was innately drawn to identify with me. My dad had never said that I needed to skip a grade in school like he did. He never said I needed to be a starter on the basketball team. He never said I needed to be the funniest guy in the room. He never said that I needed to be more spiritual or more knowledgeable or more likeable. He didn't have to. I knew it without him having to say it. However, because I struggled with my undiscovered ADHD so much, I struggled with all of these things that seemed so natural to him. I had come to believe that I would inevitably disappoint him. And so, as my car plowed upside-down through the mud and weeds in the bottom of a ditch in North Langley, my most vivid thought was of how my dad would react when he found out that, once again, my judgement had led to disaster.

As I lay upside down in the car, I tried to take some deep breaths and told myself to just stay calm, that everything was okay and that I wasn't hurt. Just as I told myself that everything was okay, I felt the water start to trickle through my hair. Oh yeah, I was upside-down in a car in a ditch full of water. That's not okay. I abandoned my calm, trading it in for some panic strength. The driver's side door was wedged into the bottom of the ditch, so escape was impossible in that direction. I crawled to the other side and tried to open the passenger door. It was also wedged into the side of the ditch and would only open a couple of inches. Well, I knew that there was no way I was going out like this and channeled my survival rage, using it to bend the door frame and expand my escape route by a few inches. I managed to squeeze through, out onto the wet, grassy field above, from which I looked down at my car. Without any delay, I walked up the driveway of the nearest farm house, knocked on the door, and asked to use their phone. This was many years before cell phones were a thing, which is probably good, because I would have been speeding and texting at the same time, for sure. I called my mom and told her what had happened and where I was, and she reacted calmly and said she'd be right there. In my weak defence, the homeowners said that this kind of thing happened all the time on that corner.

I made my way back out to the car, but by now there was a large number of vehicles that had stopped and pulled over, and people were down in the ditch peering through the narrow gap I had crawled through and calling to see if anyone was in the vehicle. I felt incredibly sheepish as I called out that it was my vehicle and that everything was okay. The guy who had gone down into the ditch looked up at me with some relief on his face, but mostly annoyance, and again, despite my near brush with death or devastating injury, the emotion I felt most prominently was shame as I attacked myself for putting these people in this situation. Someone suggested that I turn the car off, as I had left it running in my mad scramble to escape. So, I went back in through the narrow opening to turn the keys, and I kid you not, this part of the story actually happened. Well, I mean the whole thing happened, but my crashing a car while driving like a maniac doesn't really require me to assure you that I'm not lying. However, when I went back into the car, the radio was playing. It was tuned to an oldies station that played music from the 50s through the 70s, and it was playing one of those dramatic songs about a boy and girl who stole daddy's car and went for a joyride. As I grabbed the keys, the singer said in a dramatic voice-over, "No one knew why the car overturned in flames that night...." I had to laugh to myself at the incredible coincidence of it all. In both of my accidents, music had provided the punchline. The police, fire and ambulance all arrived, and I sat in the back of the ambulance feeling more embarrassed than anything.

My only injury was a bruised thigh. I wasn't even wearing my seatbelt that night, but in the end, that might have been what saved me. If I'd been unable to unbuckle for some reason, I would have been stuck upside down in the car as it filled with water. As it was, I walked away unscathed. After my mom came and picked me up, she drove me back home, and I lay down in front of the TV and finished watching the Seattle Supersonics basketball game, as if nothing had happened. Nothing else was even said about it. My dad wasn't home that evening, and I have no recollection of his reaction other than that he was calm and told me that I would have to pay for all of the repairs out of my own pocket because he didn't have collision insurance on the vehicle.

Okay, one more story involving cars and poor decision-making. It even involved the same car, which took a real beating in the short time I drove it. To be honest, I'm getting kind of bored of car-crashing stories, but I think they're important because they knit together so many elements of what made me me. Impulsivity, recklessness, feeling stupid and full of regret, and in this case, crying for attention. We used to play basketball up at the church once a week, and I'd invited one of my friends from school to come. After the games were finished, my friend and I, along with two of my younger brothers, piled into the car and prepared to go home. Of course, this was also a prime opportunity for me to show off, not only for my friend but for my brothers, as well. I knew that they looked up to me, and I wasn't about to waste this chance to demonstrate the coolness that comes with having a driver's license, so instead of simply pulling onto the street, I decided to have a little fun in the wet parking lot of the church. Luckily, everyone else had already gone home, so the parking lot was empty; otherwise, this story could have been a lot worse. As I sped around the parking lot, cranking the wheel and slamming on the brakes, nothing seemed to quite achieve the rush I was looking for, so I decided to up the ante. The parking lot had an upper and lower section, and connecting them was a narrow lane, wide enough for only one car to pass through at a time. On the side of this lane was a small lawn and then a steep 30-foot bank that dropped down onto the road below. This lane was also a curve. So, of course, with my lessons in speeding around wet curves tucked safely out of memory, I raced towards this curve and realized too late that I was going way too fast and tried to steer out of trouble. Instead, the car skidded sideways (finally!), and I smacked my wheels into the curb, popped up and landed all four wheels on the narrow lawn--chewing it up and spraying it out as I bumped over the curb again--and landed back in the parking lot.

We yelled and laughed and thought it was the greatest thing ever until I noticed that the car was leaning to one side. I put it in park and got out to inspect. I saw three troubling things. First, I realized how close I had come to driving the car over the bank, where we would have crashed into the road below. Second, I had a flat tire. Third, the flat tire had not come from puncturing the rubber but from smashing and bending the rim of the wheel against the curb. This was a much bigger deal than I'd thought. I had to sheepishly poke my head back into the car--where my eager audience awaited to applaud—and tell them that I had no idea how to fix the car. I realized I was going to have to face my dad and tell him, once again, that I had brain-farted my way into another memorable situation. As I found the spare tire in the trunk of the car and jacked the car up to replace the damaged wheel (once again in the pouring rain), my mind raced with possible scenarios that I could tell my dad that ranged from complete lies to slight exaggerations and minimizations. As I dropped my friend off and drove my brothers home, I decided that dishonesty was the best policy and that complete fabrication was my ally. I parked in the driveway and went in the house, guts twisting with the knowledge that my performance would need to be impeccable. As I mounted the stairs to my parents' bedroom, where I knew they would be waiting since it was relatively late at night, I steeled my resolve and rehearsed my story. Much to my surprise, however, when I entered the room and saw my dad sitting up in bed reading, I found myself blurting out the entire story, the truth unaltered. "Dad, I was driving like an idiot in the church parking lot, going too fast around the corner, and I smashed the car into the curb and wrecked the rim." I was shocked to hear myself say it. I was a prolific liar, after all, and this would have been fairly easy to cover up, but for some reason, I didn't do it. Perhaps somewhere in my unconscious brain, I had learned my lesson that my dad was a safe person. Fortunately, he didn't dispel that belief when he calmly asked if anyone was hurt. When I said no, he said that I would need to pay for the damage and thanked me for telling him. I actually felt more elated than stupid as I bounded downstairs to the kitchen, feeling grateful that things had gone better than I could have imagined.

THIRTY-SEVEN

BARELY WORKING MAN

My great joy in graduating from high school was short-lived as within a few weeks I found myself carpooling with my friend Len and his mom to work in Vancouver at a furniture warehouse owned by Len's uncle. While this technically wasn't my first job, it was my first real job. My first actual job was when I was 15 years old. My neighbour had been working at the corner store up the street and was quitting for a better job and asked if I wanted to take over at the store. My duties would include stocking the milk cooler and sweeping, mopping, etc. I said sure and was excited about the prospect of being a working man. I hated it. It alternated between extreme boredom and extreme stress, and my boss was not a patient man. I routinely helped myself to snacks off the shelf and milk from the cooler and did the minimum, but I felt justified in doing so because he was such a jerk. I remember saying to him one time that there wasn't much point in mopping the floor until the end of the night because then people would just walk over the wet floor with their dirty shoes and make it even filthier than before I mopped it. Without listening for even a second, he insisted I mop it right there and then. So, I dutifully obeyed and proceeded to sweep and then mop the entire store. This particular day was nasty outside, like a rain and windstorm kind of day, and so, of course--as I had predicted--people kept tracking dirt in from outside all over the floor that I was mopping. By the time I got to the end of the floor, it looked worse than before I had started. Just then, the boss popped by for a visit and got mad that the floor was so dirty and demanded that I do it again. I'm sure I did it, because I didn't want to get fired, but this is one of the reasons I had no problem helping myself to some cheesy snacks and washing them down with some illicit chocolate milk. I worked there just long enough to raise the money to buy an electric guitar from my guitar teacher and then quit. I don't remember if I handed off the job to someone else or just walked away, but it was worth it to get the guitar. I later sold the guitar to my friend Keith for the same price I'd paid for it because ... never mind. I'm not going to talk about rock and roll right now.

As I was saying, I was in Len's mom's car on the way to work at my first real job. Len's mom worked on the showroom floor, and Len and I worked in the warehouse as all-purpose grunts. One of the things I did the most when I was there was watch the clock. I started at 8 a.m., and I remember one time starting a task and then walking over to check the time on the warehouse clock and being disgusted to see that it was only 8:04. I was already counting down the hours, four minutes into the day. I knew it was going to be a long one. Even on a good day, it was a long day. I lived in Walnut Grove, a suburb of Langley, which is about a 30-minute drive to Vancouver on a sunny Sunday morning. During the week, however, it takes much longer than that. Although I had my driver's license, I didn't have my own car, so I got to work with a combination of public transit and carpooling. Eventually, Len's mom's shift time changed and didn't line up with mine anymore, so I was a full-time rider of the bus and Skytrain. This required me to catch the bus at 6:30 a.m. in Langley, ride it to Surrey, get on the Skytrain and ride it for 30 to 40 minutes, then get off, catch another bus, ride it for 15 minutes, and then get off and walk for 10 minutes. I did this for minimum wage. I spent many of those transit rides fighting the overpowering urge to sleep, but I'm proud to say that only once did I actually let my head rest on the shoulder of a stranger, who politely notified me of the violation. I had seen it happen many times to others and judged them for being fools, so when it happened to me, that same judgment was self-reflected. Of course, it had nothing to do with being a fool; sleep is a biological drive that can only be resisted for so long. We can starve ourselves to death, but we can't sleep-deprive ourselves to death. I know 6:30 a.m. doesn't sound too early, but you have to realize that I often didn't go to sleep until 2 a.m., so by the time I was tucked in the traveling sardine can known as the Skytrain, with its gentle rocking and dim lighting, staying awake was a lost cause.

I got to work before the warehouse actually opened, so I had to sit outside on the pavement for 20 minutes. This wasn't so bad during the summer months, but during the winter, when it was -20°, those were some of the most painful moments of my life. I remember shivering so badly I felt like my bones were going to break. You would think that after having this experience more than once I would make a point of dressing warmly, maybe even spending some of my hard-earned money on a pair of gloves, but instead I just wore the same thin coat and shivered painfully. What I spent my money on was food. I ate at McDonald's, sometimes three times a day, and every morning for breakfast I ate a bag of taco-flavored tortilla chips, drank a litre of milk, and sometimes threw in a Mirage chocolate bar for dessert. So, in a way, I was working on building a layer of insulation in the form of a significant increase in bodyfat. But needless to say, budgeting and planning were not my strengths. Only now as I enter my early forties am I beginning to form good habits in these areas, which is typical for ADHD folks. I have read numerous times about the social and emotional developmental delays in ADHD brains but have always reviled against it, thinking of myself as someone who was mature, but as you read through this compilation of attention-seeking and impulsivity, it becomes apparent that I am, in fact, a very typical ADHD person. Recently, I came across an article that claimed we are not only delayed in maturing in those areas but that the ceiling for our development is actually lower than for most people. Again, I resent that statement and question the research, and then I realize that in my early forties, I'm still working on the same things I was working on as a teenager with my first job. Yes, I have come a long way, but I definitely struggle more than the average person.

Oh man, we had more adventures at that warehouse than I think you would have the patience to listen to. We raced on our pallet jacks, talked subtle trash to the drunken truck drivers, and were excessively rude to the entitled customers who spoke no English. We broke furniture, made beating sticks out of cardboard tubing and packing tape, and climbed and ran through the warehouse racking like characters in a video game. We muttered under our breath at the managers, knowing our jobs were secure as long as Len's uncle owned the company. One time Len had a nosebleed, and rather than elevating his head and pinching it off like he was supposed to do, he leaned over a Styrofoam cup and kept blowing his nose so that he filled half the cup with snotty blood, which we then took outside and threw at the wall, creating a nice-sized blood spatter that looked like someone had been shot there. It was next to what appeared to be some poop but was, in fact, a chewed-up Mirage chocolate bar. The chocolate bar was there because I had noticed that I was getting really fat and decided to try an experiment where I would take a bite of the chocolate and then let it melt in my mouth but instead of swallowing, I would spit it out. I wanted to know if it would be just as satisfying. That way I could have the taste but not the calories. It wasn't just as satisfying. Which is weird. The taste comes from the sugar and fat and all of the chemicals that appear in the chocolate bar, but the feeling of satisfaction comes from actually ingesting the substance. So those movies set in the future that show people eating a pill that simulates a three-course meal would actually result in a lot of people feeling very unsatisfied. In fact, that is kind of what is going on right now, though not necessarily with food. People are tasting connection, tasting pseudo friendship, but not actually ingesting the bond that comes with meaningful relationships. This leaves people feeling predictably unsatisfied. I just realized the parallel while I was writing that story out.

Anyway, I remember one particular day in the warehouse that stands out from the monotony of make-work projects that were forced upon us by the young assistant manager who resented our free reign. A customer had called from out of town to reserve the showroom model of a dining room hutch that had glass shelves. The customer didn't want the showroom model, but it was the only model that we had in stock, and it was probably discontinued or something and thus the last resort. It had to have been discontinued because, otherwise, why would someone drive from out of town to buy the floor model? Was there a hutch emergency and the person needed something desperately? I don't know. These kinds of issues were above my paygrade or my level of caring. All I know is that my job was to go out to the showroom and put the hutch on a dolly and wheel it back into the warehouse for safekeeping until the customer arrived. Why is a dolly called a dolly? I mean, it couldn't be any more different from a doll, so what's the history there? I'm looking it up.... That was an unsatisfying search. The answer seems to be that we don't know. The best explanation was that it resembled the word "trolley." Also, it could have been used as a synonym of servant, because many young female servants were referred to as Dolly. I'm sure you don't care.

Anyway, I went dutifully to the showroom, found the prized hutch ... I'm resisting the urge to look up the origin of the word hutch ... and put it on my dolly, then started wheeling it back to the warehouse. All was going well until I opened the warehouse doors. This was accomplished by pressing a button that would open the doors and hold them open for a very brief period of time. Probably the best thing would have been to ask someone for help, but I kind of have this thing about asking for help. I hate to do it. It runs in my family, probably both the origin of my dad always insisting that everything is fine and also the result of that insistence. Anyway, I really could have used the help on this occasion. Instead, I pressed the button, raced back to the dolly, hefted the load and tried to quickly wheel it through the open doorway. All was going as planned, and my efficiency and independence were on display for all, when I hit a little bump. It was a small strip of molding separating the carpeted showroom from the concrete warehouse, and at the speed I was travelling, it was just enough to jar loose the precious glass shelves of the hutch, which I had efficiently neglected to remove before wheeling it away. The end result was a mighty crash of glass as the shelves all fell from their precarious perches and shattered, one on top of the other, on display for all to see. The customer was already on the way to the store from a location over two hours away, and this was before the days of cell phones, so the poor salesperson just had to wait for the inevitable squirmy conversation when he would explain that the purchase, for which the customer had travelled so far, was, in fact, garbage. At least he could blame it on someone else. I could only blame it on myself.

THIRTY-EIGHT

WHO NEEDS SLEEP?

As I MENTIONED, during this phase of my life, sleep hygiene was not really one of my priorities. As a matter of fact, hygiene in particular was not a priority, but that's another story. Okay, fine, one time in high school, Keith and I decided that we needed dreadlocks, and we decided to accomplish this the old-fashioned way: by not washing our hair until it was matted in fine punk-rock dreads. I held out for almost a month. My hair was so nasty that I could mold it into pretty much any shape and it would just stay like that. One day when I was looking at myself in the mirror, at my dark peach fuzz sideburns and chin scruff and my disgusting hair, I thought to myself, "This, more than anything else, is why you don't have a girlfriend, you moron." So, I washed my hair and shaved my sideburns and chin, and then I still didn't have a girlfriend. Anyway, as I said, when I was working after graduation, I made a habit of staying up too late, getting up early and catching a few Zs on the morning commute, sometimes to the chagrin of my fellow passengers. One night, however, I took it to extreme lengths.

My old high school was hosting a fundraiser for something and planned to have a basketball marathon, a game that would run for 24 hours. I don't know what the money was for, and I don't think I contributed any cash to the cause, but it was a good opportunity to go back to my high school and feel like a full-grown man. By this time, I was sporting a nice two- or three-inch punk-rock goatee, and I walked around like I owned the place. Okay, maybe not quite, but it does feel good to go back to your high school and feel above everyone who is still stuck there. I really just wanted to play some basketball, since I was obsessed with the sport. Plus, there were girls there that I liked. Anyway, my original plan was to go and play a few games, stay into the evening, and then go home, since I had to work the next day. But sticking to plans ... not really my thing. So, I played more than a few games, found myself still there at 2 a.m., and decided that I would just stay the whole night, keep playing basketball, and call in sick to work in the morning. Then the thought occurred to me that I wouldn't be able to call in sick from the school, for no other reason than that they would hear basketballs bouncing in the background of the call and know that I was faking it. So, I decided that I would go home and call. This decision was made around 6 a.m., after I had stayed up all night. So I went home and changed my mind again, planning to get cleaned up so I could go to work after all, as Len and his mom had planned to pick me up that morning and I wouldn't have to ride the bus and train. So I came home, got changed and ended up staring at myself in the mirror again. I know that sounds like I spent a lot of time checking myself out in the mirror, but when I wasn't making kissing faces, I was usually counting the millions of zits that occupied my chin, cheeks, and forehead. Anyway, I was staring at myself in the mirror, and somewhere in my sleep-deprived brain, I decided that goatees were overrated. So I shaved it off. Then Len and his mom came and picked me up, and off we went for a day's work in the salt mines. It wasn't until I got to work and felt the cold air on my chin that I noticed something was different. I felt my chin with my hand and realized the gravity of my impulsive decision. Keep in mind I was an 18-year-old kid, and growing a three-inch goatee was a significant investment in time and patience. And it was gone in an instant. It hit me what I had done, and I felt sick to my stomach.

Now, this job had plenty of down time and lazy days, but those were interspersed with days and hours of intense activity and pressure. Usually this came from massive trucks that needed to be unloaded or loaded, and sometimes both. I remember one time I was so angry with my boss that I went into a trailer, lifted a sofa-bed over my head by myself and carried it out of the truck, slamming it onto the ground in what can only be described as hulk-rage. Man, did that feel good. Anyway, this particular sleep-deprived day was one of those crazy days, as luck would have it. And by luck I mean Satan and his angels. We were back in the far wing of the warehouse, unloading a truck driven by a man who resembled Jack Skellington from *The Nightmare Before Christmas*, except he had a large, protruding pot belly. Sometimes the drivers helped us with the loading or unloading so they could get out of there quicker, but not this guy. He liked to come in and just chill while we worked. Anyway, it was while unloading this dude's truck that I realized the wonderful potential of sleep-deprivation for mind-altering. I kept catching a glimpse out of the corner of my eye of something but could never quite capture it until one time my sneaky side-eye caught sight of a tall, thin elf, straight from Santa's workshop, if Santa's workshop had been located in the bowels of hell. He had long, gangly legs that hung over the edge of the box on which he sat, and he was watching me but wouldn't make eye contact. It startled me that there would be an evil elf in the warehouse, and it took me a few minutes to realize that this wasn't really happening and that perhaps it would be a good idea if I lie down for a few minutes. Which I did. I didn't sleep, though, and part of me was really hoping that I would see him again, or something even better. Alas, I was disappointed, because I just got my second wind. I ended up staying up until 11:30 that night, bringing my total sleep deprivation to 37 hours. I wish I could have put that on my resume, because it wouldn't be much longer before I would need to be looking for a new job. See, even though my friend's uncle owned the company, he wasn't *my* uncle. I'm sure the manager had complained loud and long about our antics in the warehouse, including the time when Len had brought his pellet gun pistol to work and we'd made a cardboard cut-out of the manager, propped him up in the parking lot, and shot it repeatedly. I remember that at one point, Len was chasing me behind the building shooting at me, but I'm sure it was provoked in some way. Anyway, I think his uncle's solution for the Ted and Len problem was to divide and conquer. He promoted Len to a sales position and offered me a transfer to the main warehouse in Coquitlam, working with a bunch of dudes I didn't know. The alternative was for him to lay me off so I could find another job. I checked my options: continue in a job I hated with people I didn't know for minimum wage, or stay home and collect employment insurance while pursuing a new and exciting career as a rock star? I will take the second door please.

THIRTY-NINE

NOT REALLY A CAREER ARC

MORE LIKE A LINE

Now, about that rock star thing. As I have mentioned previously, I got my start in music pretty young. I was signed up for piano lessons along with three of my brothers and enjoyed banging away on our old piano. When I say old, I mean it was really old. We originally had this terrible little organ that had only half the keys of a full-size piano and these little buttons that you pressed to make chords, I think. My Grandma Leavitt was a piano player (I always hate to say the word pianist), and she wanted us to develop our musical talents. I didn't know I had any musical talents. So we signed up to go and see Mrs. Schreiner at her little house in Fruitvale every Saturday. One of my favourite things about piano lessons was that while we were waiting for each other to finish, we were allowed to watch cartoons on a little colour TV in her front waiting room. I don't remember what I watched, but I remember that I felt like I was in Disneyland when she said we could do it.

As you can probably imagine, I was not the most conscientious piano student. After learning some basics, I set out to create my own compositions, which were very simple and very repetitive and very fast and very loud. Luckily our house was big. Oh yeah, my grandma and the old piano. So one day, my grandma made a proposal to my parents that she was going to be getting a new piano and that we should trade our beloved organ for her old piano. Of course, she had no use for the old organ, but it was probably just her way of making it seem like it wasn't the charitable donation that it was. I remember thinking that Grandma got kind of ripped off in the deal, as we now had an upright grand piano with genuine ivory keys that was built in the 1890s, and she had a crappy little organ with weird buttons. So, yeah, piano lessons. I think the teacher tried to teach me about notes and time signatures and finger positions, but it just went in one ear and out the other. This was not particularly noticeable, however, as it turns out I was a natural. Again, though, I didn't know I was a natural until I was eavesdropping on a conversation between my mom and Tim's mom. They were talking about another friend who had begun taking piano lessons and was really struggling to learn. I blurted out, "What's so hard about it? It's easy?" Tim's mom replied, "Of course it's easy for you, Ted. You're a natural." What's interesting about this exchange is the layers of emotional response that I had. On one level, I felt embarrassed that I had butted into the conversation, impulsive as a toddler, and said something so arrogant. On another level, I felt proud that she had thought I was really good at something. On another level, I was surprised that someone thought I was good at something. On another level, I was confused that someone thought I was good at something but that no one had thought to mention this to me before, to let me in on this confidence-building secret. I also felt like her compliment was backhanded, combining rebuke and praise into a single delivery. Finally, because of this backhanded delivery, I felt angry at her for confronting me in a way that I felt was rude and undeserved. I wonder if all 11-year-olds experience emotions this complicated and layered, and if they do, I wonder if they know that they do, and if they do know, I wonder if they can name them-- because you might be thinking that all of these layers have appeared with the benefit of hindsight, coloured by the bias of experience and artifacts of revisionist history. You might be right, but as I recall this event, these waves of emotion that wash over me don't feel like revelations or new information; they feel familiar.

Anyway, this musical ability must have been recognized by Mr. Yule, my Grade 7 teacher, because he recruited me for the band that I talked about before. In Grade 7 our school also put on a production of a musical called *Sky Happy* about the history of man's attempts to fly. Seems like a bit of an odd choice of topic, but whatever. The main character's name was Rock, also an odd choice, but in context it made sense. The play began during caveman days and required Rock to wear a leopard-print caveman costume, complete with giant, leopard-print furry slippers, because that's what cavemen wore. Obviously. Why am I telling you about Rock? Because my good friend Garnet and I were both cast as Rock. One of us for each performance. This means that I have a photo of myself, mid-puberty, singing on stage wearing the aforementioned caveman costume. I have to believe that I was self-conscious about it, but it was the 1980s, so the costume probably wasn't a big stretch, wardrobe-wise. So even though Garnet and I were really good friends and hung out together at and outside of school, since we both had the same part, a natural rivalry was created, at least on my insecure end. I needed people to know that I was the real Rock. My voice was a bit lower than Garnet's at the time, so some of the higher notes were a struggle for me, leading me to sing an octave lower in parts. I also remember one particular song where I was adopting a jazz-style swing rhythm to my vocals (like a lounge singer), and Mr. Yule put a stop to the rehearsal. I was confused about what I had done wrong and waited nervously for his feedback. He pulled me aside and said that while my jazzy stylings were a sign of my obvious talent (again, news to me but also a shot of confidence), the backup choir was not able to adapt to this twist on the arrangement, so I should probably just keep it simple so they could follow along (another shot of confidence, but this was quickly followed by self-criticism as I scolded myself for not being able to predict this outcome). At one point, however, during the many hours of practice and lead-up to the production, I had done something else to get the girls mad at me, especially Jennifer. She threw a zinger at me that was totally out of context, completely unrelated to the topic of conflict, and clearly designed to hurt my feelings. As we argued, she spat out one last thing, "Oh yeah, and Garnet is a way better singer than you!" Ouch. But I don't think he was. Whether he was or not, the remark stung and left a mark. Even worse, continuing what would become a decades-long trend of near misses, the local newspaper covered the play's performance, complete with pictures and a write-up, but they came on Garnet's performance night instead of mine. So, I got no glory outside of the audience that was there during my performance, which was, by all accounts that I care about, just stellar.

Following our family's exodus from Salmo to Langley, we were given the option to continue with piano lessons or quit, since we wouldn't be able to afford for all of us to keep going. I took the first chance and quit that thing like a good habit. I use that expression because it seems much easier to quit good habits than bad ones, and this was really easy to quit. Not being harassed to practice against my will, not having to perform with gut-wrenching anxiety at the year-end recital, not having to take up my valuable fantasy time with real-life talent development, that sounded like a win to me. The performance anxiety in particular was a welcome subtraction from my life. I could stand on stage, play the drums, sing, act, and generally attract attention, but when it came to sitting down at a piano in front of an auditorium of strangers and performing a piano piece with shaking fingers, I felt like I was being asked to walk the plank. And I wasn't alone, either. All of us had anxiety-initiated meltdowns prior to performing each year, with Mike, of course, setting the bar highest as he not only resisted going on but actually fled out the back door to the parking lot. I'm not sure how my dad cajoled us onto the stage every time, but I doubt it was with validation.

After piano was abandoned and Mr. Yule's band was left behind, my involvement in musical pursuits experienced a sharp drop off. We did get a drum set for Christmas one year, and we have a great photo of my grandma playing the drums on Christmas morning. I think that kind of rowdiness is found consistently throughout my family history. I come from a long line of pioneers, adventurers, farmers, and risk-takers. Also known as the natural pursuits of the ADHD brain. This is one of the things that led to the delay in anyone noticing that ADHD was causing problems in my life, because everyone around me was similar. More on that later. I played the drums in the basement for a while, but with no band and no audience, my interest waned significantly. My time became more occupied with weightlifting, wrestling, and trying to fit in. It wasn't until Grade 10, when I was at my friend and neighbour's house, that I picked up his dad's old guitar and found that I could now play bar chords, which I had never been able to master when I was 12 years old. This new ability, combined with the attention that it got me from those in the room, led me to regain an interest in music. I asked my parents if they would buy the guitar for me, and they agreed. It was actually a true piece of crap that was probably bought from the Sears catalogue. The strings were terrible, and they hurt my fingers really badly, but I had wandered into a cloud of motivation, and nothing would dissuade me from my pursuit of neighbourhood glory. The first song I taught myself was "Ghostriders in the Sky." I honestly have no idea how I even knew that song existed. I just picked it out by ear, mostly while my family was on a vacation. I remember repeatedly going to my mom to ask her how the next part of the song went and then proudly coming back to show her what I had figured out. Remember, I was 15 at the time, not 8. It seems odd that as a teenage punk with popularity on my mind, I was so excited to show my mom what I could do. It also reminds me of one of the most cringe-inducing memories of my life, when I took my older brother's little ghetto blaster (which is really a questionable name, if you think about it) and forced my parents to sit in the living room while I pressed play and performed a song and dance interpretation of Michael Jackson's "Bad." When I picture my dad watching this spectacle, I feel like crawling under a rock, but I also love him so much for not saying anything negative about it.

Anyway, Grade 10 was also the time I met my best friend Keith, and—as I mentioned before--we both joked about becoming rock stars. Because I could play the drums, I sold my electric guitar to Keith, and we borrowed a drum set from a friend and played the most obnoxious garbage you could imagine. I mean, I'm serious. Listening to us makes me want to punch me. After this introduction into stardom, just as we were about to take off, I had to move to Nanaimo with my family, scuttling our dreams. I asked my parents for a 12-string guitar as they continued the tradition of trying to soften the emotional blow of moving by distracting us with presents. They bought me the guitar, and as much as I loved the rich sound of 12 strings, for some reason I took six of them off. This was where I rocked out by myself under the green light of my bedroom. When I found out we were moving back to Langley, I was primarily excited for the chance to get "the band" back together. By now, Keith's older brother's friend Scott had joined the fray as a drummer and wannabe lyricist and singer. Keith and I both played electric guitar, and we had no bass player. We usually jammed at Scott's house, since he was older than we were, already out of high school. When it was just Keith and me, we jammed in my basement or Keith's garage. We came up with some real sweet tunes, including one about a girl in our school that we loved to hate, another one about a friend of ours named Jeremy, making fun of his wardrobe and attempts to be cool for the ladies, and my personal favourite about the Millennium Falcon. It featured this award-winning lyric: "Han's in the front with Chewie by his side. You can say what you want, but this baby's got drive." Grammies here we come.

Looking back, I feel a bit bad for Scott. How badly must he have wanted to be in a band to agree to be in a band with us fools? He kept trying to write song lyrics that were meaningful, but Keith and I just shot them down time and again, calling them cheesy. My lyrical style was heavily influenced by Kurt Cobain and Beck, both of whom were known to write words that fit the rhythm, rather than write for a message. This worked well for me as my stream-of-consciousness style fit rather nicely into meaningless songs. In the end, the band couldn't survive because Keith had no rhythm and Scott ran out of patience.

We found out that we had a gig, which is a weird word. Why is it called a gig? I'm looking it up.... Once again, the internet has let me down, and no one seems to know. Anyway, someone was tricked into allowing us to play at their party or something like that, and we decided we'd better tighten up our performance. We met at the pizza restaurant where Scott worked and hung out until the place closed. Then we brought in our equipment and set up, feeling like true punk-rock superstars, jamming in a pizza restaurant at midnight. It all came to a crashing halt, however, when Keith kept missing his cue. Keith would be the first to tell you that back then he had almost no rhythm. So we kept our songs simple and used almost no technical music terminology, mostly because we didn't know any. So, Keith kept missing his cue, and finally Scott, exasperated beyond containment, yelled, "Geez Keith, you've got to be able to hit that!" Keith was probably embarrassed by repeatedly screwing up and was not in a place to be getting this kind of feedback, so he started packing his stuff up without saying anything. Since he was my ride, I started packing my stuff up, too. I didn't agree with either of them. I thought Scott was right but that he should have kept his comments to himself. I also thought that Keith was being too sensitive, but he was my best friend, so I didn't want to argue with him. So we drove home. What could be more punk rock than that? Quitting the band and ditching the gig.

I didn't speak to Keith for about a week, I was so annoyed with him for ruining our chance at glory. It wasn't until a girl I really liked found out that we weren't talking and threatened to not talk to *me* again until I patched things up that I found the humility to call him. All I said was, "Hey, it's Ted," and he interrupted me to apologize for the way he'd acted. He said that he had felt so embarrassed about it that he was afraid to call me. I told him that all was forgotten, and who needed Scott anyway? We could just find another drummer. This launched a series of really awkward encounters with awkward people and a lot of close calls with marginally talented dudes. Of course, who were we to talk? We were not great, but we had a very specific style we wanted, and no one seemed right. We even made a poster to pin up at the music store, with two main criteria. We wanted someone who could play fast and specified that we wanted "no stinky losers." Unbelievably, this poster didn't generate any leads. Somehow, however, despite our terrible marketing skills and being really unappealing, we found the most amazing dude. He was the perfect fit for us. The first song he played with us, we just about hugged each other for joy. He was amazing, so skilled, so technically sound, so fast, and totally seemed to get what we were going for. Even better, he was a couple of years younger than we were and would do whatever we said without question—and we could shoot down his ideas and he would just take it. As I write this, I wonder, what happened to that kid who won all those citizenship awards in elementary school? Then I remember all of the times I hurt people's feelings, betrayed friends, and generally acted like a jerk and think that perhaps this punk persona was not a role I was playing, after all, but a genuine part of me. I stop short of saying "the real me," because I think it's not healthy to have a static sense of self, anyway. I think all of us have multiple facets that can be displayed depending on the situation. I think this is especially true with ADHD folks as we are often described as social chameleons. I mentioned earlier that throughout school I was friends with such disparate groups that the only thing they had in common was me. The thing was, I was never faking when I was with these groups. I could talk with the smart kids and play sports with the jocks and sound like a burnout with the stoners and smash stuff with the punk delinquents, and all of it was me.

As for my career as a rock star, it was as short as my attention span. We played two gigs worth talking about ... actually it was three, but I only really remember two ... nope, now I remember all three. The first one was some sort of group bill, and I have no idea where it was or how we got it. I think it was through Todd, the drummer. It was such a thrill to move from the garage or Todd's bedroom to an actual community hall and see people moshing to our stuff. I really don't like the word mosh. It seems like such a stereotyped view of the 90s punk-rock grunge scene, and I also think it doesn't really capture the aggression that exists in a mosh pit. Anyway, reflecting the diversity in our intrapersonal interests, our set list ranged from slow and mellow to extremely loud, angry and fast. My singing could not easily be classified as singing, but I didn't really have a good voice for the genre, anyway, which was frustrating to me. I couldn't sing very high, but a bass voice doesn't really carry over the instrumental chaos. I also didn't have a very good Cobain-like scream, more of an angry-dad yell. I remember after that first gig, even though it was in a run-down community hall in rural nowhere, I felt like we were really doing it!

Our next gig was at a grad celebration for the class a year younger than us. We knew and were friends with some of the kids who were on the organizing committee, and when they had the idea of having a live band at the party, one of them suggested us. I'm not sure that the rest of them had any idea what they were signing up for. We weren't a cover band—we only played original stuff, and most of it was punk or really heavy smashing music.

One of the songs was about a girl I liked who just happened to be a part of this grad class and the organizing committee. I won't tell the long story of our almost relationship, but it felt a bit like a teen movie to sing this punk-rock anthem about how awesome she was, almost a year after we had stopped talking to each other. It was like this really dramatic, scripted moment where she realized how I really felt about her, but then it had this very anticlimactic moment where she smiled at me, made some conversation, and then we continued to not speak to each other anymore. Looking back years later, with the benefit of hindsight, experience, and an education in mental health, I realize now that she was experiencing much of the same as I was. She couldn't accept that someone really liked her, because she didn't really like herself, and the closer I got to getting past her walls, the more threatened she felt. The bigger the gesture, the bigger the push-back. I hope she eventually dealt with that and found happiness. It's a really frustrating thing for people who are trying to help us. All of their efforts to encourage us and reassure us only serve to have the opposite impact. Trust me, if it's frustrating for the helpers, it's just as frustrating—if not more so--for those being offered the help. I wish it would work. Anyway, the looks we got at this gig were priceless as people could only really laugh in disbelief at our intensity and how out of place it was at this lighthearted celebration of graduation. In a way, I valued that impression almost more than I valued people liking our stuff. I wanted to be seen as different, weird, not caring about what other people thought, which is of course quite paradoxical in that I cared a lot about people thinking that I didn't care at all. I needed them to know that about me. This has helped me many times in my life and career to connect with people who are insistent that they don't care what anyone thinks because they are practically wearing a billboard that screams, "I'm okay, right?"

The next and last gig we played together was not for a few years. In the meantime, I had learned a lot about myself and my life and had grown up a fair bit (relatively speaking), but I'll go into that later. At this gig, there was a battle-of-the bands type thing going on at a local community centre in Langley, and once again, we knew someone who was on the organizing committee who offered us the opportunity to relive our glory days. We jumped at the chance. We got our old set-list together but had to use a new drummer because Todd had long ago left the group to pursue drugs and electronic music, so guess who we found to fill in. None other than Scott, our one-time friend and then nemesis and now friend again. He had got a lot better but was still nowhere close to Todd, but we only planned to play a few songs, anyway. At this particular gig, there was a band called Gob that was supposed to be the headliner. They actually had a record deal and a few videos that played on Muchmusic (the Canadian equivalent of MTV). We were scheduled to go on right before them and were getting psyched/nervous as our time approached. Then we were thrown a curveball when someone from Gob told the organizers that they had to go right away because they had somewhere to get to. I imagine the place they had to get to was anywhere but this particular gig with these particular hacks. In any event, they got their wish and bumped us out of our place on the bill, but this had the unintended effect of pushing us to the last spot, which looked to late arrivers as if we were the headliners. It also meant that many of Gob's fans who had shown up just to see them play stuck around to watch our short set and inadvertently gave us our biggest crowd ever. Many of these people watched our set with a look of confusion, however, as they probably wondered who we were and how we got to be the headliners. We were received well, but that was it for me as a punk-rock musician. I found that it just didn't quite have the same payoff for me as it had when I was younger, and Keith and I were up to different things in our lives and had different priorities that made getting together and jamming very difficult. In a way it's the classic tale of what could have been. Guys meet in math class, dream of punk-rock stardom, have very little talent, make poor music, play bad gigs, decide it's for the best to break up, and then spend the next 25 years talking about how fun it was. I kind of like that story arc.

FORTY

SPIRITUALLY SCATTERED

AFTER HIGH SCHOOL, as you might have gathered, I lacked direction. In a sense, I had goals in mind, but they were a tad unrealistic, given my inability to stick with anything, exercise self-control or overcome my hidden anxiety enough to find a decent job. I bounced around, making bad decisions and going down dead-end roads. Skateboarding, playing music, and dreaming of glory were fine through high school, but as I entered chronological adulthood, I definitely felt like I was missing out on life. Before I go further with that, let me give you some context. I am a member of the Church of Jesus Christ of Latter Day Saints, also known by the nickname, Mormons. I was born and raised in the church and always went. We were taught the principles of the religion in the home, and our family tried hard to live them as best we could. I don't want this story to distract from the rest of them (how's that for irony), but I think it's important that you know that about me because so many of my experiences and the formation of my self-concept came from living in a religion that has defined expectations and requires more than a passive commitment to ideals. Think, for example, how it might impact someone who believes that his standing with God is impacted by his diligence in following His teachings but whose brain is incapable of consistency. Think of someone who belongs to an organization that connects worthiness with the willingness to resist temptation but whose brain struggles with impulse control. Think of a culture that tends to lean toward perfectionism and keeping up appearances and how that might be experienced by someone who is publicly very imperfect and often tells more truth than is socially desired. The dissonance that I experienced as a Mormon growing up believing these things to be true but struggling to live them led me to begin a process of rejecting my faith during my teen years. I rebelled against my parents and the leaders of my local congregation. I found fault with their reasonable guidelines and attempted to ease my discomfort by convincing myself that it was all just made-up garbage. Those of you who are reading this who are not religious might agree with me on that point. My parents remained patient with me, seeming to know intuitively that I needed to push back and find my independence and make my own mistakes and learn things the hard way. What made this process all the more painful was that my dad was a leader in the church for as long as I could remember. He was not just a leader, though, he was a bit of a legend. He was charismatic, well-spoken, hilarious, and totally followed the rules. He was all of the crazy fun parts of my personality but didn't seem to struggle with toeing the line in the church. Not only that, I was constantly compared to him with that curse word, potential, thrown around liberally. People did not intend to make me feel bad, I'm sure, but that was the impact. It was just another way that my dad seemed to have set the bar unattainably high.

Being a Mormon was also another thing that set me apart from my peers, as if I needed something else. I couldn't watch the same movies, listen to the same music, make the same dirty jokes or find them funny, and "dating" was off limits until I was 16. This made for some serious repressed energy as there were girls who liked me and "asked me out" in that Grade 7 way, but I always had to say no. This was a constant source of frustration for me as a young teen. I don't want to portray a negative image of being raised as a Mormon. It just made things harder for me. In the church, there are many expectations, and I was someone who never dealt well with expectations. One of those expectations is that when Mormon boys turn 19, they will serve a mission for the church. This means that we are expected to fill out an application and send it off to church headquarters in Salt Lake City, where church leaders assign a mission to us and then send back a letter telling us where and when we are expected to leave. We do not have a say in where we go, other than whether we are going or not.

As you can imagine, young Mormon men serve missions for a variety of reasons, not the least of which is cultural expectation. Many of them serve missions because they sincerely believe the church's teachings and want to spread the news to the world. Some go because they want to see a different part of the world or experience a different culture. These poor boys are often disappointed when they find out they have been assigned a mission in southern Utah or Toronto. Many of them go because of the social stigma that would be there if they didn't. I must say that the church culture has changed considerably in this area, but it still has a way to go. People in the church are generally more understanding of individual barriers to serving missions, such as social anxiety, depression, or not having a solid belief in the teachings. For me, though, there was so much pressure to go, and much of it was not subtle.

My uncle was also a leader in the church, and it seemed that as I approached my nineteenth birthday, all conversations with adults centred on whether or not I was going to go. That might not be an accurate description. The adults' position was not one of curiosity or understanding but generally one of prescription and direction. I was supposed to go. I should go. I needed to go. As you have also gathered from my story so far, I have a fairly strong don't-tell-me-what-to-do reflex. This reflex combined with my self-doubt and feelings of unworthiness to create a solid defense mechanism of defiance and refusal. Eventually, I refused to even discuss the subject and made it clear to anyone who wondered that I would never, ever serve. In the meantime, I kept jamming with my band, hanging out with Keith, and trying out some drugs that I was promised would expand my mind and allow me to fully express my creativity. For the record, they did not do that. Marijuana made me laugh one time, and then it just made me paranoid. I tried mushrooms a couple of times with absolutely zero results, while the people around me seemed to be getting good value for their money. It's probably a good thing that these experiences where underwhelming because I was desperately looking for something to take me away from the intersection of failure, underachievement, frustration, and hopelessness, and if drugs had helped, I probably would have just kept going until it ended badly. As it was, I just sat idling at that intersection, with frustration growing every day.

I remember one time coming home late at night after another potential gig for the band had fallen through, leaving me and Keith going through our usual routine of sitting at McDonald's on a Friday night exchanging an increasingly exasperated flurry of "What do you want to do tonight?" "I don't know. What do *you* want to do?" until we gave up and parted ways. Because my dad cared, he waited up for me. He had previously threatened to kick me out of the house because of my negative attitude, rudeness, and unhealthy influence on my younger brothers, but my mom had talked him out of it. He had recalculated and instead wrote me a letter telling me how much he loved me and how he really hoped I would remember who I was and what I had been taught, and that I would live accordingly. This letter had planted seeds in my mind that had begun a process of re-evaluating the path I was on and where it was leading. This particular night, I remember slumping down on the loveseat opposite the couch where he was sitting in his bathrobe. Tears rolled down my face as I told him that nothing ever worked out the way I wanted it to. Ever! It wasn't fair and I was getting sick of it, but there was nothing I could do about it. He then gave me some of the best advice that I've ever received, saying, "Ted, the issue is that you are a world-class high-jumper who is trying desperately to be a sprinter. You are meant for one path but insist on forcing your way onto another one. As long as you continue to do that, you will continue to feel this way." I didn't argue with him.

Through the influence of some other important people in my life at the time, I kept in contact with the church, attending services on Sundays and occasionally other activities, but also keeping a distance from the teachings and full acceptance. I won't go into detail because you probably aren't reading this book to learn about my spiritual awakening, but eventually I'd had enough of struggling against what God seemed to want from me and for me and lowered my defences, agreeing to go on a mission. My dad was in a leadership position in the church at the time. He literally hugged me and then went downstairs to his office to start filling out the application. In the Mormon church, they don't ask you where you want to go; you ask them if you can go. If the answer is yes, they send you either to where you need to go or where you are needed; usually it works out to be both. It's a bit like a really meaningful raffle. You don't have to buy a ticket, but once you do, the outcome is not determined by anything you have any control over. I then had to break the news to Keith and Todd, because we were still rocking and rolling on a regular basis, and leaving for two years would probably cramp our style. Because Keith is a wonderful person and a great friend, he was disappointed that I would be leaving but also totally supportive, saying, "If that's what you need to do, then you better do it. I understand."

Four months later I found myself in the Missionary Training centre (MTC), ready to embark on a life-changing adventure. My first task, though, was not to cry when saying goodbye to my parents. I'm not sure why I set that as a goal, and after I accomplished it and they drove away, I really regretted playing it cool and tough. I had received my assignment, and I was going to be serving in Atlanta, Georgia, learning to speak Vietnamese because those were the people I was assigned to work with. Keep in mind that my only experience with Vietnamese up to that point was hearing my Vietnamese friend Cliff's mom yell at him, so I was a little intimidated by the idea that after nine weeks of language training, I would be ready to not only carry on a conversation but actually talk about important things. I remember that first night, after I had met my partner, Elder Wright, moved into my little dorm room and had some good unhealthy food to eat in the cafeteria, I sat down on my bed to begin writing in my journal. As I did so, I added up the number of days I had left: 730. The number stared back at me like the diagnosis of a debilitating disease. I suddenly felt the weight of what had been a five-month-long impulsive decision. I immediately began to cry. What had I done? Why was I here? There was no way I was going to last that long. What was I thinking? These were the thoughts that rocked me off to sleep that first night, but things got better the next day.

I had a good bunch of mostly like-minded missionaries in my group in the MTC, and we had a lot of fun, but we didn't really focus a lot on the rules. When people outside the church hear how strict a mission is, they often think that the church should lighten up a bit, but you have to realize two things: 1. We volunteered for the job, and 2. When you have 50,000 boys and girls across the globe aged 19-23, it's necessary to keep the leash a bit tighter than usual. Anyway, we had lots of fun, and we were learning the language pretty quickly. At least some of us were. I always had a good ear, and my musical background was handy since Vietnamese is a tonal language, meaning that a word can have totally different, completely unrelated meanings depending on the tone with which you say the word. In English, we tend to ask questions with a rising tone at the end, but in Vietnamese, if you use a rising tone, you change the meaning of the word entirely. It definitely took some getting used to, but we had good teachers and they gave us a good system, so we progressed pretty well.

On top of the hours and hours of language training every day, they were also trying to prepare us for dedicated missionary life. They taught us how to teach and how to talk to people, and they taught us the teachings we would be sharing with the world. At one point, about six weeks into this adventure, one of our instructors, Anh Loc, stopped the class because he had something to say. Now, keep in mind we somewhat tortured this poor guy who was teaching at the MTC while attending university nearby. We would intentionally say things wrong, we would joke around constantly, and we even came up with a fun little game that he never caught on to. Because we were so rowdy, he instituted a rule in the class that you could only speak if you were holding the hacky-sack. It was like the conch in *Lord of the Flies*. If you wanted to say something, you raised your hand--he would toss you the hacky sack, and then you could speak. Someone (Okay, it was me), came up with the idea that we would never actually catch the hacky sack when he threw it to us, but we would always make it look like we were really trying to catch it. It was so fun, and we stuck with it for quite a while. This was just one of the ways that we gave him a good-natured hard time.

Anyway, this one day he stood at the front of the class and told us, "Guys, I have to say, I have been teaching here for a while now, and I have probably never had a class that learned Vietnamese as quickly and as skillfully as you guys." We interrupted him to congratulate ourselves, and when the noise had died down, he then added, "However, in all of that time, I have probably never had a class that was less spiritually minded." This was not a compliment. It stung a little bit, and I remember thinking, "Oh yeah. That's why we're really here. How could I have forgotten about that part?" After that, we decided to try harder to be more mature, but as you are probably aware, maturity isn't a decision or an event. It's a developmental process, and it takes a while, but we did do better for the short time that we had left.

After nine weeks of this training, we were ready to be sent out to our assigned field. The MTC is located in Provo, Utah, in the heart of Mormon country, and we were very sheltered during our time there. Nothing but language and missionaries and Mormons as far as the eye could see for nine straight weeks. When my traveling partner (Elder Peacock) and I landed in Atlanta, I felt like I had teleported straight to Babylon, and my senses were jarred. The first thing I noticed was there was something weird about the skyline. After a few minutes, I figured it out. There were no mountains. Not even one. I had grown up in places where mountains were a ubiquitous part of the horizon, if not part of my actual daily life, but as the song says, I never really knew how much I appreciated them until they were gone.

I neglected to mention that as a Mormon missionary, you are assigned a partner, or companion, by the mission president, an older man who supervises the missionaries in the area with his wife. The mission president is the older man. Not the companion. The companion is a young person like yourself. When you first get to the mission, your companion is known as your trainer, and it is his job to show you the ropes, teach you the rules, and bail you out when you have no idea how to speak the language, which you quickly realize is the case as soon as a real live person starts talking to you. My trainer was Elder Broadbent. All male Mormon missionaries are referred to as Elder, by the way. It's not just a remarkable coincidence that all of my companions had the same name. He and another missionary, Elder Baillie, had come to pick us up at the airport (You are never supposed to be out of sight or sound with your companion, unless you are in the shower or otherwise using the bathroom), and it was good to see their friendly faces. The comfort of familiarity wore off quickly, though, with this exchange:

Elder Baillie: "Are you guys hungry after a long day of traveling?"

Us: "Man, so hungry!"

Elder Broadbent: "So you guys want to go get something to eat?"

Us: "So bad, yes!"

Elder Baillie: "Well, we sure can, as soon as each of you has contacted someone."

In Mormon missionary language, contacting someone means trying to strike up a conversation about religion with a stranger. For the stranger, being contacted means being interrupted or annoyed. As soon as Baillie gave us this challenge, I felt weak in my legs. The tambourine-banging, school-rock-band- drumming, punk-rock-living, fire-starting, vandalizing maniac who was never short on words or opinions was actually terrified at the prospect of getting real with a stranger. At least I wasn't alone, because Peacock had gone just as pale and silent as I was. We had a long train ride ahead of us on the MARTA, which is Atlanta's large light-rail transportation system. We both stood there, completely paralyzed, avoiding eye-contact with anyone for what felt like forever, until some mercifully curious woman asked me, "Is that your uniform or something?" She was referring to the fact that all four of us were wearing dark suit pants, white short-sleeve dress shirts and dark ties, with matching black nametags on the shirt pockets. After she broke the ice, I instantly felt comfortable explaining who we were and what we were doing there. She had a few more curious questions that I answered, and we had passed the first test. For my prize, I nostalgically ordered a McChicken sandwich at the nearest McDonald's after we got off the train, only to discover that McChicken sandwiches in the United States are quite disgusting. That might sound like a generalization from one sandwich, but I've tried repeatedly, and I can honestly say I have never had a good McChicken in the U.S. I don't know why. Maybe because food laws are different down there and the chicken is even less real than it is back home, but I have learned my lesson and given up the quest.

Anyway, Broadbent quickly set out to teach me the ropes. It's funny because we seemed to be very much alike, which worked for us and against us. We had some good times, and he did body-check me through a wall in our apartment one time when we were wrestling with each other, but he also patched the hole. Mostly, though, I felt like he was just impatient with me. Because, of course, he was. He was a lot like me. He was also 19 years old, had been on his mission for about nine months or so, and was given the responsibility of training and babysitting an overconfident, lazy kid who was also inse-cure and defensive and homesick. That's a hard enough job for a full-fledged parent, let alone a fellow teenager. I didn't have that perspective at the time, though, and my self-confidence began to decline rapidly. I had some good advice from a Vietnamese man who saw me at a social gathering and asked me in English, "Why aren't you talking very much?" I told him that I couldn't understand anything people were saying, and I certainly didn't know how to say anything myself. He validated my feelings and then told me to carry a notebook—that way if someone said something that I didn't understand, I could write it down and later look it up in a dictionary. If I then used that word or phrase in a sentence a few times the next day, I would learn the language in no time. Emboldened by his advice and support, I started filling notebooks at record pace, and my language skills took off to the point where after only two months of training, I was assigned to a new companion, one who had only been out a month or two longer than I had. He was not super happy that my language skills were better than his, but as far as I know, I never made mention of it. I didn't have to. The Vietnamese people have a strange sense of politeness. They would have no problem at all telling you to your face that your Vietnamese was terrible or that you were fat, but they were very reluctant to tell us that they were not interested in hearing what we had to say about religion. This led to a lot of awkward conversations in which it was quite apparent that they had no interest, but they insisted that they did.

Anyway, I eventually overcame my fear of annoying other people, and we walked and biked through the slums and ghettos of Atlanta like we fit in. Except we didn't. In the neighbourhoods where we lived and worked, we were often the only white people for miles. This was a unique experience that I don't think a lot of white people encounter. For the first time, I felt judged for my appearance. I felt helpless to change people's opinions of me, even though they were based on something someone else had done wrong in the past (or present, to be honest). The racism was extreme in Atlanta, and it flew in both directions. I hated it. I wanted people to know that I wasn't like that and that I never had been. One of the ways I tried to do this was through basketball. I had become much better at basketball after high school, although that's not really saying much, and I was a decent athlete. In Atlanta, you're never far from a basketball court, and whenever we were out walking around in our white shirts and ties, I would take the opportunity to get in a game. We found that this was a great way to break down walls and show people that we were friendly, normal dudes who just wanted to talk about stuff. However, it was also against the rules. Mormon missionaries are on the clock 24/7. The only exception to that is Monday, during the day, which is know as Preparation Day, or P-Day. During that day, we were supposed to do our laundry and grocery shopping, write letters home to our family or friends (this was in the days before email), run other errands, and maybe, if we had time, see some of the local sights or play some sports.

Basketball was a P-day ritual for many missionaries, and I saw it as harmless to play outside of P-day, especially in areas where the locals were not terribly friendly. However, not all missionaries saw my reasoning, and it came to the mission president's attention that I was not following the rules. Of course, this is just one of the rules that I wasn't following, but none of them were particularly egregious, and if I was back home, not living as a missionary, they would have been considered normal daily teenager stuff to do. However, this mission president was not very understanding. He called me into his office, lectured me about obedience, and warned me to shape up. I was not impressed by how unimpressed he was with me. Defiance-protocol activated. My dad was notified by the mission president that I was on thin ice, leading to a pretty scathing letter from him, reminding me that my family was paying for me to be on this mission and saying that I was out there not taking it seriously--and that I needed to straighten up and fly right. I did not want to read this letter, and I certainly did not want to listen to either of them.

I had a lot of unsanctioned fun on my mission, like the one time I was having a serious wrestling match with one of the three other missionaries who lived in an apartment. He was 6'4" and over 200 pounds, and he was going to play college basketball after his two years were over. Elder Roberts was lots of immature fun, and he reintroduced the word "yo" into my vocabulary, as in "What are you doing, yo?" He was intentionally being very white while saying something more commonly heard from our black neighbours. Unfortunately, he wasn't my companion. My companion was a white boy from Utah whose efforts to come across as urban were not tongue in cheek but quite genuine and, therefore, quite embarrassing. Man, I could tell some stories of close calls walking around the streets of inner-city Atlanta with a white wannabe homeboy. Anyway, the area I was serving in was very racist, and I didn't like it there at all. We had white members of the church telling us to avoid certain areas and refusing to go into certain housing projects with us. One older guy who we were riding around with was bragging about his emergency preparedness (something many Mormons obsess over) and said that the most important part of his stockpile was his AK47 rifle. We thought he was kidding, but it turned out that he wasn't. He was deadly serious.

In hindsight, it might not all have been driven by racism but by a recognition of the established invisible boundaries in the area, decades in the making. As missionaries, we were naïve to that history, and so we would blindly go wherever the people were. I remember one time waiting for a bus outside a particularly bleak housing project, and some young people came up to us, staring at us as if we were exhibits in a museum. "What are y'all doin here?" one girl asked us. When I tried to explain what missionaries do, she interrupted to make her point more clearly. "No, what are y'all doin' *here*?" I answered that there was no reason not be there. She then asked if we were trying to get ourselves killed. She was alluding not only to the fact that this was a violent, crime-ridden area, but that it was especially dangerous for white folks. We heard this kind of thing all the time, so we kind of laughed it off. They wandered off shaking their heads only to return about 20 minutes later. "Y'all still here?" she asked with awe in her voice. "Y'all crazy."

Anyway, Elder Roberts was also a white boy from Utah, but he was self-aware enough to know to make fun of himself for being a fish out of water, something that won him credibility in the city. After serving and rooming together for only about six weeks, my prayer was answered and I was transferred to another area, deeper in the city. For our last night in the apartment together, Roberts and I decided the best way to celebrate was with an impromptu wrestling match. This match was going really well for me until he slammed our 420 combined pounds up against the wall and I felt it give way behind me. As we staggered away from the scene, we looked in shock at the hole that was roughly the shape and size of my torso. We were due to be transferred the next morning, which meant that our apartment would be inspected. How could we hide the damage? Interesting that that was our first and only consideration. We didn't even think about telling the truth. We only thought about covering it up. Roberts came up with a genius plan, taking pages out of several church magazines and taping them up to the wall, creating a makeshift wallpaper out of church posters and pictures. We ironically and joking called it *The Wall of Truth,* and it served its purpose as we passed our inspection the next morning and were transferred without anyone ever mentioning it to us. That apartment was widely considered to be the nicest one in the mission before we moved in there, but by the time we left, the place was crawling with cockroaches and featured the *Wall of Truth* along with another smaller hole in one of the bedroom walls from when I spear-chucked a plunger at Roberts, which he ducked and dodged just as the handle pierced the wall with deadly force.

As you can imagine from this small sampling of action, it wasn't long before I was in the mission president's office again being read the riot act. At this point, I told the mission president that I just wanted to go home, if it was all the same to him. I had just passed the halfway point of my two years, and I'd had enough. I'd had enough of the judgment, the racism, the rules, the loneliness, the structure, and the lectures, and I just wanted to go home and not have to worry about it anymore. I then asked him for his opinion on whether I should go home or not. His answer perfectly summed up the reason for my feelings. When faced with the opportunity to empathize, comfort, guide, and care, he instead grimly stated, "Well, I think it would be a pity if you followed up one stupid decision with another one." That was all I needed to hear to know that my mind was made up. Now, you have to understand that this was really against the grain. People don't serve half a mission unless they get sick or something terrible happens--or they break the really serious rules and get sent home. I was *choosing* to go home. I was quitting. When my dad and uncle heard about this, they called me on a conference call, imploring me to stay and stick it out, to give it another try. My uncle offered to get on a plane and fly to Atlanta to meet with me, but wouldn't you know it, my mission president said that was against the rules. I then called my mom and talked to her, and after getting off the phone with her, I felt more than ever that I needed to leave and be back, safe at home.

The next day, I was on a plane, heading back across North America, excited to reunite with people who liked me. Also, I saw Larry King in the airport in Chicago during a layover. He was coming up the escalator, and he looked old and wrinkled and the same as he did on TV, which is weird, because don't people usually wear tons of makeup on TV to hide their old wrinkliness or other imperfections in their appearance, because normal, imperfect people really don't want to watch other normal, imperfect people on TV? So, why did he look the same in person as he did on TV? Either he wasn't wearing makeup on TV, or he was wearing makeup in the airport. Anyway, that has nothing to do with this story. It's funny, when I look back on this day, how clueless I was to my family's experience of the same events. My parents had celebrated (with relief, I'm sure) my turn-around from wayward son to dedicated missionary, and I had not lived up to their hopes and dreams. I'm sure they tried to be happy for me when I came smiling out of the international arrivals gate at the Vancouver airport, but inside they must have felt very conflicted. They would have felt that I was missing out on a great opportunity and might even have wondered how they would explain my premature reappearance to their friends at church. I, however, was oblivious to their feelings and experience and just felt overjoyed that I was home, back with people who appreciated my presence. Sometime later, I heard someone say that at times in life, we all need to be "warmed by the fires of home," and I think that described my experience perfectly.

We drove in two separate vehicles to a pizza restaurant, where everyone ate with a mix of happiness, confusion, and awkwardness. No one was really sure what was going on except me. I was looking forward to resuming my normal, pre-mission life. My dad, however, had other plans. He was confused about what had gone wrong, about how I had left with such promise and how that promise had fizzled out. He spent the next day asking me questions and trying to understand the sequence of events from the time I'd arrived in Atlanta until the time I'd left, and as the conversation progressed, it became clearer to me what the issue had been. I can't tell you how validated I felt to hear my dad describe the mission president in uncomplimentary terms. When he talked about how rigid and inflexible he was and how it contributed to my struggles, I felt like someone was actually listening to me. Then he made an interesting proposal. He suggested that I be reassigned to a different mission for the remainder of my time and said that if that mission turned out the same way, then I would know that missions just weren't for me. However, if the new mission was better, then I would know that the issue in the other mission was the president. I agreed to give this experiment a try.

He asked me where I would want to go, and for some reason, I suggested Tacoma, Washington. I've never understood why I chose Tacoma. It was a three-hour drive from my front door in Langley. I could have chosen a big city like Dallas or Los Angeles or any number of places, but I chose lowly Tacoma. As I think of it right now while I'm writing this out, I think it must be that I still needed to feel the warmth of home and family and found comfort in being so close to them, even if I never saw or interacted with them. So, after spending the weekend at home, I was dropped off at the new mission and met the new mission president. My dad's gamble paid off in some ways, because the new mission president was awesome. My behaviour and maturity were no better in Tacoma, and in some ways were even worse, but the new mission president was spectacular in his ability to be patient with me. He was grandfatherly, relatable, fun, funny, and forgiving. When I stepped outside the lines, instead of punishing and lecturing, he listened and validated and then guided me back. One of the most profound experiences I had with him was when I had gone to see him to tell him about a rule that I had broken. We talked for quite a while, and he told me that the next time I had the inclination to make the same decision, to please call him and talk to him first. This was revolutionary for me. However, that wasn't the experience that I was referring to. As we shook hands and I headed for the door of his office to leave, he said, almost off-handedly, "You know, I think it's possible that you might suffer from some depression." It was like a flash of light had pierced the darkness of my mind, and the feeling of relief that washed over me was subtle but intense. The best way I can describe it was that this insight felt familiar, as if I had always known it was there but had never had the words to articulate it. When he said the word 'depression,' it connected the dots for me, and in an instant, I saw not just the missteps of my mission but of so many misadventures before it explained. This was my first experience with a mental health label, and it brought such relief to me that it is no wonder I gravitate toward such labels in my own work with my clients. This mission president was no mental health professional; he was a lawyer who had struggled with depression in his own past and could recognize its signs in me.

I'd love to say that from that point on things got better, but of course they didn't. In the Mormon church, missions are often described as the "best two years of your life," but for me they were the hardest, the darkest, the most taxing, the most revealing, and the most disappointing years of my life. There were times when I was going from house to house, trying to tell people about the happiness of believing in God, that I would go back to our apartment at night and wish I was dead. I would stand on the rooftop of our building and gaze out at the city lights and wish I could go to sleep and not wake up. Then the next day, I would drag myself out of bed, put on my white shirt and tie, and do it all again. Then, gradually, toward the end of it all, something shifted in me, and I began to like being there. To this day, I don't remember what it was that changed, but maybe I was just maturing. Whatever it was, I went in to see the mission president for a routine meeting, prepared to tell him that I would like to extend my mission by an extra month. Instead, he told me that he thought I should probably go home a month early. I was shocked. I felt like I had just turned a corner and could finally see what it was all about, and now I was going to have to leave? I was disappointed as I left the meeting, knowing that I would only have six weeks left instead of the usual 12, or my hoped-for 16, but as those six weeks progressed, I began to see how inspired he was to make that decision for me. I was so ready to be done with being a missionary. I was ready to go home and get a job and move on to the next phase of my life. This time, my homecoming was fantastic. Not only was I thrilled to be home and see my family and friends, but they were equally happy. The first time, my own happiness was not enough to cover everyone, but this time, our shared happiness was more than enough, and the feeling of peace that came from surviving my darkest two years was worth it all.

FORTY-ONE

GOING NOWHERE SLOW

ONE THE FIRST things I did when I got home from my mission was watch some movies. I don't even remember what. My friend Len, whom I had worked with at the furniture warehouse, had a connection at a video store, which is a really funny way of saying that his dad worked at a video store. I think I called him "a connection" because I've been binge-watching spy shows on Netflix--because I want to, okay? Anyway, because his dad worked in a video store, he received advanced copies of new movie releases for him to view in order to decide whether to order copies or something like that. If you think about it, isn't that really putting a lot of trust into one person's individual taste for movies? What if he was a hipster snob and willed himself to dislike popular movies and instead only chose abstract arthouse and minimalist "films"? Wouldn't that cut into the bottom line of the video store? Or what would it say about the guy if the video store had a higher-than normal proportion of low-budget action movies with buxom ladies on the cover? Actually, I don't imagine that would cut into the profits very much. What would it have been like to be a video store owner in the early 2010s? Is that what you call that time period? The 20-teens or 2010s? Is that even when video stores started to go out of business? If you owned a big chain of video stores, I suppose you would probably have had smart people who could have forecast that kind of stuff happening, but if you just owned a little independent store, then it might have caught you by surprise, and then all of a sudden no-one was coming to your store to look at your low-budget skin movies, and you'd have to go get a real job selling cell phones at a kiosk in the mall or something.

Anyway, Len's dad was that guy, and he didn't send me a bunch of dirty shows, but now that I think of it, a high proportion of them were violent. Actually, now that I remember, there was a stack of videos at Len's house, and I got to choose from the library, and I chose mostly violent shows. Nothing like showing the spiritual growth of my mission than choosing violent gangster movies. That first week home I probably watched close to 30 movies in the basement by myself. They were not all created equally, that's for sure. It reminds me of when Keith and I used to rent movies every weekend when we were younger. We would rent one decent-looking movie and one that was guaranteed to be a B-movie disaster. The worse the better. They were hilarious to watch for the first 30 minutes or so, and then the sheer horror and boredom would usually overtake us and we would eject the tapes. I can't remember the last time I wrote or said that phrase, and my kids will probably never say it in their lifetimes. I remember one time Keith and I rented the movie *Papillon,* and even though there are probably some who would consider that movie wonderful, we found it painfully boring. We got it in our heads that night that we would not be defeated, though, no matter what, and forced ourselves to watch it to the end. I remember at one point almost writhing on the ground in the agony of disinterest but vowing to conquer the movie. We did it, too, lasting to the bitter end. Ah, those were much simpler times, but it was also the kind of hollow existence that led to my crisis that landed me on my mission, from which I returned two years older but not much more mature, as attested by my week-long movie binge.

To bring my life full circle, I even got a job at the same furniture store that I used to work at with Len before my mission. This time, however, he was employed on the sales floor, and I was the warehouse grunt. Without my partner in pranks, the job was much harder to bear. It was also apparent that I had been given the job as a favor from the owner, and some of my fellow grunts seemed to resent my presence from the start. I mostly kept to myself as I was not interested in these guys at all, especially the warehouse manager. He was a short guy with a long ponytail, and he would always sit in his office poring over orders that we were supposed to fill, though he never actually lifted a finger to help out. I swear he thought he had perfected the "stressed out about my really complicated job" act and made sure that anytime I walked past his open office door his great burden and mental prowess were both on display, evidenced by lots of deep sighs and temple-rubbing. Except one time when I caught him looking at a porn magazine.

I ended up injuring myself on the job, which also didn't help them to have a good opinion of me, because how dare I? They probably thought I was faking because I clearly didn't want to be there, and I'd made no effort to befriend or socialize with anyone, and then I came up with a back injury. I don't blame them for being suspicious. I was otherwise a very fit young guy, but I had a pre-existing back injury that was aggravated one day when I was trying to lift a sofa bed onto a dolly. There's that word again. Dolly. To be honest, we never called them sofa beds growing up. We called them hide-a-beds. I actually had one for my bed when we lived in our first house in Langley until we had a flood in our lower floor, which led to my bed cushions floating away in a foot of water and the eventual replacement of my bed by another, which I would have until I finally moved out of the house seven years later. That's a long sentence that is also pretty boring. I don't know why I call it a sofa bed now. Probably just because it's easier to type but also because it seems like the thing most people would call it.

Anyway, my bad back went all the way back to high school basketball. I don't remember ever really injuring it, but I do remember it hurting and spasming so badly at a basketball practice that I couldn't keep playing--but of course I kept playing, anyway, because when you're that young you have no idea how these things will come back to haunt you later in life. I never let my injuries heal properly, whether it was my back, sprained ankles, sprained fingers, or torn knee cartilage. When I got my wisdom teeth out, I was told to take it easy for a week or two, but instead I went straight from the dentist to the gym and played basketball for two hours. I remember telling people at that age that when I was older I would rather be in a wheelchair with 50 great stories than to be in perfect health with nothing to talk about. Well, here I am. Lots of stories but also lots of chronic, nagging injuries that will only get worse as I get older. Listen to me complain.

So, my back was hurt. I filled out the necessary paperwork and went home to rest and start physiotherapy, which I only ever found to be completely useless. I spent most of my time in physio sitting around waiting for the physiotherapist to come back and tell me what to do next. Physios seemed to work like waiters. They would have five or six patients at a time and just rotate among us, checking in to see if everything was okay but not actually doing anything that was helpful. It was while I was thus disabled that I met a girl who would go on to be my girlfriend and almost my wife. I won't name her, even though the likelihood that she ever reads this is extremely low. I will give her a pseudonym. This will be fun to pick a name. I'm torn between giving her a realistic name or a completely unrealistic name like Zaphod Beeblebrox, who was the president of the galaxy in Douglas Adams' *Hitchhiker's Guide to the Galaxy*. I can't call her that because it would probably be some sort of copyright infringement, so I'm back to square one. I don't want to pick a name that could be interpreted as any sort of judgment toward her in case someone knows who I am writing about, but do I really want to just pick a name like Mary or Sally or something like that? I guess so. I will call her Fake Sally.

FORTY-TWO
NEVER JUST STRAIGHTFORWARD

So, I originally spotted Fake Sally at a church event and fully intended to introduce her to Len, since we were both returned missionaries on the prowl for a companion that we would actually want to spend our time with. However, after I started talking to her, I realized that Len's main competition would actually be me and that he would, in fact, be losing this battle. I ended up asking her out on a date for the next day and met her at her house to go for a walk. We ended up driving to a local lake and talking for like five hours. Then we went back to her house and kept talking. All told, our first date was around nine hours long. There was an obvious chemistry between us, so I abandoned all pretense of setting her up with Len and very shortly found myself with a girlfriend. Despite this chemistry, there were problems almost from the start. I won't bore you with the details because they aren't really relevant to this story, but the end of the relationship is very relevant.

One time when we were driving somewhere, she was reading something to me out of a church magazine. Whatever it was, it ignited my idea machine, and I began pondering something else while she continued to read aloud. When she finished, she said, "Isn't that beautiful?" referring to the quote she had just shared with me. I hadn't heard a word of it, and I sheepishly told her so. She slowly folded the magazine closed, placed it on her lap and stared out the passenger window in silence. "You're not mad, are you?" I asked with some irritation. "No," she replied in what felt like a very condescending tone, "just disappointed." I just about pulled over right there and let her out. Instead, I said nothing and drove her to the place where I was supposed to drop her off and left her there. Not long after that, I broke up with her. I didn't want to take on the role of "disappointing boyfriend." I had already spent too much of my life playing disappointing son, disappointing friend, disappointing student, disappointing missionary, and was currently off injured from a job I hated where I was only looked at as disappointing grunt. The one place in my life where I had some choice and control was in my relationship, and I was not going to be with someone who was disappointed in me for being myself. I told her that it wasn't working, that we should see other people, all the clichés that were true. She was upset but accepted what I'd said.

One of those people that I wanted to see (actually the only one) was a girl named Tina, whom I had also seen that same night I met Fake Sally. The next church dance I was at, I watched Tina dance with so many different people, smiling and laughing and having fun while I sat moping against the wall on the floor. I also watched Fake Sally doing the same. It's hard to say why I didn't approach Tina and ask her to dance, but I think maybe my self-confidence was pretty low, having been such a disappointment to Fake Sally. I saw Tina enjoying the company of so many people that I figured she wouldn't be interested in a guy like me. Then, suddenly she was standing in front of me, asking me to dance. I agreed and we started to make our way to the dance floor. Right at this moment, another dude came up, grabbed her hand and tried to drag her away from me, saying he wanted to dance. She told him that she had already asked me, and I started to back down, saying it was okay, I would get the next one. Instead, she pulled her hand away from the intruder and insisted that

I come and dance with her. Unlike my first dance as an 11-year-old, I didn't run away crying but followed her out to the floor where we slow-danced through two songs and had a conversation where I dazzled her with some Vietnamese and asked her out on a date. She said she was busy on Saturday, so I asked about a different night. She said she was busy that night, too, so I asked for a third night. This was one time where my inability to read social cues was actually helpful, because I later found out she'd just been making excuses. It turned out that she had just come out of a very painful breakup, and she was afraid of the feeling that she had when we were dancing and talking, afraid that we would actually work and that she was setting herself up for disaster. Fortunately, I was blind to this and just kept forging ahead until she agreed to go to the movies with me.

If you think about it, going to a movie is almost the worst activity for a first date. Of course, there are worse options, like taking a girl to meet your parole officer, but sitting next to each other for two hours without talking is a terrible way to get to know someone. After the movie, we went out for ice cream, and I talked about myself for an hour straight, it felt like. By the end of the night, I was in love with her and the feeling seemed pretty mutual. As I hugged her goodbye, I gave her a kiss on the cheek, which makes me cringe when I think about it. As soon as I did it, I felt like a dummy. It seemed like such a grandfatherly thing to do, but I didn't want to be more forward than that. As I drove away, I thought, "Well, she's seen the real me. If she isn't scared away by that, then maybe we have a future together." I couldn't wait to see her at the next church dance that weekend. However, when I did see her, it did not play out as I had hoped.

It turns out she had carpooled to the dance with a few girls, including none other than Fake Sally, which must have been fairly awkward for everyone. Once she got to the dance, she barely spoke to me. When I was sitting down with an empty chair next to me, she sat a few seats away and talked with other people. I was gutted, seeing her so close but feeling so distant. I really didn't want to say that she was so close but so far away when I was writing that sentence. I really dislike clichés, but sometimes they are actually the perfect way to say something. I guess that's why they are overused to the point that they become clichés. Anyway, while I was feeling so forlorn, I looked out onto the dance floor and watched as Fake Sally laughed and smiled, enjoying her time away from me. Suddenly, I forgot about all our fights and incompatibilities and how disappointing I was, and I walked up and asked if she would be willing to dance with me. She was willing, and we talked as we danced and then we kissed and made up. Somehow, we were back together.

Looking back on it, I just didn't want to be alone. Growing up in a big family had left all of us kids with the same core deficit in getting attention. I wanted to be noticed and wanted, and Fake Sally noticed and wanted me. In my moment of loneliness, that was enough to blind me to everything else. However, after that night, things continued to go as they had before, with her being all serious and grown up and me wanting to play basketball on the street with my younger brothers. I didn't want to talk to her on the phone, and I didn't want to travel the 45 minutes from my house to hers. You know, basic things that a boyfriend should be willing to do. Finally, her birthday approached, and for it, I bought her a beautiful gold watch because I'm the kind of guy who sometimes says, "I love you this many dollars." I drove out to her house and gave it to her and had dinner with her and her family. That evening, I was lying in a hammock in her backyard as we talked, and suddenly I found myself on the ground, the wind knocked out of me. It turned out that I was a bit heavy for the hammock, and it had snapped, dropping me to the dirt. We laughed about it, and for some reason, the next day, I broke up with her again. Well, I know the reason.

It turns out, Tina had had just as good a time on the date as I had, and she, too, had looked forward to seeing me at the next dance. However, one of Fake Sally's friends was intentionally running interference at the dance, keeping her away from me and encouraging her to play hard to get. She was then dismayed and disappointed to see me rekindling things with Fake Sally. In the few weeks that followed, she agonized over whether she should call me or not, as she wasn't sure whether I was with Fake Sally. Finally, one evening in desperation, she sat by the phone and debated for a long time, while her family all encouraged her to be bold and make the leap. Finally, her dad said he would go upstairs and leave her all by herself to make the call, and she agreed. I answered the phone and was shocked to hear her voice, as I'd thought she was not interested. She cut right to the chase, I'll give her that, as she asked me if Fake Sally and I were officially dating. I told her that we were, and she said, "Oh." At that point, she wanted to get off the phone as desperately as she ever had in her life, but I just kept talking to her and laughing with her, and I didn't want to hang up. When I finally and mercifully let her end the conversation, I sat there wondering what had just happened. The thought occurred to me that while I couldn't stand talking on the phone to Fake Sally, I could have talked to Tina forever. Why wasn't I dating her? This led to my calling Fake Sally and asking her to meet up so we could talk. She came to my house, and I told her that we were just not compatible and that the chemistry we had was not enough to sustain a relationship. I told her that when two people are just dating each other, if they can't get along then, how on earth would they get along when they were married and things were so much more real? I told her that when we were dating, we should seem perfect in each other's eyes, and that we clearly didn't see each other that way. She cried and begged for me to reconsider, saying she could change and be different. I told her that she didn't need to change for me, and I didn't need to change for her. I told her that there were people out there who would think that we were perfect the way we were and that we each deserved to be with those people. She reluctantly agreed with me, saying that her mother had told her the exact same thing earlier that day. After she left, I went inside the house, down to my room, sat on my bed and bawled like a baby. Even though it was my idea to break up, it was still hard. Then I talked to my mom about what had happened, and she agreed with my reasoning. Then I picked up the phone and called Tina to ask her on a date for that evening.

She was understandably floored and asked, "Aren't you and Fake Sally dating?" I told her that we had broken up. Tina changed her plans for the evening, and I drove out to pick her up. This was another sign of our connection. She didn't live much closer than Fake Sally, but I would have walked there if I'd had to. Anyway, needless to say, we hit it off again. After a few more dates, we were officially a couple, and I had never felt so happy. I wanted to marry her, and she wanted to marry me, but we agreed to not talk about it because I didn't want to put pressure on the relationship. So, of course, she was surprised when after six weeks of dating, I impulsively suggested that we get married. It was not exactly a classic marriage proposal: "So if I asked you to marry me, would you say yes?" We were sitting on the couch at my house, and she had her head on my shoulder. She responded, "Yes, of course." I then said, "Okay. Then let's get married." She sat up and looked me in the eyes. "Are you serious?" I said, "Yes, of course I'm serious. Let's get married." We then hugged and kissed and smiled until our faces hurt. And then the dog farted, and it smelled so bad, but we didn't even care. At the end of this long and convoluted journey to happiness, we had found each other, and we were going to be together forever, and we didn't care about anything else. We didn't care about what was normal or what was expected or what was prudent. We just wanted to be together. When we told my parents, my mom rejoiced and my dad, ever the light drizzle on the parade, smiled and said, "But neither of you even has a job." Ahh, romance.

FORTY-THREE

ALMOST A MURDERER

As UNROMANTIC AS my dad's response was, he was correct. Since I had got home from my mission, I had basically been off work injured and not trying terribly hard to get back to it. Soon after I impulsively quasi-proposed to Tina, we realized that although we were both going to be in school in the fall, with her going into her third year of nursing and me starting my first semester of university, we would need to pay for a place to live and food to eat and all of that fun stuff. So we both went out and got the first jobs we could find. Tina got her job at the movie theatre back, which sounds pretty cushy, but she had worked there as a teenager and was now coming back at the age of 23, which took some humility on her part. However, as low as she felt working with teenagers and dishing up popcorn, she was in the clouds compared to the job I came up with. A kid from church was quitting his job to leave on his mission and asked if I wanted to take over for him. Because I was not organized or motivated enough to go out and look for something better, I said yes without asking a lot of questions. I learned later that if heaven is a place on earth, then hell is the pork processing plant that I worked at for the next two months before school started.

My job was to spend the morning making hundreds of cardboard boxes that would later be filled with various cuts of pork and loaded onto trucks. Neither of those duties were the hardest part of this job, although the monotony of both was almost fatal. The hardest part of the job was not even the smell of the burn bin, which was exactly what it sounds like. All of the leftover unusable or unwanted parts of the pigs were discarded into a giant bin and incinerated. The stench of this bin was unlike anything I had experienced before or since. My only involvement with the burn bin was when I was dragging a couple of garbage cans past it to throw regular garbage away. The burn bin was down at the bottom of a sloped parking lot, and right beside it were two regular garbage bins. Many times, before I could take a deep breath and hold it, the smell invaded my nostrils and left me dry-heaving, eyes watering and wondering why. Just why. Usually, though, I could hold my breath as I sprinted down the ramp, quickly emptied the cans, and sprinted back to the top where I would let out a mighty exhale and get away from this wormhole into the bowels of hell as fast as I could. As I said, though, this was not the worst part of my job. Which says something. When the worst part of your job isn't the giant bin of burning pig parts, that's a pretty terrible job.

The worst part of my job was not even the giant slabs of slaughtered pig that I had to haul from one hook to another. The pigs were really cold, floppy, and heavy, and they left my coveralls (and my clothes underneath, I later discovered) soaked in pig blood and juices, which I then had to wear for the remainder of my shift. I remember walking past a giant wheelbarrow-shaped bin, which was full to the brim with eyeballs. I guess some Chinese restaurant or something wanted them. One of my great regrets in life is that I never took the opportunity to help myself to a few eyeballs that would have never been missed. Just think of the fun I could have had with them. But no, this was not the worst part of my job, either. The worst part of my job was the guy who picked on me relentlessly, calling me stupid, idiot, moron, and much, much worse. I can't even remember his name, which is ironic, because I have never been exposed to such a tormentor in my life. He actually told me at one point that he felt that it was literally his job to make the new guy quit, and I was the new guy. I literally spent hours every day fantasizing about beating the crap out of this guy. I didn't want to get fired from my sweet job, though, so my fantasies would always include a way to make him take the first shot so that technically I would only be guilty of retaliating in self-defence.

This fantasy was delusional on two fronts. First, a decent workplace wouldn't care if it was self-defence or not if I beat the ever-loving crap out of a co-worker; I would probably not be kept on as an employee. Second, this was nowhere close to a decent workplace. This was the kind of workplace whose benefits package included not firing you if you showed up drunk. They would just send a guy home and tell him to come back the next day when he was sober. I heard tales of previous management supplying cocaine on lunch breaks to keep the monotony of assembly-line animal slaughter at bay. Guys were routinely smoking weed just outside the lunchroom, and nobody cared at all. The reality is, I probably could have walked up and smoked the guy with a hammer, and nobody would have lifted a finger. But I was naïve, so I just dwelt on my violent fantasies to pass the time. Then my animosity escalated to scouting out locations where I could launch a secret anonymous attack without anyone knowing who the assailant was. This was hardly the first time I had harbored violent fantasies about coworkers or bosses. Len and I, while we worked at the furniture warehouse, would often pass the time thinking up violent things we could do to the manager. When I was in high school, I was the kind of kid who made up lists of people I wanted to hurt. The kind of lists that if current school administrators found them, they would be locking down the school. It was a perverse sign of how much I had grown when I was on my mission and feeling very down and decided to comfort myself by making a list of people I hated and I couldn't do it. For every name that came to mind, I could think of an extenuating circumstance that would ease my hard feelings for them.

With the guy at the meat-packing plant, however, I could conjure no such circumstances. I guess that's the difference between anger when you read scriptures every day and anger when you watch violent movies every day. Anyway, because I had tasted more peace of mind and grown up a bit from my high school days, I couldn't fully enjoy and take comfort in violent fantasy and was very distressed about what I would do for the last the month or so that I had left before I quit this job to head off to school. The miracle cure was never a deliberate plan, as far as I recall, but it unfolded perfectly. It was disappointingly simple, too. All I did was stop arguing. When he would give me helpful feedback like, "What did you do that for you #$%#$ idiot?! Are you #$%# stupid?!" I would simply apologize and then ask him how he would like me to do it instead. I basically gave him no ammo to fight back with. He kept trying to stoke the flames, and I kept robbing them of oxygen. You can't light a fire in a vacuum. I think. Let me check. Okay, that was a bit of a rabbit hole, but I think the answer that I came up with is that you can light a match in a vacuum because chemical reactions are what cause ignition, but the fire will quickly burn out because the gases that are created from the fire do not rise, and there is no oxygen, anyway, to rush into the space created from the rising gas. As if you care. I probably could have just said my original statement and you would have just said, "I get your point, Ted," but I needed to know that what I was saying was accurate and true, because I hate it when I say stuff that is inaccurate. It probably ties back to so many memories as a child of saying or doing the wrong thing and setting myself up to look dumb. Also, when I think about lighting a fire in a vacuum, I think about lighting a vacuum on fire, because ... destruction.

Anyway, my strategy of not fanning the flames worked perfectly. All I had to do was tuck my tail for a couple of hours, and he was satiated and moved on to a different employee with his savagery, even inviting me to join him in his assaults, which I politely declined without any negative consequences. I often tell this story to clients who are dealing with aggravating people because it was so effective and also a living illustration of the advice that so many parents give to their kids who are getting picked on, "just ignore it." This wasn't exactly ignoring it in the sense that I responded to his words, but what I ignored was the meaning that my brain was attaching to it, instead supplying a different meaning. He needed to feel like he was in control of the situation, and the degree to which I resisted, his need became even more blinding. When I let him believe he had control, his need was satisfied and then displaced to another target. The key realization there is that I LET him believe that he was in control, which means that it was actually me in control. It was actually I who was in control. That's the proper grammatical way to say it, but almost nobody speaks like that. Isn't it interesting how a language has rules that almost no one follows. If that's the case, how is it still a rule? Who makes the rules? Don't the people make the rules? Anyway, instead of relying on power to win, I took control of the situation by taking control of my reactions.

One of my most standout memories from my time at the plant was on my last day when I showed up for work, to the utter shock of one of the more senior employees. He asked what I was doing there. I told him it was my last day. He said, "I know, that's why I'm wondering what you're doing here. I've never seen anyone, ever, show up for their last day here." The thought hadn't even occurred to me to not show up for my last day of work. What a strange sense of pride filled me as I felt like I should brag but the subject of my boast would only sound empty if I said, "Guess what? I showed up for work today!" The other thing that stands out from the conversation is when we were loading a truck with pig meat together and he said, "Why are you quitting, anyway?" as if loading a truck with pig meat wasn't reason enough. I told him that I was quitting to start university, and he said without pausing his rhythm, "That's good. Get the hell out of here and don't come back." This may sound like more rudeness, consistent with the culture of the place, but the tone in which it was delivered was a combination of encouragement and sadness, as he probably wished that he, too, could leave and never come back.

FORTY-FOUR

FOURCHETTE DANS LA RUE

A SHORT TIME before I got engaged, my mom interrupted my TV watching to ask me an annoying question about what I planned to do with my life. I was 21 years old, living at home, unemployed, and lacking some direction. I had nothing to tell her. My plans of being a professional wrestler, skatepark owner, and rock star seemed to have reached the end of the line, and I had no backups. She asked me if I planned on going to university, and I told her that I was open to the idea but that I had no idea what classes I would even take. She told me that people usually start with classes like political science, sociology, psychology, etc. I said, "Sure. I'll take those. But also, sign me up for French because I'm good at French." So even though I was an adult, my mom signed me up for classes. I should mention that when I was 16 years old, my grandpa told me that he thought I should be a doctor. Since at that time I was failing almost every class in high school, the thought was laughable, and I actually laughed at him. From that time, the thought of going to university never really crossed my mind again until my mom mentioned it to me that summer. My high school grades were never going to be good enough to get me into any kind of university that I knew of, and besides, you don't need to go to school to know how to rock and roll.

I don't remember anything about my first experiences in sociology or French or political science. It didn't take me long to learn that I would rather be run over by a team of sled dogs (which is a weird thing to think about) than to study political science, so I withdrew from that course before the deadline so it wouldn't show up on my transcript. I have to say that I really had no idea what a transcript was or why it would be bad for a W to show up on it, but I got the heck out that class as soon as I found out that I could. As for psychology, I remember my first class very well. I don't think I'd ever heard of psychology before that day, and if I had, I didn't really know what it meant. But I remember that first class, the professor standing at the front of the room, asking students to prove to him that the table that he was leaning on actually existed. They resorted to the usual arguments, relying on the five senses. In fact, it probably wasn't all five, because I don't remember anyone suggesting that he taste the table. I think I would have remembered that. After each argument that was made, he was able to create doubt as to our ability to trust our own perceptions and to accept them as objective facts. I thought it was funny how angry students were getting with him for shooting down their incomplete theories. It dawned on me that he was correct. That we really had no way of knowing if this was all just a delusion if all we relied upon was our subjective experience. I was hooked after one class.

I remember as the semester wore on, my excitement grew with each new concept or theory or piece of data. I remember thinking, "This is amazing. We can actually answer the question of why people behave the way that they do!" Once I was hooked, it was not difficult to retain my attention and to get me to work outside of class, two things that were a distant dream to my high school teachers. I remember we had a weekly quiz, just a short, 10-question chapter-summary quiz, and I studied for the first one, reading the chapter and reviewing it, and then got 100 percent. I felt proud of myself. I did the same thing the next week and got 100 percent again. Now I was on fire and made it a goal to get 100 percent on all of the quizzes through the whole semester, which I was able to do. It wasn't hard, because the material was fascinating and the teacher was both interesting and interested. I ended up with an A+ in the class, the first time I had ever had what felt like real academic success that meant something. However, before I could get my head too pumped full of pride, I had to write my French final.

French was another class that I found incredibly easy, and I was going into the final exam sitting at nearly 100 percent in the course. However, university is different from high school in many ways. No one is chasing you to make sure you do your homework, you have way more time on your hands, way less structure, way more choice in what and how to learn, and your final exam is not held in your usual classroom at your usual time. This is something that probably everyone knows who has gone to university, but I did not. So, I showed up at my usual classroom at my usual time and was surprised that no one was there yet. I waited around for 15 minutes and still no one had shown up. I was starting to panic, wondering if I had the day or time wrong, but I had nowhere to look because I didn't have my course syllabus with me. Of course I didn't; that would have required organization skills. After around 30 minutes or so, I abandoned hope in a cloud of confusion and went home. There I found out that the final exam was indeed on a different day and at a different time. Unfortunately, I also found out that that day and time had already come and gone. That's a fancy way of saying I'd missed the exam. It felt like a bit of a punch to the gut but not nearly as bad as one might expect. After all, high school had been just one long, continuous sequence of events like this, so why should I have a different expectation for university? I figured my A+ in French would be history, to use a terrible pun. I hate puns. Like, they actually make me mad sometimes when people use them. Except for one about Ghandi, who was a super-calloused fragile mystic vexed by halitosis. Say it out loud. It's funny.

Anyway, imagine my surprise when I checked a week or so later to see that I had finished with an A+ in the class. It turns out, my French prof, looking at my performance in the course all semester, made the educated and merciful judgment that I probably would have aced the exam as well and just gave me the A+ that he knew I deserved. It was an act of mercy that may have changed the course of my education. If I had started my university career with a consequential brain fart, maybe not even my success in psychology would have been enough to buoy my spirits enough to continue on. As it turned out, I finished my first semester with two A+s and a B+. Not bad, considering I had no study skills and no confidence and no sense of the scope of a university education. Also, I got married halfway through the semester.

FORTY-FIVE
NEVER A DOUBT

Following my surprise proposal, Tina and I had both got humbling jobs and prepared to go to school in the fall. For Tina, it was a return to school, and for me, it was an initiation. I had no concept of what it took to plan a wedding, and so when we set the date for the wedding for four months from the date of our engagement, I thought of nothing more than that it was going to be on a long weekend. In the Mormon church, the wedding ceremony itself takes place in one of our temples, and it is not the same kind of event that it is outside the church. It is a simple religious ceremony, accompanied by family and close friends who are also active members of the church. It's over relatively quickly, and it is completely uniform, so no planning is required. The real work is for the reception. I couldn't decide on who to pick for my best man, and Len and I had unfortunately had a bit of a falling out during the four months of my engagement, so I asked my older brother Spencer to be my best man. He had been dating his girlfriend, Irene, for a long time before Tina and I started seeing each other, but I moved much quicker, and Tina and I got engaged first. After I had opened the door, Spencer was emboldened, and it wasn't long before he was engaged, as well. Then they picked their wedding date, and it was before ours. Then Len did the same. I regret that I didn't have Len in my wedding party. We'd had many adventures together, and he really was a loyal friend. It was probably me who had let him down more than anything. In any event, there weren't a lot of spaces available in the party, anyway.

I told my parents that I wanted all of my brothers to be included, so they were, except for Mike, who was busy terrorizing/preaching in Russia on his mission. I also included Keith, of course, and our friend Cliff. Tina had to match numbers, of course, so she included her three sisters, Lisa, Sheri, and Anita, her best friend from college, Kristie, and my sister, Carrie. It never occurred to me that there was a significant cost involved in having such a big wedding party. Of course, our wedding paled in comparison to some weddings that I hear about, but for my parents to drop $700 on tuxedos was not insignificant. Tina's mom sewed all of the bridesmaid dresses, and a woman from our church made the wedding dress. We used the church gymnasium for the reception--Tina's sister Sheri and her friend decorated it to look like a fancy ballroom. We had another woman from the church do the catering, and all in all, it was a relatively low-cost affair. I have to say that the moment that I was married to Tina was and probably is the happiest moment of my entire life. That is not to take anything away from other happy moments of significance, such as the births of my children, but it was the closest thing to pure joy that I have ever felt. I had spent my entire life wanting to be wanted, wanting to be important, significant, admired, recognized, valued and every other synonym you can think of. When I looked across at Tina in that moment, I really felt all of those things, with no shadow of doubt that it was real. For someone for whom doubt was a constant, I felt elation at having none in that most significant of moments.

FORTY-SIX

LIVING ON A PRAYER

WE HAD FOUND a place to rent, and it was exactly the kind of setup you would want to tell your kids about when they were complaining that they didn't have their own room or that the restaurant didn't have anything they liked. You know the kinds of complaints I'm talking about. When that stuff inevitably comes up, it's helpful to be able to say things like, "When you've lived in a little three-room shack where you bedroom smells like a combination of rubber and fish, your couch was previously owned and used by a wet dog, the water pours through eight holes in the ceiling into buckets, and your washing machine is located in a shed outside, then you can complain." That was our first place. The cost was low, it was in Langley, close to Kwantlen College, where I had begun my education, and it would allow me to keep going to the same congregation that I had been attending since I was 13, with the exception of my mission and my one year detour to Nanaimo. It's interesting that as I list the reasons why we lived there, they all centre on me. Tina's school was located an hour away in Chilliwack, her family was half an hour away in Abbotsford, and she had no roots in Langley at all. I'm not sure how she agreed to all of that.

Anyway, the place was an absolute dump, and I'm sure that my parents knew that, so on our wedding night, which was the day before the reception, instead of relaxing, my parents, sister, and youngest brother went over to the new shack and cleaned and painted and tried to make it look like a little home. It was a bit like putting lipstick on a pig, but I loved them for making the effort. As I mentioned before, one of the bedrooms just reeked like fish. And rubber. We couldn't find what caused the smell, and we couldn't mask it or get rid of it. Good thing I had the ability to just compartmentalize and ignore. One of our wedding presents, easily the best as far as I'm concerned, was a little kitten that we named Katie. If not for the whole 'different species' thing, I would have sworn we came from the same family. She loved to wrestle, she was full of energy and love, and she was very attached to us. When we were driving down the road approaching our house, we would always make a bet with each other, "Kate or no Kate?" What we were referring to was whether or not we would see her tiny little kitten head pop up in the window when we pulled into our driveway. More times than not, she would appear and then race over to the front door to meet us and greet us with love and affection and a little bit of clawless wrestling. She was an endless source of entertainment for us, better than TV.

As we entered the rainy season, which in the Lower Mainland of B.C. is approximately nine months out of a year, we started to notice little bubbles appearing on our ceiling, and I made the rookie mistake of poking one of them with my finger. The result was a steady stream of water pouring from the ceiling, which we scrambled to contain with a bowl or mop-bucket, whichever was closer. Of course, from this first bubble I learned that when subsequent bubbles appeared, it guaranteed a satisfying bubble-popping experience. I don't know what the standard handyman procedure is for leaky bubble ceiling, but I think poking it is probably not high on the list of options. Soon, we had multiple streams and multiple containers full of water. We existed like this for a few days before we finally went to the landlady and told her what was happening. She apologized and said that she would get her son to come and take care of the leaky roof for us. Even though we were many miles and many years from the Kootenays, imagine my surprise when I came home from school to see a genuine "Salmo Job" of roof repair. The handyman's skills were almost parallel to mine, evidenced by the large tarps that were draped over the roof of the shack. That was it. The landlady assured me that her son would do a better job eventually, but he never did.

Although we only lived in the shack for about five or six months, there were many memories associated with it, including one time when we came home from an outing, parked the car on the dirt lot that passed as a driveway, and met Katie at the front door. We then went inside and were shocked by a loud thump against the outside wall, coming from the direction of the driveway. We raced outside to see what had caused it and saw that our car, which we had left in neutral with no brake on, had slowly rolled forward down the slight incline, gathering steam until it came to a stop up against our shack.

At our wedding, lots of people brought gifts of cash to us, which was really fantastic, since neither of us was working while we were in school, because obviously love is enough and all you need. When the money ran out as we reached the end of the semester, we got desperate enough to go back to the bottom of the job-hunting barrel, with Tina getting a job at the mall in a clothing store and me somehow convincing myself that I could wake up at 5 a.m. in the dead of winter to go suffer at the meat-packing plant again. Tina was in her third year of nursing school, and as the semester came to an end, she was informed that she would not be passing and would have to take the whole semester over again. They also told her that she wasn't really RN material, which was not very nice to say three years into a four-year program, but it was also super accurate. She was much more apt to sitting with patients, listening to their stories and helping them feel important, which, as you may have noticed, is not typically in the job description of an RN. They suggested that she challenge the LPN exam instead, since she was already overqualified for it. So, instead of finishing the semester going to class, she studied at home to write the exam and picked up a part-time job selling clothes at a store in the mall. I love her for her willingness to do what was necessary for our family.

I got a job stocking shelves at the grocery store on the graveyard shift and lasted two days before I stopped going back. I didn't even call to quit. I just stopped showing up. I never even got paid, but I didn't care. I was not going back there. I did get a ghoulish photo ID out of the deal, though. Together, we answered an ad in the classified section of the local newspaper looking for people to help make Christmas wreaths and ended up working in someone's shed with a bunch of other desperate weirdos, making tacky Christmas decorations for minimum wage. We worked there until we got paid and then moved on. That's how I ended up at the meat-packing plant again. I had tried two things. Both had failed (sort of), so I was going to just go back to the devil I knew. This time, however, because I now had a few months experience under my belt, they started me at an even better position. Instead of packing boxes for the first half of the day, they had me doing something even worse than I could have imagined.

After the pigs were killed, they were strung up on a hanging assembly line. The line carried their carcasses along, stopping to dip them into a boiling bath to get the hair off. Then they went down around the corner to the burner. Not the vomit-inducing burn bin, that was something different. The burner was a little device that the pigs went through, pausing to have their flesh seared just enough to tighten it up and singe whatever hair was left. That's when the pigs arrived at my station. I kid you not when I say that I was armed with a machete and a blowtorch. That sounds like the implements of an interrogator in a third-world country, but there I was. First, I stopped the pig from going past me with my left arm, then I used the machete to scrape off the burnt hair. Then, if the burner had not done an adequate job, I used the blowtorch to sear the skin some more. That might also result in some more singed hair, so I had to scrape that off as well. Then I could mercifully let the pig move on to the next station of indignity. I was the first person in the assembly line, and no one could do anything until I had scraped, singed, and scraped, so the pressure on me was intense. Of course, the guys were super understanding and patient. Nope. They had skipped the last two years of finishing school and were the same surly lot I was working with before. I think I lasted another two weeks, long enough to get a paycheque, before I decided I would rather be the pig on the line than work there for one more second.

This left me with a dilemma, however, as all of these jobs had not put enough money in our accounts to pay our rent. Tina had passed the LPN exam, of course, and had found a job working as a care aid in a series of group homes for adults with severe developmental disabilities. She was great at it, but she was only working casual hours to start, so I needed to go get a real job. Also during this time, we had decided to start a family--because when you are poor, uneducated, and unemployed, it seems like a good time to take on something simple like birthing and raising a child. However, as happy as we were to be expecting our first, Tina unfortunately had a miscarriage just before she reached 12 weeks of pregnancy. I was away all day working in my new job as a carpet cleaner when it happened, and this was in the days before cell phones, so there was no way for anyone to get a hold of me. The territory I covered was immense, so my hours were very unpredictable. As a result, Tina reached out to my family, and my dad came rushing over and picked her up to take her to the hospital. I came home to an empty and darkened house, with no explanation until Tina came home. I'm sure I did a poor job of consoling her. Of course for the woman, the mother, a miscarriage is a very different experience than for the man, but for me, I just felt bad for her. She was told that it was basically a group of cells, not even a real baby, and so for me, there was no person to mourn. However, I know now that it was not just the baby that was lost. It was the perception that she had lost her chance to be a mother, the thing she had wanted more than anything in her entire life, for her entire life. Tina's life goals were to be a mom of six children. Nothing else. I intentionally said "nothing else" instead of "nothing more," because I can't think of anything "more" than being a mother.

FORTY-SEVEN

ACT LIKE YOU UNDERSTAND

So, the carpet cleaning job was another one that I hated, but this time I stuck with it because I literally had no choice. There was this guy at our church, Dennis, who fancied himself an author and director, and he had decided to put on a little dinner theatre fundraiser and asked me if I would take a role in the play. I said sure, because after all, I had played Rock in Salmo Elementary and never felt that I got my due as a star. I ended up with the male lead in a spoof of western movies loosely based on (and sometimes blatantly stealing lines from) *Blazing Saddles*. I played a gunslinger in love. It was following a rehearsal for this play that I came home to find Tina sitting on the front steps waiting for me. I was so happy to see her that I knelt down and took my cowboy hat off, producing a little ring box that contained the engagement ring that she still wears to this day. I think this made up for my lack of romance with the original proposal.

Anyway, the play was such a smash hit that Dennis followed it up with another script spoofing murder mysteries, loosely based on (and sometimes blatantly stealing lines from) the movie *Clue*. In an early example of fanfiction, however, he had also written a part in for Inspector Clouseau of *Pink Panther* fame. After taking the lead role in the first play, I wanted less pressure this time around, so I decided to go for the Clouseau role. In fact, it was a role I was born to play. I love doing funny accents, and Clouseau is a difficult one for many people to nail, but I was a natural playing the role of bumbling idiot. The role also allowed for some ad libbing, which was also something that I loved. In a way, my character stole the show and fed my need for attention and admiration. I guess when it comes to acting, I'm a natural, which is a funny paradox in words, if you think about it. I'm a natural at pretending. I guess when you grow up with the curse of two shadows (potential and underachieving) hanging over you, you are always kind of acting like you know what's going on and that you're doing better than you actually are. In addition, I find it easy to get into a character because I think my mirror neurons are especially tuned in to observational learning. I'm able to mimic facial expressions, accents, body postures, and even walking gait and do it quite effortlessly. It's this micro-awareness that can be a gift and a curse at the same time, as I can't turn it on and off when I want. It wouldn't even be accurate to say that I can turn it on when I want, because while I notice all of these little things, I also had (have?) a difficult time sometimes with missing obvious cues.

Anyway, how did I get here from talking about carpet cleaning? Oh yeah, so one person who was in the audience was a friend of my dad's who ran a chain of carpet-cleaning franchises across Canada. He approached my dad after the play and asked if he thought I would be a good manager for the newest franchise. My dad, in his classical supporting role, said no. Granted, he might have been correct, but still, it would have possibly been a good opportunity for someone who was lacking direction and confidence. But it's an interesting phenomenon, if you think about it. My dad pointed out the human tendency to overgeneralize a person's competence based on their skill in one area. I was really good at acting and being funny, so this guy assumed I would be a good manager of a carpet-cleaning franchise. I'm not sure those skillsets dovetail very well, but that impression of competence was generated effectively enough that when I got tired of coming home covered in burnt pig hair and blood, I called this guy up, and he offered me a job as a carpet-cleaning technician. The product was great and worked really well, but I was not interested in upselling, which, of course, is the lifeblood of so many of these kinds of businesses. To be honest, I had spent two years as a Mormon missionary trying to sell people on something I believed in, and I was tired of it. I could have made much more money at that job if I had been willing to go outside my comfort zone (and sell my soul to the devil), but I didn't care enough. The base wage was enough to cover our bills, and so I settled for that.

Around the same time, Tina's grandma's dementia was getting quite serious, and she was moved into a care home in Abbotsford. For some reason, being a homeowner somehow contributed to paying the expense of living in the care facility, so her children, including Tina's mom, didn't want to sell the townhouse where she had been living for many years. So, they came to us with a pretty sweet proposal. We could move into the three-bedroom townhouse, fully furnished (straight from the 1970s) and only had to pay the monthly strata fee of $275. So the rent was halved and the house size was doubled. Also, there were no tarps, no holes in the ceiling, no rubber fish smell, and the laundry was indoors. We did not hesitate to say yes. Around this time, Tina found out she was pregnant again, and it was wonderful news. My brother Spencer and his wife, Irene, were about to have their first child, and the family was buzzing. I was also enrolled in my second semester of university, but because I had to work full time, I was only taking one class. Spanish 101. It came very easily to me, and I was acing the class, just like I had aced French. The prof was even the same generous guy. Then one day, I was working at some rich guy's house in North Vancouver, and the job just kept getting uglier as the day wore on. When I finally finished and packed my equipment and sore body (turns out that carpet cleaning isn't any better for a bad back than lifting couches in a warehouse) into my little prison of a van and hit the road, it was dark outside and pouring rain, conditions that I feel comfortable saying have never in the history of travel led to traffic moving smoothly. This day was no exception, and the result was that I missed my Spanish midterm exam, worth 30 percent of the course. I could have probably explained the situation to the prof and got another chance to write it; after all, he had done me such a huge favour with my French class. For some reason, however, I just stopped going to class. I didn't realize that the F in the class would a) count against my GPA, and b) show up on my transcript even if I retook the class. Why didn't I know these things as a 22-year-old university student? Because I was still just cruising along, mostly clueless as to how the world worked and how things all fit together.

FORTY-EIGHT

JOB CAROUSEL

So, I quit school to work, and not long after we had arrived in our new house in Abbotsford, I quit my carpet-cleaning job. I just couldn't handle the grind, the people I worked with, the people I worked for, and it was killing my body. So, in a move that I would almost always advise my clients against, I quit a good job before I got a replacement. Luckily our rent was almost non-existent, and Tina was working full-time hours now. While all of this was going on, my Vietnamese language skills were slowly going to waste, something I swore would never happen. I started looking for work as an interpreter, both for the money and also to keep from getting rusty. I found out about a program through Abbotsford Community Services where they would provide interpreting services to low-income clients. It was quite the racket they had going, too, paying us around $20/hr with a half-hour minimum, while they got paid $30/hr from the provincial government to run the program. However, as I said, I wasn't just doing it for the money, so I signed up for the training, anyway. I'm glad I did. It opened some doors for me that would prove to be life changing and not just for me and my family. One of the things I learned in the training was that when working as an interpreter, a person should be careful not to adopt the role of spokesperson for a culture. It seems like a no-brainer, but you'd be surprised how often I was asked questions about what Vietnamese people were like, as if they could all be painted with the same brush.

My first interpreting assignment was to go to a doctor's appointment with a client who was off work with a back injury. I needed to study up on my anatomy vocabulary, and I was very nervous that I would not be able to do the job well enough to justify my wage. It was just another case of feeling like people's expectations of me were unrealistic and that I was a fraud. Actually, though, the fact that I, as a white guy, could speak even one word of Vietnamese was endlessly impressive to the Vietnamese and Canadians alike. The assignment went well, and I found myself with another one soon after. This time I was to go to the local welfare office to interpret for a man during his appointment with a social worker. This also went well, as I explained to the social worker that the man did not have enough money to buy food for his family and hadn't for quite some time. When she asked how they were surviving, he told her (through me) that he was just racking up his credit cards. The social worker looked at me and shook her head slightly, sending a clear message of disapproval of his actions, but did she think that he couldn't see her? As if this subtle body language would not be immediately understood? I felt uncomfortably in the middle. As the interpreter, my role was to say his words in the first person and to say her words in the first person. I was not to embellish, explain, or assist the communication process in any way. This was an impossible task, but I stuck to it as well as I could.

My third assignment was to accompany a man to see a psychologist who had a contract with the Workers Compensation Board. The man, in his 50s, had injured his neck at work and was being re-trained for a new job. Seeing a psychologist was part of his rehabilitation. The psychologist was terrible. I had seen a counsellor on my mission and knew how good it felt to get pent up feelings off my chest, even though he never followed up with me and things quickly settled back into the clinging tar pit of depression. All this psychologist did was ask the man how his neck felt, how he liked the new job, whether it was difficult or not, and other sundry and meaningless checklist-type questions. He was the stereotypical government-fed professional who did not even look up to make eye-contact with his client until he dismissed him from the appointment. After this appointment, I stood in the parking lot as this proud Vietnamese man, survivor of war and prison camps, broke down and cried as he asked me, "Isn't he supposed to ask me about my feelings?" I wasn't sure what to say, so I broke protocol and said, "I think they usually do." Then I talked to him about his feelings, his injured pride of no longer being able to provide for his family in this new country, of his fear in starting a new job and whether or not it would work out better than the last one. Then I gave him a ride home. This role did not feel awkward. It felt natural. I made an unconscious mental note of it. I say an unconscious note, because at the time I didn't recognize its significance, but later in my life, as things unfolded for me, I came to recognize it as a pivot point.

After that appointment, the interpreting job went downhill. Eventually it was simply going up to the police station on Friday nights to explain to some frightened grandparent that they had been arrested for the possession of a controlled substance for the purpose of trafficking and that they would need to sign this Promise to Appear in court in order to be released from jail. They would protest their innocence to me, and I would pass their words on to unsympathetic, unbelieving police officers. I remember one giant, hulking cop looking down at me with a confused cloud behind his eyes, grunting out the question, "You speak Viet-manese?" I answered that I did and feared for the welfare of the tiny crying grandmother who was either actually innocent or just scared for what the authorities would do to her now that she was in jail. After all, back in Vietnam, encounters with the authorities were never pleasant. Why were they all being booked for the same offence? The answer is that many Vietnamese in the lower mainland were involved, either directly or indirectly, in the illegal marijuana trade, usually running grow-ops in a variety of settings. The task of watching the grow-op would often fall to an aged parent or grandparent because it would be less suspicious, but the result was that it was often that same aged parent or grandparent who ended up scared, confused, and alone in jail looking up at a hulking, confused cop who couldn't pronounce the name of their language, let alone speak a word of it. After a couple months of this routine, I told community services that I wanted to be taken off the list of interpreters to call. As this was my side job while I was hating carpet cleaning, there were no real repercussions to quitting, other than losing the opportunity to practice my Vietnamese. After I quit the carpet cleaning job and hadn't found anything else for the period of a month, I got a surprise call from another carpet-cleaning franchise, a bitter rival to the guy I had worked with before. They were in desperate need of an experienced technician and would give me better money and better working conditions. I really hesitated because I hated the job so much, but in the end, I took it because I couldn't justify sitting around the house playing my guitar while Tina worked full time. The job was just as bad as I remembered it being, and I still had no interest in upselling, but at least these guys had more integrity and were not interested in ripping customers off. I worked for them for a few months, but when September came around, I quit again to go back to school full time.

FORTY-NINE

WE HAD A BABY

ALTHOUGH I WAS BACK in school, I was just taking odd courses, mostly electives, trying to figure out what I wanted to do with my life, so I had an inordinate amount of time on my hands to be around Tina and support her through the seemingly interminable final weeks of pregnancy. On February 28, 2000, we got up at 5:30 a.m., put Tina's packed bags into the car, said goodbye to Katie, and headed off to the hospital for a scheduled C-section, due to the baby lying in a transverse position. Other than the epidural, Tina didn't get any real pain drugs because she couldn't feel anything below the waist, anyway. She just kept saying, "It feels so weird...." over and over and over again. It was a surreal feeling to hear that first cry and to hear the doctors say, "It's a girl!" Coming from a family of almost all boys, and being an uber-masculine, aggressive-type guy, the thought had never even occurred to me, not even once, that I would have a daughter. Granted, growing up I probably never thought for more than a minute combined about having children, though I did spend weeks' worth of hours thinking about who I might have children with. Despite never giving it any thought, apparently I had built up an unconscious expectation of having a son, because when the doctor excitedly announced that I had a daughter, I paused to see if he had made a mistake. He hadn't, and I stood up and gazed upon my progeny for the first time in the flesh. She was big and pink and had blood all over her head and was screaming in a very healthy way. One of the great things about a C-section delivery is that the baby's head doesn't get misshapen by getting squeezed through the birth canal. She looked perfect. She was big, too, as we had suspected, weighing in at 9 pounds, 4 ounces. It turns out that the blood on her head was, in fact, her own, because the surgeon, in his haste, had nicked her scalp with his scalpel. This wasn't discovered until she had been fully cleaned off.

I came floating out of the operating room while they were sewing Tina up and met members of both of our families in the hallway to deliver the news. We had decided ahead of time what her name would be, so everyone was excited to meet Amanda Caroline. Tina says that when she first heard Amanda's cry, she thought, "That's *my* baby! She's a real person!" for 9 months, Amanda had been theoretical only, and finally the vision had come to life. It was one of the most exciting moments of my entire life, but I also felt the weight, almost immediately, as it had occurred to me some weeks before, that this little human would only ever know me as Dad, not as Ted. She wouldn't know the punk-rockin, greasy-haired, skateboarding, irreverent guy; she would know me as her protector and the person who was supposed to have all the answers. I had expressed the angst of this realization a week before in the lyrics of a song I wrote, called "One Week Left."

> *Doesn't seem too long ago*
> *We decided to bring you home*
> *We thought maybe, having a baby*
> *Would be too much, but we have grown*
> *People tell me I can't force you*
> *In the direction I want you to go*
> *I hope I can show and teach you*
> *So that you will go on your own*

You can see me, you can hear me
Whatever I say, you'll believe.
I hope I can say all the right things
So you will always be with me
One week left, one week to wait
Will I be good will I be great enough for you?
Will I be half as good as my dad?
Will I give you the life I had?

I HAVE to say that I feel like this song was a gift from God. It so perfectly sums up my feelings toward being a parent, and as my first born--"the experimental child" as her younger siblings jokingly refer to her--turned 18 and graduated from high school, I couldn't even sing two lines without emotion choking out any hope I had of singing. But I love crying my way through the song. This is one of the things that having a daughter has done for me.

Speaking of crying, I remember the first night that Amanda came home with us. Because Tina had had a C-section, she wasn't discharged from the hospital for three days. I slept at home on those nights, since there was obviously not much I could contribute in the way of breastfeeding. The first night Amanda was home with us, I fully intended to play my part as the dutiful father and husband, and each time she awoke crying during the night I would get up along with Tina to lend moral and emotional support. It only took three times of Amanda waking up crying for me to feel hopeless, desperately trapped, and exhausted. She was waking up every two hours, and despite my great feats of sleep deprivation as a teenager, this was a different matter entirely. I remember saying to Tina, "I can't do this. I can't live like this. I need to get my sleep in more than two-hour chunks." Needless to say, I survived.

Amanda was not an easy baby; however, because she was our first, we had no one to compare her to, and we didn't know that. She didn't really sleep through the night until she was probably two or three years old. Because the townhouse we were living in was old, it was afflicted with squeaky floors that made an already difficult situation almost impossible. If we could miraculously get Amanda to go to sleep, we had to delicately and slowly tiptoe across the squeaky minefield of her bedroom floor, ever-so carefully place her down on the crib mattress, and if that didn't wake her up, make the equally slow and treacherous journey back across the room to slowly close the door behind us. Of course, it almost never worked that smoothly.

It's funny as parents how we feel so entitled to things like sleep, time to ourselves, and not having to explain ourselves. It's straight-up delusional. Why would we expect a baby to sleep through the night in a crib in a separate room from us when she'd spent the last nine months literally inside her mother's body? Granted, some babies do, but most don't, and when they don't, the parents often feel like they're failing--and if they don't point the blame at themselves, they can actively resent the child. Now that my kids are older, it's easier to recognize the ridiculousness of the position, but when you are a rookie parent, you just don't know any better. Being a parent, especially of a newborn, requires so many of the traits and skills that an ADHD person lacks. It requires selflessness, patience, follow-through, organization, motivation, self-awareness, self-care, and even a good working memory. We always laughed (inwardly) at my dad when he was getting after one of us and had to cycle through all seven of our names before he got the right one out, but of course, I end up doing the same thing now. My kids don't laugh inwardly, though, so maybe I'm less intimidating.

FIFTY

OVEREATING, BUT NOT ANONYMOUS

ANYWAY, when Tina was pregnant with Amanda, she gained a serious amount of weight. I never put any pressure on her to watch her weight when she was pregnant because I really didn't care about it and because I'm not a jerk or an idiot. I wanted a big, fat baby, anyway. There's always been a preoccupation with big things in my family. I'm sure it comes from my dad, but he was always impressed by tall people, strong people, big trucks, big trees, but not so much by my big mouth. So, when it came time for me to procreate, of course I wanted the baby to be big. It's not like I was feeding Tina a diet of protein shakes and amino acids, but I could recognize that being pregnant is hard enough without having to worry about what you look like. Of course, to help Tina transition to this newer, bigger version of herself, I chipped in where I could and gained 35 pounds, myself. My weight up to that point had fluctuated wildly following my graduation, but it was mostly intentional. I was a lean 185 pounds when I left on my mission, but the Missionary Training centre is known for feeding the missionaries a bit too well, so it was no surprise that I gained about ten pounds in the nine weeks that I was there. How could I not? There were long lines in the cafeteria, so they put freezers full of ice cream sandwiches halfway down the line, just to help us pass the time. This was the case for all meals except breakfast, which means I had at least two ice cream sandwiches every day. I also discovered a love of peanut M&Ms and kept track of how many bags I had eaten over my time there. The total ended up being somewhere in the 80s, which is pretty impressive, given that I was only there for 65 days.

On my mission, we were riding terrible bikes and doing a lot of walking and sweating, so I could pretty much eat however I wanted without having to worry about the impact on my waistline. When I got transferred to Tacoma, however, and discovered the joy of a bench press in my apartment, I correctly reasoned that in order to put on enough muscle to achieve my goal of bench pressing 315 pounds, I would need to eat a lot more protein, and in order to have the energy to work out that hard, I would need to eat a lot more carbs. However, on my limited missionary budget, I was not able to buy fancy supplements and shakes, so I just ate everything in sight and as much of it as I could find. This led to me getting my weight up to 230 pounds again. I ended up achieving my goal, as I mentioned, but when the weights were taken away after someone in the mission damaged their apartment by dropping weights on the floor, I was just left as a fat guy. I split my pants and broke chairs by sitting on them and had to buy new clothes at the Goodwill store because I couldn't fit into anything I owned anymore. I decided at one point that I was not going to go home looking like that, so I started to change my ways. I stopped eating desserts and took smaller portions. We were still riding around on bikes, and by the end of my mission, I was back down to 200 pounds. When I got married, I was a solid 195 pounds. I started powerlifting again shortly after that and gained my 35 pounds back. Once again, I was incredibly strong but had a face that looked a bit like it was carved out of a marshmallow, so I decided that something needed to change. I stopped eating like crazy and lost the weight again. Then when Tina got pregnant, I gained 35 sympathy pounds. I've seen this funny meme going around on social media that says, "I wish I was as fat as I was the first time I thought I was fat." I laugh, but it's so true. When I was 18 years old and working at the furniture warehouse, I was horrified that my waist had grown to a number that was a good eight inches smaller than it currently is at the time that I write this.

Most people wouldn't equate ADHD and obesity problems, but if you think about it, the requirements of maintaining proper weight are skills like impulse control, delayed gratification, goal setting and follow-through, emotion regulation, and self-awareness. These are not my areas of strength. Anyway, after Amanda was born, Tina started working on shedding the baby weight, and I followed her in the process. We didn't do anything dramatic or trendy; we just ate healthier and exercised. For some unknown reason, I decided to try running on the treadmill at the gym. That might not seem weird, since I had had such a sports-involved youth and still played basketball on a regular basis, but that was purposeful running. I was running after something or away from something. Running just to run was the thing I hated the most. I'm not built for it. I'm full of fast-twitch muscle fibers, built to lift stuff and smash stuff, not glide along like a gazelle. When I was in Grade 12, I had a chance to get an A in my P.E. class. All I needed to do was get a decent time in the 2400-meter run. Instead, I decided to walk the whole thing and took the B. So, I'm not sure what I was thinking the first time I got on a treadmill and decided to see how far I could run in an hour. Actually, I think I might have some idea.

My brain is attracted to extremes. Even though moderation is much more sustainable, in almost all activities in life, moderation cannot sustain my attention and dedication because the reward is not as immediate or noticeable. I'm also attracted to the kinds of feats that make people say, "You did what?!" It's rooted in my need for attention, I guess. No one is impressed when the fat guy does 15 minutes on the treadmill. They might say, "Good for you" or "You gotta start somewhere," but I want them to say, "You're the most impressive guy I've seen in my life. You did a thing that I didn't think anyone could do, least of all you." I ran 8.4 kilometres that first time. I was shocked. In high school I couldn't even do a quarter of that without wanting to die. The next week I went back and ran 9.4 kilometres in the same amount of time, and I was hooked. It was extreme--I saw immediate results, and I could brag about it. So, with eating better and falling in love with running, the weight started to drop off. Approximately six months after Amanda was born, I found myself, once again, tipping the scales at 200 pounds. Probably the most intoxicating thing about losing weight is the feeling of control that you have over yourself. The ability to say no to things that you felt helpless about previously is a great way to balance feelings of powerlessness elsewhere in your life. You know who else says that? People with anorexia. It was this realization that I had while losing weight that allowed me to see eating disorders as having only a tenuous relationship with body image and a much stronger link to trauma and powerlessness.

FIFTY-ONE

NOT SO FAST, GENIUS

THAT SEMESTER AT KWANTLEN COLLEGE, I was taking some more filler courses, building up elective credits and not really knowing what I wanted to do in psychology. The thought came to me one day that I loved sports and I loved psychology, and I wondered if there was any way to combine the two into a career. So, I went to the internet (this was pre-google), searched the term "sports psychology" and was overjoyed to find that this was a growing field that I could actually be a part of. I immediately decided that this was going to be my future. However, in the meantime I still needed to take geography, computer science, and Spanish (to erase the F that I received when I stopped going to class). Spanish came easily to me, and the computer science class was really simple but taught me the basics of Microsoft Word and Excel, which skillset would be incredibly handy throughout my education and beyond. I found that geography was also pretty easy, and I really loved the prof who was a very friendly older guy from Nigeria who had a heavy accent and a twinkle in his eye. Because I was doing well in my classes, I was able to reassume the role that I had in elementary school of "the kid that the teacher liked." It was a great feeling. I got two A+s and an A, a semester that most people would be ecstatic with, but I ended with a nasty taste in my mouth due to my ADHD rearing its ugly head again.

I was going into my geography final with 100 percent in the class. That's not a typo. I had not missed an answer on any test or assignment the entire semester. That's the kind of grade that you would think would sit in direct counterevidence to my inner feelings of stupidity and inadequacy, but, in fact, it kind of worked in reverse. The grade was so extremely different from my high school experience that I figured there must be something wrong with the class, the school, the professor, or anything else that might explain how I could be doing so well in my education. One of the brain's little cognitive shortcuts is called the confirmation bias, which I referred to back at the very beginning of this book, so you probably don't remember what it is. It's the tendency to pay attention to and remember things that confirm what we already think and to screen out everything else. When we can't screen it out, like having 100 percent in a class, the brain is very adept at twisting or reframing the information so that it still fits into the pre-existing bias. For my brain, it was easy to argue that this was just a small school, that the prof liked me, or that I was graded relative to my classmates, who were mostly a few years younger than I was.

In any event, I had 100 percent heading into the final exam, and by the time it was over, I knew that I had aced it. I mean, really aced it. There wasn't one answer that I didn't know. Not only that, but I did the whole thing in about a third of the allotted time. I don't remember one single thing that I learned in that class, but I remember that during the final, this girl who was sitting behind me opened a crinkly bag of chips and would occasionally take one out of the bag and slowly crunch away on it. Because the room was so quiet and my ADHD senses were so tuned in to my irrelevant surroundings, it sounded like she was tap-dancing on the desk. I remember that they were Sun Chips because I kept turning around to glare at her. I mean, it was like a comedy sketch. She wasn't just eating chips, she was slowly crunching away at them, one single chip at a time, dragging out the process for as long as possible. It's like she was eating them *at* me. Wait, do most people eat chips one at a time, or do most people shove them into their mouths by the handful like I do? I'm going to ask that question on my Facebook page right now.

Anyway, I somehow survived her chewing assault and strutted up to the front of the class to drop my exam booklet onto the prof's desk. I enjoyed the idea of my classmates looking at me in awe as they continued to struggle with the test and sauntered out of the classroom, noticing on my way that my crunchy, crinkly friend actually had two bags of chips, with one remaining unopened in the event that she was in there for the long haul. I almost took the bag with me, but my impulse control worked that time, and I left. A week or so later, I checked my grades online and was shocked to see that I had finished with an A in my geography class instead of the A+ that I was absolutely certain I would see. I quickly went to my backpack to grab my geography binder to get the syllabus out to get the prof's contact information so I could email him and ask what had happened. As I opened the binder, I saw the answer to my question. It was the multiple-choice section of the exam. The exam had been divided into two sections, contained in two separate booklets while we were writing it. The multiple-choice section and the written section. When I had strutted up to his desk to drop off my finished exam, I had mistakenly only taken the written booklet with me. When I came back to my desk, perhaps distracted by the crunching sound echoing in my ears but more likely distracted by my own ego, I had mistakenly put the other booklet into my bag and left. As such, I only got 50 percent on the final exam. Unlike my French professor who had taken mercy on my scattered mind during my first semester, my kindly Nigerian friend gave me no such credit and slashed my mark down without prejudice. These are the kinds of experiences that lead a person to go into a class with 100 percent and still feel like an idiot and a fraud. Of course, now I know that the two things are completely unrelated, but at the time I didn't, and it just fueled my self-image of the "Almost-Champ."

FIFTY-TWO

GIVE ME AN INCH

AFTER MY THIRD successful semester of university, I got a better job. My dad was working for the provincial power company, and they were having a lot of problems with illegal marijuana grow-ops stealing power. During a meeting with a security consultant, my dad mentioned that I spoke Vietnamese, as many of these thieves were Vietnamese. The consultant, a former member of the Royal Canadian Mounted Police, couldn't believe his ears and gave my dad the number of someone who would really want to speak to me. My dad passed the number along to me of a special RCMP unit that performed various forms of surveillance. It turned out that they were working on a Vietnamese file at the time and were in sore need of interpreters. I guess it was uncommon to find a white person who could speak Vietnamese, but it was also important that I be able to pass the high-level security clearance check that the RCMP conducts on employees who have that level of access to information. I mean, this is the kind of security check where they talk to everyone who's been your neighbour in the last 10 years, as well as all previous employers and immediate and extended family, then ask you really probing personal questions to find out if you're a bad guy or not. To have a Vietnamese speaker who was also fluent in English and could pass the security check, they thought they had struck gold with me.

I showed up for the interview and was told that I would need to complete a typing test. Nobody had told me about a typing test. This was back in the late 90s, and writing papers on computers was still a relatively new thing to me. I was strictly a two-finger typer. They left me in a room with two paragraphs displayed on the upper part of a computer screen. All I had to do was type out the two paragraphs as many times as I could in three minutes. Seemed simple enough. After they came back to see my results, I was not surprised but still embarrassed that I had not even typed out one of the paragraphs one time. I figured I had just blown my chance at a sweet job and was prepared to be given a gracious thank you for showing up, when they essentially told me when my first shift would be. I was shocked. It turns out that if you have one skill strong enough, it can make up for the ones you lack. I suppose that is true in many areas of life, especially as someone with ADHD. For example, my creativity could often make up for my lack of attention to detail. My ability to hyperfocus under pressure would make up for my lack of organization beforehand. The fun, generous and thoughtful parts of me would make up for the attention-seeking, jealous, and selfish parts of myself. I think it's really important that we always see ourselves and others in a balanced way, as dynamic, fluid, hybrid people who, while prone to being trapped in the moment and thus seeing ourselves as only one way or the other, are actually kaleidoscopes.

Anyway, I showed up for my first shift and began listening to other people's lives on the phone. Obviously, I can't tell you anything about how it works or what I heard or saw, but let it suffice to say that the job of voyeur was perfectly suited to my ADHD brain. I was a people-watching professional long before that job or my current career as a therapist. Whether it was staring at people in a restaurant, the classroom, at church, or--my personal favourite--at the mall, I loved sitting and watching people and wondering about their lives. I know that I'm not alone in this tendency, but landing this job in the summer after my third semester was a blessing in so many ways. I only worked on the Vietnamese file for a few weeks before they closed it down, but they transferred me over to a different file that was just English speaking. What a break I caught. If I hadn't had the Vietnamese, they wouldn't have looked at me twice for a hire, but it turned out that that was only the key that unlocked the door. The job paid decently well and had good benefits, holidays, sick days, and pretty decent coworkers from very diverse backgrounds. My two main partners in crime (prevention) were Chisen and Sean. Chisen was this really smart Japanese woman who was saving money to finish her university degree, and Sean was a university football player who could have been my own brother for how alike we were. We were all pretty close in age and left fairly unsupervised to do our jobs. As you might predict, Chisen was the most mature of the bunch and took on the role of fun mom, while Sean and I were the unruly teenagers who made mom roll her eyes and shake her head on a regular basis.

It was a job that had periods of both intense excitement and mind-numbing boredom. Our office was located in the RCMP head-quarters in Vancouver, so across the complex there were gyms where we could work out or shoot hoops. When it was time for me to take my break or my lunch, I would head over and hit the treadmill, continuing my weight-loss journey. It was a long commute to Vancouver, but I found a way around it by leaving extremely early in the morning. That way I could beat the traffic on the way in and out. We didn't have a super-specific shift time, as long as there was always coverage on the phones, so I would often arrive at work before 6 a.m. and not have to do any actual work until closer to 8 a.m. Eventually my supervisors realized what was happening and told me that I couldn't come in that early, so it was back to the traffic. The highways and roads around Vancouver are terrible, for the record. Like, world-leading terrible. I could drive the 60 kilometers from my house in Abbotsford to the freeway exit on the edge of Vancouver in about 40 minutes, and then it would take me another 40 minutes to go the last 10 kilometers. This is the kind of math that leads people to commit acts of violence.

Traffic is the bane of my ADHD existence. Being able to see your destination but also being prevented from reaching it for no discernible reason is among the most frustrating experiences on earth. Well, in my life, anyway. I'm sure seeing your much-needed food relief diverted by corrupt government leaders while you and your family starve in temporary cardboard housing is much more frustrating than bad traffic, but I don't live in that place. I live in the place where it takes 40 minutes to drive 10 kilometers. In a way, this issue is very representative of the internal traffic in the ADHD brain. Often you know where you want to go and even how to get there, but something just keeps getting in the way. The time slips by, and you end up scrambling at the end without any explanation for what was causing the delay in the first place. I was reading recently about different executive function problems that can occur with ADHD and autism, and I came across one that explained so much. It's called "initiation," and it's the step between intending to do something and actually doing something. For most people, this process seems to have only two steps. You want to do something, so you do it. In actual fact, though, it's a three-step process. You intend to do something, you start to do the thing, and then you do the thing. For people whose brains struggle with that middle step, there ends up being a mental and emotional traffic jam that is as inexplicable to the actor as it is to the audience.

Anyway, I remember this one time when it took three hours to get home from work. It was a smoking-hot day, my car had no air-conditioning, and it was a standard stick shift, meaning I just about wore the clutch out that day during the stop and go, but also meaning that I could never really just zone out because I had to stay mentally engaged enough not to stall my car. At about the halfway mark, I heard a commotion to my right and looked over to see another guy who was in my position but who was not handling it as well as I was.

He was losing his mind. I kind of expected him to pull a Michael Douglas move like in the movie *Falling Down,* where the guy has just had enough and goes on a violent crime spree. The guy was screaming, cursing, and attempting to beat his steering wheel to death with his bare hands. He had lost any sense of caring about how this might be perceived by his fellow sufferers and had completely given over to the dark side. While I had a little chuckle at his expense, I could also completely relate. Since that day, I am proud to say I've had a few of those moments of my own, but knowing what I know about the importance of expressing emotion, not just feeling it, I see it as a positive thing.

Of course, this setup was a bit too good to be true, and since I epitomize the old saying about giving someone an inch and they will take a mile, I pushed my luck until I lost the trust of my supervisors. Because, of course, it wasn't really okay, even if it was technically within the rules, for me to get to work two hours before there was any action. It basically meant that I got paid to do nothing for two hours, and while that wasn't my intention, that was the reality, so, as I mentioned, they asked me to come in a bit later. Also, I had the bright idea of combining my breaks and lunch and taking an extended lunch break over at the gym, which didn't really cause too many problems until I convinced Sean, and even Chisen, occasionally, to join me. Anyway, at a certain point in the file, the active investigation was closed, and our duties changed to transcription of selected pieces of evidence. This meant that we didn't need to cover live calls, and thus we had much more flexibility in our workload. Basically, as long as we got everything done that we needed to do, we were left unsupervised. Technically. However, because every once in a while all three of us ended up over at the gymnasium for a free-throw contest, we increased the chances of an actual supervisor coming to our work room and finding it empty during the middle of a shift. Which happened. Also, it happened that they stopped by one other time when it was just me that was gone. This did not look good, and it was my second "strike." The supervisor was not impressed, but because I hadn't technically (gotta love that word. It's an annoying rule-break-er's bread and butter) broken any rules, they could only be annoyed with me. Which they were. It kind of reminded me of a time in Grade 3 where I made an assumption that landed me in some hot water.

FIFTY-THREE

JELLY TOTS FOR EVERYONE

My Grade 3 teacher was Mrs. Dunne. I don't know much about her other than that she had long, fake nails that were always brightly coloured. She would often wear colourful hoop earrings and had a strong 80s game going, style-wise. She could be really nasty to us kids, because why not be a teacher and then be mad at kids for a living, almost as if she was surprised at how much we didn't know? So many adults are like that, I find, when it comes to the frustrating things that kids do. We bark at them and ask incredulous questions like, "Why would you do that?" instead of remembering that they don't know anything, and it's our job to teach them--and that same question, delivered with a tone of curiosity instead of condemnation, would actually go a long way in helping us understand the way they think and thus put us in a better position to help them learn. I realized this when my kids were young, and I put up signs that said "Teachers. Not Taskmasters" all over our house, but they eventually just faded into the background and became visual white noise; the thought has never left me, though, even if I can't always practice what I preach and know to be true. That was a long sentence. You might need to read it again.

Anyway, when I was in Grade 3, the boys in my class all became obsessed with eating kippers, which are like sardines, but they aren't actually sardines. I don't know the difference, and it doesn't really matter. What matters is that they are gross. Salted fish with the skin on, served in a gooey juice from a tin can. They cost a dollar for a can over at Piper's corner store, which was just across the street from the elementary school. At recess and lunch, kids who had a few cents would head across the street and pick out some penny candy or some potato chips for 50 cents. During the 80s, it was so awesome that Hostess potato chips included little stickers of WWF wrestlers in the bags, and I ate many bags of pizza-flavored chips in hopes of completing my collection, which all ended up stuck to my desk at school. Pizza-flavored chips don't taste like pizza. Who decided that that's what pizza-flavored things should taste like? Anyway, kippers.

Mrs. Dunne always seemed like she didn't belong in the redneck crowd of Salmo, and I'm pretty sure she didn't actually live around there. So you can imagine her delight when the boys in her class all started to ingest such a large quantity of stinky fish snacks that the room began to smell like stinky fish. Finally one day she had had enough and told the class that kippers were no longer going to be allowed unless the boys who bought them also brought their tooth-brushes to school to get rid of the smell. I imagine that was an issue that they didn't cover in her professional-development program during university, but there she was, delivering the edict to us with all of the dignity that she could muster. As cold and harsh as Mrs. Dunne could be, she had a strange habit of giving out little candies called Jelly Tots for a job well done, either academically or behav-iourally. Occasionally I managed to land a jelly tot, but the most memorable prizes were a half tot, because she would literally put the tot down on my desk and then cut it in half with one of her long fingernails. Which is gross. But at the time, I just knew that I was getting some sugar, and that's all that mattered.

An even greater honour than getting a Jelly Tot was being trusted to be the kid who got to run across the street to Piper's during school hours to buy a new package for Mrs. Dunne. Every time, the kid who was selected for this task was told to keep the change and buy a little something for themselves. It was really a double prize. You got to leave class. You got to be important. Also, you got a treat. So, that's a triple prize, even better. One day, I'm not sure how, but I won the lottery and was given a dollar to run across the street to Piper's and buy the next bag of Jelly Tots. I did so and used the leftover money to buy myself something, which I ate on the way back to class, of course. I proudly came back into the classroom, walked over to Mrs. Dunne's desk, and handed her the package of Jelly Tots. She thanked me, and then when I turned to walk back to my seat, she shocked me by asking, "Where's the rest of the money?" I stopped in my tracks and stammered out, "I spent it on something else." Her eyes narrowed as she contemplated the best way to skin me alive. "Why would you do that?" she hissed, and not in the curious way that I was suggesting above. "Um, because you always tell the kid to keep the change," I answered.

"Did I tell you to keep the change?" she asked, as if cross-examining a serial killer on the witness stand.

"No," I had to admit. "But you always tell the kid to keep the change, so I assumed that you would be okay with it."

"But I didn't tell you to keep the change, and you just assumed that, didn't you? How am I supposed to trust you now?"

"I don't know. You always tell the kid to keep the change...."

"Well, I guess I won't be asking you to do that favor for me again."

This was a long time before the concept of a verbal mic drop became an overused trope, but it definitely qualified, and I hope she felt good about shaming me and setting me up to fail and then taking advantage of the opportunity. I walked back to my desk and sat down with my face red-hot with righteous anger and shame. It felt so unfair, but I also was kicking myself for being so dumb as to assume that she would be okay with me spending her money. Chalk up another incident of being misunderstood due to my own misunderstanding.

Anyway, when my supervisor mentioned that perhaps I should spend more time working at work and less time goofing around, I had a very similar feeling. I was happy to leave that job to go back for another semester of university.

FIFTY-FOUR

WE HAD ANOTHER BABY

AMANDA (WE CALL her Manda) had settled down from her challenging early months and revealed that she was incredibly smart. I know that lots of parents see that in their kids, but she was (is) legitimately intelligent. Think of it this way: the typical 18-month-old kid has a vocabulary of around 60 words. Manda had a vocabulary of 250 words. We counted them. She was able to speak in sentences and tell us what she wanted some of the time, which is always a bonus with a whining toddler. When she was almost a year old, halfway through my semester, Tina got pregnant again. While it wasn't planned, it also wasn't prevented. Mormons have lots of kids. It's kind of a thing that we're known for. So even though we were poor, Tina's maternity leave had just ended, I was in school, and we were living on borrowed time in the townhouse, it was a very happy thing. I always feel bad for people who get pregnant when they don't want to be because something that could be such fantastic news is coloured with disappointment, if not total devastation.

Because of this development, I decided after the semester to go back to the RCMP since the job paid well, I knew what to do there, and surprisingly they wanted me back. I guess I probably fell into the, "he's already got the security clearance" category of qualifications. In any event, I was back in familiar territory, although my coworkers were all completely different. I don't think Chisen was even there anymore, and they intentionally split up Sean and me because we got along too well. Isn't that what they do to the "overly social" kid in elementary school? Too bad for them (and me) that I'm like that meme that was going around Facebook that says something like, "Hey teacher, I talk to whoever I'm sitting next to, so moving my desk won't make a difference." Except I was a 25-year-old man, not an 8-year-old kid smelling of kippers with a pocket full of illicit change. I made fast friends with the employees and even some of the RCMP members that I worked with, and I had learned my lesson from my earlier misadventures and tried to hide my rule-breaking more effectively. Because, of course, that's what punishments teach people like me. They teach us to be sneakier.

As Tina's due date got closer, we had to make a decision about whether we were going to have another C-section (the recommended course of action) or a VBAC (vaginal birth after Cesarean), the doctor's less-preferred option. Our thinking was that if we could avoid another major abdominal surgery, that would probably be the best. The doctors preferred the C-section because I guess the risk of internal tearing can be pretty high. However, before we could decide either way, Tina's water broke and we found ourselves heading off to the hospital with some mild contractions and a lot of excited and nervous energy coursing through our veins. That's a weird way to say it. We left Manda with her favourite Aunt, Lisa. She's Tina's oldest sister and at that time was single and had lots of time to devote to being Manda's aunt, something that would come back to haunt us in the near future. I'm sure that a lot of women would find it funny that I said mild contractions, as if there is such a thing. That's like saying I was mildly kicked in the junk, I would imagine. Of course there are degrees to such a thing, but even the mildest degree is extremely unpleasant. Tina's contractions were progressing as normal, and so we headed to the hospital. They checked Tina to see if she was dilating, and she was, so everything was going as normal, but as is usually the case, everything is normal until it isn't. She dilated to about five centimetres and then stopped. The contractions kept coming, but she would not dilate any more than that, no matter what they did to help the process along. To top it off, the terrible Abbotsford hospital (long since demolished to build a newer, better one) only had one anesthetist on duty that night, so after Tina's first epidural wore off, there was no one around to give her another one. "The epidural wore off?" you might wonder. Yes, because we had already been at the hospital--with Tina in some form of painful distress--for 20 hours at that point. They tried to bring her to happy land with some nitrous, but it didn't work at all. In hindsight, I should probably have strapped on the mask to see if there was an issue, but also in hindsight, it's probably good that I didn't, just in case there was no issue. In any event, the time wore on and the medicine wore off.

Did I mention that during a VBAC, if a woman has not dilated past five centimetres after four hours, they are supposed to proceed with a C-section? No? Well, no one mentioned that to us, either, and here we were entering hour 22 with no progress. Granted, the repeated checks of the baby's vitals did not indicate that there was any fetal distress, but still, I imagine those rules exist for a reason. To make a very long night into a much shorter story, it was finally decided to proceed with the C-section, and after 27 hours of terrible pain, we headed to the operating room together. During this entire ordeal, our doctor showed up to the hospital to check on Tina exactly one time, and his visit lasted less than five minutes. This was strike two. Anyway, on November 5, Tina gave birth to another baby girl, whom we named Rebecca. She looked a lot like Manda and was almost the same size. She managed to escape the slicing of the wayward scalpel, unlike her older sister, but she had put in 27 hours of stress along with Tina and really just needed to rest. Unfortunately, in this old dump of a hospital, that was not to be, because they were renovating at the time and were literally using a jackhammer in the hallway outside the hospital room where Tina and Becca (which

I've called her from the beginning) were left to rot, er, rest. So every time this little bundle of newness was finally able to calm her nervous system down, a jackhammer would explode 15 feet away from her bassinet, causing her startle reflex to be on display repeatedly.

As terrible as the birth process and the recovery was, what became equally difficult was the hard time that Manda had warming up to her little sister. She showed no interest in seeing her, holding her, or talking to her, and had little regard for Tina, either. Now that I think of it, the long night of the delivery was the first time she had ever spent a night away from us, and she was never a good sleeper to begin with, so it was probably kind of rough for her, too. Then at the end of the tunnel, instead of a light, there was her mom in a hospital bed, on pain medication, holding a baby and loving her. This was not a good couple of days for Manda, and it took her a long time to not want to leave Becca at the bus station. She didn't actually suggest that, but she did have the vocabulary to do it if she had thought of it.

Making matters even harder for Manda was the fact that Becca was colicky for three months. To this day, there are few sounds in the world that have the capacity to make my blood steam (like, past boiling) like a crying or fussy baby that cannot be soothed. Of course, it forms a vicious cycle in which the baby's crying stresses out the parent, whose stress is sensed by the baby, causing it to cry. Poor Becca and I went around this cycle so many times it could be named in our honor. I was not at my dad or husband best during this phase of my life. When Tina was able to sneak out for any length of time, she would almost invariably come home to me standing on the doorstep with a screaming baby in one arm and a scowl on my face, pronouncing edicts like, "You are never leaving me with her again!" When I think back on this, it is with a mix of compassion and anger. If I saw another dad acting like this, I would smack him in the head and tell him to grow up, but then I also realize that I was 25 years old, stressed with school and a screaming baby and a toddler, and I had no coping skills whatsoever. It's a miracle that we all survived those three months, but I also know that we didn't come away without scars.

Becca struggled with anxiety off and on for years and has always been overly mindful of the emotional state of Tina and me. Manda is a perfectionist who has a hard time seeing herself in a positive light, although she has made great strides in this area. It's kind of too bad that we have kids before we're ready, but I guess no one is really ready, no matter how many times they've read the book about what to expect. Becca was also prone to ear infections, suffering through 24 in her first year of life. It was rare to see her without an infection in one or both ears, and she cried a lot. However, at the three-month mark, pretty much to the day, the colicky crying seemed to vanish, and she just became a normal crying ear-infected baby. Poor kid. This was also the time we finished with our terrible doctor. The final straw was when we asked him whether Becca was colicky and he said no, that colic tended not to start until the three-month mark, which is the exact opposite of the truth. After that, we let him go and switched to a different doctor. We also gave up on the Abbotsford hospital and decided to have our kids in Langley from then on.

FIFTY-FIVE
AND BACK TO SCHOOL

LEADING up to Becca's birth, I had gone back to work with the RCMP, and although Chisen and Sean were gone, it was just as interesting and fun as it was the first time around. I understood the boundaries and expectations better than before, and I did a much better job for them this time around. I was taking another semester off to work, though, and if I'd kept this pace up, it would have taken me 10 years to graduate, which reminds me of the line from *Tommy Boy* when Tommy says to Richard, "Lots of people go to college for 10 years," and Richard answers, "Yeah, they're called doctors," and then Tommy says, "Shut up, Richard." That's a funny movie. Anyway, I don't remember the reasoning as to why I decided to take another semester off, but during the fall, as Tina got closer to having the baby and I was getting really tired of the commute to Vancouver, I decided to switch schools to the University of the Fraser Valley, out in Abbotsford. At the time, it was a University College, like Kwantlen, which is probably the equivalent of a junior college in the United States. This meant that it offered academic degrees but also trades programs. It also meant smaller class sizes, cheaper tuition, and more accessible instructors. These were all critical things for me, even though I didn't really realize it at the time.

Because the RCMP is a federal government institution, the employee benefits packages are ridiculously good, even for civilian employees like myself. I took full advantage of this when Becca was born and took some time off for parental leave. This turned out to be no holiday, as I mentioned above, but it also led to a classic Ted moment. As my return-to-work date in December creeped closer, and things were not getting any easier at home with two small babies and a stressed-out wife recovering from her second C-section, the thought of leaving them behind became increasingly unbearable. Of course, I didn't let my boss know what was going on, and so they continued to believe that I would be returning to work on a particular date. Imagine their surprise when on that date, instead of arriving at work, I called to tell them that I would not be coming back at all and would be returning to university in January. They were not happy with me, but at that point, I didn't care, because my family needed me more than the RCMP. The part that is classic Ted is that this decision was discussed with Tina and ruminated about with myself for weeks, but I didn't actually make the decision until 6:00 in the morning on the day I was supposed to go back to work. It was another example of calculated impulsivity; the appearance of a last-minute, split-second decision that was obsessed about for a long time beforehand.

Deciding to go to school at the last second also meant that when it came to registering for courses as a new student, the choices were very limited. This is how I ended up taking macroeconomics as a course, when in any other circumstances, I would rather have eaten a live snake. Maybe not. I hadn't touched anything math-related since Grade 11, when I mercifully escaped with my 50 percent passing grade and rejoiced at the prospect of never having to do math again, and here I was having to calculate all sorts of things that I didn't understand or care about. This was the first real test of my academic ability, and I wore that professor out, meeting him in his office on a regular basis and asking question after question. It's a good thing that I had no friends at school, because I needed my entire mental capacity to wrestle with that class. I was also taking Spanish and a psych class, both of which came pretty naturally to me, so the economics class was definitely the chief occupier of my mental energy. In the end, I managed an A- in the class, which was another revelation, a broken glass ceiling for me, as I gained confidence that I could actually do hard things and learn. Of course, my already well-ingrained belief that I was stupid didn't let that feeling hang around for long and quickly reframed my grade as one based on the professor's pity and being a student at a small school that wasn't even a "real university."

At UFV, which was then called UCFV, but to this day I want people to take my degree seriously so I call it UFV, I took a variety of courses including kinesiology, philosophy, psychology and language courses. I ended up registering for Japanese for some reason. I guess I reasoned that they were arts credits that would count toward my degree, and I loved learning languages and they came naturally to me, but in hindsight, those credits might have been put to better use in other areas more relevant to my future profession. However, it could also be argued that the confidence I gained by excelling in language courses paid dividends in my core courses by demonstrating that I did have some natural capacity to learn. My Japanese course was particularly fun because it taught me a completely different grammatical system from that of any other language I had studied. The similarities between Spanish and French almost made me feel like I was cheating in my Spanish class, but Japanese was a totally different animal. It also gave me a glimpse into what my brain was good at: making connections. I remember lying in bed one night, going over some Japanese vocabulary and grammar in my head, because, of course, that sounds like a normal thing to do when a person is trying to go to sleep. In my brain, it was like a curtain was drawn back and I could finally understand this grammatical principle that we had been trying to cover in class. From there, I created a logic equation that presented a corollary of the original principle. In other words, if this is how you say this, then this must be how you say that. I remember feeling excited at the prospect that I was basically watching my brain do this on its own. When I went to school the next day, I pulled aside a Japanese exchange student who was in my Spanish class (we had made a deal that I would help her with Spanish and she would help me with Japanese) and asked her if what I had figured out was correct, and she looked at me with a stunned look on her face and confirmed that it was. She asked how I knew that, and I told her, which stunned her even further. I remember that conversation to this day, because it was the embodiment, in many ways, of what I had always wanted. I wanted to be exceptional so that I could be notice-able. Her shock at my learning pace validated this innermost desire and gave a great boost to my confidence. This was the odd thing all along my university journey. I would achieve amazing results, which would on some level confirm and build a belief in my intelligence and competence, but then I would commit some blunder that would remind me of my roots as an idiot.

For example, in my second semester of Japanese, I was cruising along at an A+, acing almost every single assignment, quiz, and test that was thrown my way. On the day of our final exam, we also had to hand in a final project, which I had worked hard on and knew would garner a top mark. I wrote the exam, knowing I had aced it, and confi-dently strode (borderline strutted) out of the classroom and went home to await the GPA glory that was soon to follow. Imagine my surprise when I checked my mark a week later to see that I had only got an A in the class. Does this sound familiar? I couldn't understand what had happened, so I went into my bag to get the professor's email address from my course syllabus and what do you think I found? No, it wasn't the exam. It was the assignment. It was sitting there in pris-tine condition, because I hadn't handed it in and hadn't opened my bag since that fateful day when I was supposed to. I mean, the parallel here is astounding. This was a virtual replica of my earlier experience in geography, and I felt even more moronic for having repeated my performance. As George W. Bush so eloquently said, "Fool me once, shame on you. Fool me twice ... you can't fool me twice."

FIFTY-SIX

SUCCESS DESPITE BEING MYSELF

IN A NUTSHELL, that event encapsulated my time in university. I generally did exceptionally well, scoring at or near the top of the class in almost all of my classes. I had come a long way from the distracted kid who forgot his homework, but my successes didn't cancel out the ghosts of those earlier days, especially when they showed up alive and well every once in a while. My usual process, especially early in my education, was to underachieve early in the semester and then create a spreadsheet on the computer (thanks to my computer science class at Kwantlen) that told me exactly where I stood and what I would need to do to escape the class with no less than an A. That sounds familiar, too, now that I think of it. It's basically what I used to do before all my final exams in high school. The difference was that in university, I was a bit more proactive about it, waiting only until the first month had gone by. One semester, I remember drawing upon an increasing reservoir of evidence that I could succeed at school. I looked at my spreadsheet, at the stark reality of what would be required for me to recover from my usual disorganization and procrastination, and formed my motto, which I wrote on my workbook: Plan, Work, and Ace Everything. I had learned that if I did the first two, the third was within reach. Then I went out and proved it to be true.

Throughout all of my university career, I only got two B+s. Everything else was an A- to A+. I feel uncomfortable saying that out loud, my old roots coming back to haunt me. I can hear my dad's voice saying that I should be more humble. I can hear the nameless voice saying that it was a small school and that it would have been different at a big school. I can hear that voice saying that the GPA was calculated on a different scale that doesn't translate, and so it makes it seem higher than it really was. But I have to fight through those voices and recognize that I have the capacity to be intelligent and to let my intelligence show. You can't fluke out for an entire degree. I don't feel like having this argument with myself right now. Let's talk about something else. How about sports psychology?

I was told by a professor near the beginning of my education that if I wanted to get into graduate school in the area of sports psychology, I should make sure that all of my undergraduate work was in some way related to that subject area. I would also need to show my research ability and network with professors at the schools where I wanted to go. Thus began four years of hyperfocus. I ate, slept, and drank sports psychology. Ugh, I hate that expression. Ate, slept, and drank? That's so cliché and sounds like something that someone would have said in the 60s but not in the cool way, like someone saying that something is dynamite, groovy, or neato. Did they say neato in the 60s? I'm googling it. Yes, they did. They also said righteous, choice, and nifty. Don't those seem like they would have been said by very different groups of people in the 60s? Like, I can't imagine being a person who said that a new song by the Beatles was groovy and righteous also being a person who said that *The Good, the Bad, and the Ugly* was neato. I guess it's hard to come up with a list that covers all the different subcultures without dividing it into subcultures, kind of like how I can't fold laundry with Tina because I want to divide it into Manda's socks, Manda's shirts, Manda's pants, etc., whereas Tina just puts it into a pile called Manda. My way is more detailed; hers is more efficient. Anyway, sports psychology was super groovy.

I loved it. I was specifically interested in clinical sports psychology, which is like normal clinical psychology but working with athletes and coaches. But I was also interested in how the brain worked, how it perceived its environment, how it could be tricked and manipulated, how visualization was used to help athletes train without lifting a finger, and eventually I settled onto the subject of coach-athlete relationships. I was very interested in the impact a coach could have on a player outside of performance and read everything I could find on the subject. I was also interested in conditional goal setting, the psychology of achievement, and everything else I could get my hands on. It was so great to be able to study and learn about things I was actually interested in, that concerned real parts of my life, and the prospect of working in that field was beyond exciting. Along the way, I began to develop a reputation as a student. Professors knew I was serious and capable and gave me leeway to go outside the box on assignments and get creative with my topics and approaches. Soon, they were letting me know about research assistant positions that became available and asking me to help grade the exams and papers of first- and second-year students. I mean, think about that. At times, I had to shake my head because I still felt like the same kid who was falling asleep in biology class.

I remember one research assistant interview that I had with a professor whom I had never had as an instructor. I happened to mention in conversation that I tended to contribute a lot to class discussions, otherwise known as talking a lot. She nodded her head and said, "So I've heard." I was surprised and asked what she meant. She said that I was known in the department as someone who was very interested in discussing things. I didn't necessarily read this as a compliment, especially coming from her, since she kind of had a reputation for not being very nice or patient. It was another one of the seemingly endless moments of me realizing that I was being perceived differently than I thought I was. On the surface, you would think someone as self-conscious about this kind of thing as I was would be more careful, but then you wouldn't really understand how the ADHD brain works. We're full of these kinds of paradoxes and inconsistencies. I guess if you think about it, self-conscious is not the most accurate term to describe someone who is afraid of how they are perceived by others, because to be conscious of the self is to be aware of the self, and most people who worry about this do not have a very accurate awareness of themselves, so how could they be called self-conscious? There has to be a better term for it. As I run through the thesaurus in my brain, I settle on self-doubt, because that seems to be the most accurate. Interestingly, the mental act of running through the thesaurus in my brain is visualized automatically by the words being placed on a giant spinning wheel, like on *The Price is Right,* and the wheel slows down as it gets closer to the right word, and then there's some sort of game show sound and I decide on self-doubt.

One of my favourite professors was Wayne Podrouzek, who seemed bent on living up to the absent-minded professor stereotype. He was all high energy, non-conformity and personal opinion, but he was also a staunch scientist and lover of high-quality, valid research. He was interested in knowledge for knowledge's sake and not so interested in real-world applications. In some ways, this allowed him to be a bit less biased than a researcher who was looking for results that would support his or her life's work. I can see how Wayne could be intimidating to younger students, but with me, he seemed to engage the thirst for knowledge that I always carried, and he could string together a series of research studies into a format that resembled an adventure novel. At least that was how I experienced them.

Another notable instructor I had along the way was Roger Friesen. Roger was a sports psychologist, even though he did not have a PhD. He was from a less-regulated time in psychology when accreditation was less stringent, and I don't mean that in any kind of disparaging way. Roger was extremely accomplished as a sports psychologist and human being and had a very gentle, curious, open-minded way about him that immediately drew me in. He was also a great storyteller, which I am realizing now is a characteristic that I value in people, especially my friends. As I am writing this book, Tina will often comment on how surprised she is with how many stories I remember, and my explanation is that I have always been a talker and a storyteller. When I had an experience, I would tell someone and I would tell everyone, and the repetition of those stories encoded them into memories. I'm not sure what it is about story-telling, but I find that it connects with me and with other people in a way that a simple imparting of facts cannot. Thus, professors who simply read off the screen or recited endless lists of data had difficulty engaging me.

Despite all of my success in school, don't think that I had neces-sarily changed my ways completely. It was my standard practice not to read the chapters in the textbook but to read the research papers that I was interested in, usually working toward some final literature review that I found fascinating. Unfortunately, that fascinating research was not what was covered on the exams, so I had to find time to memorize terms and concepts so that I could regurgitate them for marks. This usually meant that I would head off to school on the day of the exam with anywhere from three to six chapters to read and review and memorize and understand and around six hours to accom-plish it. On paper, it was enough time, but what it didn't account for was my ADHD approach.

I would park next to the athletic building because that was where I spent most of my time. More on that later. Walking past the front lobby, I might get into a conversation with one of the basketball coaches or players or the front desk staff or the athletic director, and then I would find myself walking through the doors of the gymna-sium, where people were playing pickup basketball or just shooting around. I would watch for a bit, but because people knew I liked to play, I would end up being invited to join in a game, which I would reluctantly do, because I knew that I had so much studying to do. One game would often turn into an hour or two of basketball, and then some more conversations afterward with whatever athletes or staff happened to be in the area. Then I would think, "I have to get studying because I just used half my time playing sports." Of course I would also reasonably conclude that you can't effectively study on an empty stomach, so I would improve the efficiency of my studying by heading to the cafeteria to get some pizza or other brain food. I would find a table by myself, intending to study while eating, but I'd invariably get caught up in people-watching, or someone would join me who knew me from a class, and conversation would once again sweep away my best intentions like a wave and a sandcastle.

After I finished eating and zoning out or talking, I would make my way to the classroom where the exam would be held with around 2 hours to go before the deadline. I had learned in one of my classes that environmental cues are helpful in associative learning and memorization, so I figured that if I learned and memorized in the room where the exam would be held, it might help me to remember the information during the exam. Of course, by then I didn't have time to read all of the chapters, so I would just read the chapter summaries, lists of terms and key concepts and review my notes from class. I would identify the stuff that I would have a hard time regurgitating and come up with an acronym or some other mnemonic device to help, and as soon as I got the test booklet handed to me, I would write the memory prompt on the top of the first page so that I didn't have to remember it anymore. I would also often write "relax" or "slow down" on the top of each page to remind myself that it was not a race, because that's how I often approached it. I didn't see exams as tests of my knowledge; I saw them as tests of my prowess. I didn't just want to defeat my competitors, meaning my fellow classmates; I wanted to destroy them. It wasn't enough for me to get the best mark; I also had to get it faster than anyone else. Fortunately, that was usually what happened, but the relative ease with which I was finding success only underscored my brain's explanation of that success, arguing that in order for it to be this easy, there had to be some flaw in the system. There had to be some explanation other than my own ability.

FIFTY-SEVEN

CREATING DOORS AND WINDOWS

THROUGHOUT MY UNIVERSITY EXPERIENCE, I avoided working a real job. I know that sounds pretty lame, but I had my reasons, other than not liking to work. I reasoned that because I needed to get straight As, I couldn't afford for my time to be diverted anywhere else. This was sound logic, but of course, looking back, it was probably pretty false. If I had worked a part-time job, even 20 hours a week, it would have still equated to less time than I wasted playing sports, watching sports, or going to the gym. Maybe that's why after I had been at UFV for a couple of years, hanging around the gym most of that time, I decided to apply for a menial job sitting behind the front desk in the gymnasium, signing out basketballs to my fellow time-wasters. If I was going to hang out there, I might as well get paid for it, right? Little did I know the important role that decision would play in my development.

UFV, then UCFV, had started out as a very small college, growing over the decades into a much bigger, more professional institution. The downside of this growth was that the mom-and-pop approach that belonged to the younger version lingered longer than it should have in some areas, and the athletic department was one of them. The coaches of some of the teams were little more than community volunteers, and the athletic director at the time didn't even have that title. She had sort of fallen into the role just as her husband had fallen into the role of assistant men's basketball coach. Their main qualification for these jobs was longevity. I don't mean to disparage either of them, but it was clear, even to her, that the school was outgrowing her. She decided to retire, and an interim director was appointed to take over. This director openly admitted that she didn't really know what she was doing. She had been abducted from a different department in the school and told that she needed to cover until they could find someone else to take over full time. This worked to my advantage. I was already in place behind the front desk, and because she was so out of her element, she frequently asked me questions about how things worked, which gradually turned into her asking my opinion.

One day when I showed up for my shift, the athletic director asked me to come into her office. She said that the community relations department wanted someone to write press releases for the athletic department, and she had heard that I liked sports and wondered if I would be willing to go the games and write articles for the school. I was more than ready to agree to this when she told me that they would pay me to attend. She didn't know that I would have done the job for free. Thus it was that being in the right place at the right time, and maybe even being the right person, opened a door for me. The next thing I knew, I was getting paid to watch sports. I had up-close access to athletes and coaches and developed a familiarity that would serve me well going forward. It was in this position that I learned a very valuable life lesson as well. If you act like you know what you're doing, people generally won't question you.

At our home games, I was recognized by the staff and coaches, so I could walk in and out the doors without being checked, but when we travelled to away games in the lower mainland, I was a stranger. I didn't think it would be fair if I had to pay to go to a game when I was technically working, but UFV had made no provision for me. I took matters into my own hands by making my own press credentials. This consisted of printing out a small square of paper that said UCFV on it and putting it in a used plastic case connected to a lanyard that had the school logo on it. I wore this around my neck, but it never would have passed closer inspection. The critical component of my disguise was simply walking past the ticket-takers while looking important and busy and like I had every right in the world to go where I wanted. It was surprisingly easy to fool people, and it gave me confidence that expanded to multiple applications of this mindset. Sometimes I have advised clients of mine that if they can't actually be confident, perhaps they could just act like someone who is confident. Almost all of my press releases ended up in the local paper completely unedited, which also boosted my confidence, even though my name was never attached to the articles because they were technically issued by the community relations department. Alongside the opportunity to get paid to watch sports and talk to athletes and coaches, this job also opened another critical door for me. Well, to be specific, I created a door and barged through it.

Spending as much time as I did around the gym and athletic department, I noticed a trend that the men's basketball team would often lose players halfway through the season due to academic ineligibility. Many players were only in school to continue to play sports and had little interest in education, but because the basketball season spanned two semesters, players could lose their eligibility for the second semester if they didn't pass the first one. Because I was a student who was doing quite well and had overcome my own school struggles, I thought that maybe I was in a position to help, so I wandered into the newest athletic director's office (the third in just over a year) and made a suggestion. I offered my services as academic coach and explained that I believed that I could keep the athletes on track academically and prevent the loss of future players. The athletic director was interested and counter-proposed a trial semester after which he would re-evaluate the idea. I was assigned three women's basketball players, all rookies, who had barely squeaked past the bar in the first semester and were valued members of the team. Their coach was completely on board, which was a big help, and so I began to meet with these players on a weekly basis to follow up with how things were going and to keep them accountable. They gave me their course syllabi and reported their grades to me so that there would be no surprises at the end of the semester, and four months later, they were all on the honor roll. While the athletic staff was very grateful to me for my help, I felt guilty taking the credit because all three players were actually quite intelligent, capable students who just needed to be kept on task. I felt like my contribution was overvalued. Yet another example of desperately wanting recognition but also being desperately uncomfortable with it.

After that successful trial semester, the AD came back and proposed that I take on this role with all of the athletes across all of the teams. Within a short time, I had gone from handing out basketballs to being a part of the athletic department inner circle, sitting in on meetings and wielding some authority. It was a bit surreal to me, considering that I was still a student at the time. After a few months, it became clear to me that not all of the athletes needed my help, that some of them were doing just fine on their own. I eventually cut these ones loose after talking to their coaches. It's strange how some people just seem to have it all. One basketball player on the men's team was the team captain, Canadian player of the year, MVP of the championship and national champion. He was also taking seven classes and getting straight As, and to top it all off, he was a super nice guy. When I meet people like that, I wonder how they came to be. Some people seem to have so little to work with, and some people have so much. However, I guess there's also the opposite. I remember one of the men's team players was a little guy, only about 5'5" or so, but he somehow walked on to become a key role player off the bench; whereas another guy who was about 6'5" with a very well-rounded skill-set couldn't stay on the team for a whole semester due to academic issues and struggles with substance abuse and injuries. As I said, it was an odd position for me to be a fellow student but to be privy to this information and have some responsibility for these people.

I had many good conversations with the athletes and the coaches, which led to an independent studies project investigating the parallels between the working alliance in counselling (the relationship between counsellor and client) and coach-athlete relationships. It was so fun to design a research study from scratch, come up with my own measurement instruments, collect the data and analyze it. I can't even remember what the outcome of the study was, but I learned a lot from the experience and built my reputation even further as someone who was capable of functioning in the academic world. This led to one of my favourite on-campus, resume-padding positions where I was made the coordinator of the human performance lab. One of the kinesiology professors, with whom I'd had only one class, must have heard good things about me because he offered me the position without even really knowing me very well. The job required me to hang out in the lab and discuss potential research projects with kinesiology students, helping them think through their design, methods, analysis, etc., without actually having to do any of the data collection myself. It was perfect for me as it allowed me to use my creativity and curiosity but didn't require any of the detail-oriented stuff that I struggled with.

Other research assistant positions that I held were not nearly as interesting, with a couple of them being comprised solely of data entry. The most involved research position I had was with the professor whom I mentioned before who didn't have the greatest reputation. She was studying the sense of community that exists in what are called intentional communities, which I discovered is really just a modern term for communes. I did endless incredibly boring literature review on sense of community and what contributes to it and helped to interview and score the responses of many pleasant hippies that I met. Throughout the project, I remained curious about how a project like this could get funding from the government. If you want to do real research in academia, you need some sort of grant, and this professor had received one. I couldn't understand why this research mattered enough to enough people to justify the expense of the study. In the end, I don't even know if it was published, but I would be surprised if it was. I learned nothing except that I was sure that I didn't want to take any classes from her if I could avoid it, which I did.

FIFTY-EIGHT

BIRTH AND DEATH

DURING ONE OF my last semesters at UFV, we were blessed with the birth of our third child, Jill. She was the first of our babies whose gender we found out before the birth. As I mentioned earlier, growing up in a family full of boys and being a macho man, it hadn't occurred to me that I would have a daughter, and when Manda was born, I would be lying if I said I wasn't a little disappointed for just a fraction of a second. When Becca was born, I had the same experience. I decided that for the third child, I didn't want any such ridiculous reflex to taint the moment of birth at all, so we decided to find out the sex ahead of time. I know that doesn't sound great to say I was disappointed to have daughters, but you have to see my reaction in the context that I have described. After that split-second reaction, never once did I ever wish that my daughters were sons, and I slowly realized over time that having these precious girls sent to me gave me the opportunity to become much more aware of the struggles of women and girls in this world, something to which I was completely ignorant before this adventure began. When the ultrasound revealed that our third child was indeed a girl, I think I just smiled and said, "of course." The main benefit I found from finding the sex ahead of time was that we were able to pick a name for her relatively soon. This meant that for the better part of the pregnancy, we were able to refer to this unborn child as Jill instead of "the baby." The effect of this was that when she was finally born, I felt like I already knew her. Since Tina had already had two C-sections, the doctors didn't bother with any other option. We switched doctors to this wonderful, sweet and super-competent OB-GYN in Langley who was just great throughout the process.

Jill was born on a fairly momentous weekend in our family. My sister got married, we went to Tina's grandpa's funeral, and we discovered that our beloved cat Katie, whom I referred to as my first-born in the wilderness, had been hit by a car and killed. It was the first time that I had ever lost a pet, and it just about crushed me. She was a wild one by nature and loved to be outside, and she had even taken off missing for days before, so we hadn't thought much of it when she didn't come home for a few nights. We would call her, and I would walk around the co-op housing complex where we were living at the time, but there was no sign of her. One day as I was leaving for the gym, I had the feeling to turn right out of the parking lot instead of the usual left, and I listened to the feeling. When I rounded the corner, I was horrified to see Katie's distinctively beautiful coat on the road. She had not only been hit, she had been repeatedly run over by the busy traffic. I feel sick and sad as I write about it, the thought of her being discarded like that. I hope that it was over quickly for her. I immediately felt a hollowness in my stomach like I had never felt before.

I drove the rest of the way to the gym with shaking hands, and as soon as I got there, I asked to use their phone. I went around the corner to call Tina in private and told her what I had seen. I broke down and cried like a young child, and I told her that I couldn't bear to go and pick up the body. She cried, too, and we got her brother-in-law to go and do it for us, sparing me the awful chore. The tears kept coming for a few weeks after that, and even now when I think of her, I feel a heaviness in my chest and my throat tightens up. Because

Katie was a wild child who wanted to go outside a lot, but was also a cat and therefore stupid, rather than just go to the door and meow, she would go to the door and spray urine on the curtains. The last time I ever saw her alive, I was threatening to murder her. Of course, if I had known, I would have been happy for her to pee all over the house, but it was now just another experience of regret, a mistake that couldn't be erased.

Jill was an awesome baby. After Becca's colic, we were paranoid that Jill would be a repeat of that history, but we were so pleasantly surprised that she was an easy baby. She fell asleep well and was very smiley and chubby and so happy all the time. As she got older, she would entertain herself by sitting in a box of books and going through each and every page of each and every book, looking at the pictures intently. She would do puzzles and just sit quietly, observing her sisters and smiling and laughing as they danced and sang. Around this same time, my good friend's son, who was around Becca's age, was diagnosed with autism. He was quite severely affected, and they were unable to have even the most basic interaction with him. He avoided eye contact, wouldn't respond to any kind of cues, and had no language ability. Because of my education and my relationship with my friend, he asked me if I would be willing to be trained as a behavioural therapist and work with his son. I readily agreed, not necessarily because this was my dream job but because I was curious, and I thought it would make my application to grad school look even better. It was such a frustrating job. It wasn't even necessarily because it was difficult; it was more because it was so outside of my comfort zone. The job required me to be highly energetic, silly, enthusiastic, and to get down on the floor and play. These were not my areas of strength and skill, and I felt like I was being forced to speak a completely unfamiliar foreign language the entire time I was on the clock. I also didn't really think that this form of therapy would be very effective. Eventually, I told him that I couldn't help anymore. The strongest memory I have of baby Jilly was after a shift with my friend's son where no attempts at interaction were reciprocated. I came home and went upstairs to Jill's room, where she was sound asleep, having a nap. I crawled across the floor as quietly as I could. I crawled because even though she was an easy baby, she had followed her sisters' footsteps in being a light sleeper, and we never, ever, ever wanted the babies to wake up from their naps, no matter how cute they were. Anyway, I crawled over to her crib and peeked through the bars to see her beautiful chubby little face. The thought that I would never be able to communicate with her or interact with her, or even connect with her, filled me with overwhelming sadness. She was young enough that it was still a possibility for autism to be present, and I felt some anxiety at the prospect. However, I talked myself out of it and just decided to be grateful that she was so wonderful, whatever was to come.

What's ironic is that Jill is probably the most autistic of anyone in my family, followed closely by me. We both have sensory difficulties, high intelligence, some social difficulties and rigidities, but only rarely to the level that would be required for a diagnosis of ASD. This is not uncommon, actually, for ADHD folks, as genetic research has indicated a common underlying factor for ADHD, bipolar disorder, autism, Tourette's, and schizophrenia. The effect of this commonality is that diagnosing any of these can be complicated by the presence of symptoms from any of the others, but often not enough for the second diagnosis. Our sensory and cognitive weirdness have allowed Jill and me to bond very well, though, and I am ever grateful that she is blessed with a parent who can relate to her, because if I couldn't, she would be a bit of a challenge.

FIFTY-NINE

BUT I CAME ALL THIS WAY

LATER IN THE same year that Jill was born, I was going through the process of applying to graduate school. I only considered one program, which was probably a mistake, but I was given such strong assurances by my professors that I felt like it was a sure thing. I applied to Simon Fraser University, the same institution from which my dad, uncle, and older brother had graduated. I applied there because one of the world's leading sport psychologists was a professor there, David Cox. I had even created a reason to meet with him the year before for a research project in one of my courses. At that time, I had gone to his office and had a good conversation with him, telling him of my intentions and desire to work with him in graduate school, and he had been very encouraging. As my credit-gathering came to a close and my networking and resume-padding reached its end, the only thing left to do was to write the GRE, the Graduate Record Exam. The GRE is a test that measures your verbal reasoning, quantitative reasoning, and writing ability, and can also include a subject test for the particular area that you plan on studying in grad school. I was not too worried about the verbal or written part of the exam, but I was terrified of the math. I bought a book from the store called *GRE for Dummies,* which is really a paradox, if you think about it. Not a lot of dummies are writing the GRE. Anyway, I knew I was in trouble with the math when I had to look up what an "integer" was. That's how basic my math skills were. I went through the book laboriously, with very discouraging results. It was exactly like it was in high school, with me thinking that I understood a concept and then not getting the correct answer and having no idea how I had gotten it wrong. I was completely on my own, too. I was basically teaching myself math from scratch in order to compete against math whizzes and nerds from across North America.

The day of the exam, I headed to downtown Vancouver, found the testing centre, and settled in for judgment day. I had written dozens of practice tests with widely varying results, so I didn't really know what to expect. The GRE is one of those computerized tests that feeds you questions based on how you did on the previous question. In that way, if I got an easy question, I wondered if I had blown the previous one, but if I got a really hard one, I felt like I was doing well. The three hours passed in a blur, and then it was home to wait for the results. I can't remember how long it took to get them, but I remember the mix of pride and horror that resulted from opening the envelope and reading the outcome. In the verbal reasoning section, I was in the 93rd percentile. In the writing section, I had scored a 5/6. In the math section, I was in the 55th percentile. In context, that's actually not too bad, since the group I was being compared to included people who were literally applying for graduate programs in math, chemistry, physics, engineering and other similar fields. To be in the top half with that group of people felt like a bit of a victory, but I also knew that it was not going to help my case for graduate school. For the subject test, one of my helpful UFV professors had given me an unused textbook, which I'd combed over. Okay, I'd read most of the chapter summaries and highlighted the terms that were already highlighted. In the end, I wrote the subject GRE the same way I had done all of my exams as an undergraduate. I went in there determined to destroy, and that's what happened. I scored in the 97th percentile on the psychology test. If nothing else could validate my grades, if everything else could be twisted, this was something that my brain actually had to stop and consider for a second. There was no favouritism from professors, no "small-school" excuses, no getting lucky. Apparently, I actually knew my stuff. This restored my confidence in my chances at SFU.

The school received applications from over 600 students every year and only had room for 12. I was thrilled when I was informed that I had made the first cut and was invited to come up to the campus for an interview with two different professors, including David Cox. These interviews went really well, I thought, and afterwards, I was invited to a restaurant on campus to eat with the faculty and some of the other candidates. I felt like I was a real grown up and couldn't believe that this was really happening. Not long after that, I was informed that I was not in the top 12 but that I was number 13 on the list. They reassured me not to worry, that every year at least a few people would decline the offer and study elsewhere. I just needed to wait for these students to make their decisions, and then SFU would get back to me. At first, I was nervously excited. It was all about to pay off. However, as the days passed by, with no word from anyone at the school, I began to grow increasingly nervous. I didn't have a backup plan because I didn't think I would need one. On the final day, at the end of the day, David Cox called me at home to tell me that, unfortunately, there was no room for me that year, as every one of the accepted students had decided to attend SFU, after all. He said that he felt really bad for me, but that the final student had accepted on the last possible day to do so. He said that he had gone to the department and lobbied to have an extra space created in the program so that I could attend, but they had denied him. As he was telling me this, my academic life was flashing before my eyes, but I was still conscious enough to think, "yeah right." For some reason I doubted the truth of what he was saying, figuring he was just telling me that to soften the blow. In hindsight, he had no reason to lie to me. It was entirely possible that he'd done as he'd said. While I was crushed by this blow, I was not mortally wounded. His words gave me hope that I could get in the next year, depending on the group of students who were my competition.

It's a difficult thing when your identity, the thing you are known for, the thing that you believe defines you, is taken away from you. For around four years, I had been known as the student who had promise, potential, and a bright future in the field. I had been recognized for my abilities by others and had, against my own reflexive defenses, allowed myself to start to believe in what was being said about me, at least the positive things. I had been nominated for the psych grad of the year and attended a small reception in the psych department offices where the award would be handed out. The competition was between me and two other students, both of whom I knew well. I brought my wife and my mom with me, expecting that this was the beginning of all my work paying off. Instead, it was a harbinger of things to come as there were three students and two prizes, and I was the only one who walked away with nothing. When I think back on this event now, all these years later, I can't believe that they would organize such a thing. What is the point of inviting three students for two prizes when you know that one of them will get nothing? Even if it hadn't been me, I think I would have felt very uncomfortable with the setup, but of course I was especially sensitive to it because I was the guy whose only prize was a stale sandwich provided by the university cafeteria as refreshment for the event.

SIXTY

DON'T LET ME DOWN

Now THAT I had gone through the gauntlet and fallen short, I didn't know what to do next. I continued my duties as the academic coach but now had to inform everyone, person by person, what had happened. This was in the days before social media, when I could have informed everyone with one post. Instead, because I was so well-known as the guy who was going places, everyone I saw asked me about it, and I had to tell the story over and over. With each telling, it was drilled into me that I'd never really had a chance, that I was a fraud, and that I shouldn't get my hopes up again, no matter what. This has been my mantra for a lot of my life, when I think about it. Don't get your hopes up. If there's one thing that I can't stand, it's letting people down. I think it's because I've had so many experiences with letting people down and being let down.

I remember when I was younger, in the heyday of my wrestling mania, the WWF brought their superstars to Spokane, Washington, a city located about two hours to the south of Salmo. My friend Jeff Sims and I were both big fans and were talking about how cool it would be to go when his dad, another ADHD beacon in my childhood, generously volunteered to take us down to see it. We were thrilled. I couldn't believe that my dream was going to come true. As the day got closer, it was all I could think about. However, on the day of the event, I called Jeff to talk about travel arrangements only to be told that his dad wasn't going to be able to take us. I remember thinking, "How could something that is so important to me be of so little importance to someone else? Especially someone who is supposed to care about me." That's the thing, I know his dad did care about me. He was just prone to overcommitting to things and impulsively agreeing to help out. It was the caring that made it especially hurtful. It felt like a betrayal, and I was beside myself with anger and hurt feelings. Somehow, I ended up talking to my dad about it, and in one of the greatest parenting moments in history, my dad agreed to take my brothers and me to the event himself. This was with a few hours' notice and not a lot of extra money kicking around. He really stepped up to the plate, and I have never forgotten it. These kinds of events were not infrequent throughout my life. When I made plans with others, it was common for them to fall through, usually because the other person was not equally committed or because the event or activity wasn't nearly as important to them as it was to me. I couldn't help but feel like I wasn't important to them, either. So, when I got so close to the prize only to come away empty-handed, it was a terrible, gut-wrenching feeling, but it was also a familiar one.

SIXTY-ONE

I NEED MORE THAN THIS

NINE MONTHS after Jill's birth, we got another little surprise when we found out that Tina was pregnant again. This was a bit sooner than we'd anticipated, but we were still excited to welcome another person into our family. Tina had made a friend, one of Manda's friend's moms; this girl was psychotically motivated to go to the gym and managed to drag Tina along for the ride. I can't imagine the dedication it took for Tina to get up at 6 in the morning, fully pregnant, and head off to the gym to ride the elliptical for an hour. Do you say you "ride the elliptical"? Do you "use it"? Do you "run on it"? I don't know which one is right. It doesn't really matter, because it was impressive no matter what verb you used. Jill was nursing right up until Tina got pregnant, but when the baby-growing hormones started to show up, the milk disappeared, and Jill was not ready to be weaned. It makes me sad to think about it, because she would have had no context for the sudden change and difference in connection between her and her mother. By now Manda had started kindergarten in French immersion and was doing as great as we always knew she would. Later in the year, though, she complained to me that she wasn't doing very well in school. I told her that her report card said otherwise, that it showed that she was doing really well. She responded with wisdom far beyond her years when she said, "Dad, it shows how I'm doing, not how I'm feeling." It was, in hindsight, prophetic as she was an A student from kindergarten all the way through to graduation, but her teachers and peers never knew what a toll those results had extracted from her. ADHD can be like that. The end result looks great, but the battles won and lost along the way can take a lot out of you.

After graduating from UFV and not getting into SFU the way I had planned for so long, I wasn't sure what to do. My brother-in-law Jason was running his own landscaping business and asked if I wanted to come and work for him. Since I had no other options or plans, I said sure and began a season of grunt work that I never want to go back to. It was hard, it was hot, it was dirty, and it was monotonous. I remember one day we spent around six hours weeding in someone's backyard. They had some sort of shrub garden that was set on a steep bank, and I spent hours looking for weeds among the green plants and bushes that were supposed to be there. By the end of that day, I was literally hallucinating. I got into the truck, and as I looked out the windshield, all I could see were green plants and weeds, the same scene that I had been staring at for hours. My brain had gotten so used to having it in my visual field that it had decided to go fully automatic for me and just supply the visual input that it was expecting instead of what was actually there, which was an empty street. It's interesting how the brain can do that. That's basically what underscores all forms of optical illusion, the brain filling in gaps with what it expects based on prior experience. What's interesting is that the brain does this all the way from a sensory level to a social-perception level (i.e., seeing disapproval from others even when it isn't there) to a self-perception level (i.e., seeing failure and inadequacy when it isn't there). Dang brain.

Two memories especially stand out from my time as a landscaper. The first was at the end of a long, hot day, when we drove the truck and trailer to the local compost site to unload our clippings and weeds and leaves and bushes and whatever other treats we had accumulated. We were not alone, as it was the end of the work day for many other landscaping businesses as well, and there were several truck-and-trailer combinations unloading their treasures. I remember looking at an older guy, dirty from head to toe, obviously in physical pain, working hard and looking miserable. I thought to myself, "I did not go to school all those years and get all those As for this to be my future. This is not an option for me. I will not let it be." This was not a shot at anyone who has chosen that line of work, but I knew that it was not for me and that to settle for it would be to do myself a great disservice. The other memory that really stands out came on the end of another long, hot, dirty day. I had just come home and was so gross that I probably shouldn't have been allowed in the house. Not long after I'd arrived, there was a knock on the door. During this time, Tina had volunteered to watch another little girl from the complex, one of Manda's friends, for a few hours a couple of times a week. The knock on the door was her dad coming to pick her up after he'd got off work. When I opened the door, he stood there in his button-down, collared shirt, hair perfectly in place, no sign of dirt or sweat anywhere on his body or clothes, looking fresh as a daisy. I remember thinking so loud that I'm surprised that he couldn't hear it, "I need a job where I look like that at the end of the day." I feel like these little reminders of the distance between where I was and where I wanted to be were critical in keeping my mind focused on the long-term future.

SIXTY-TWO

WIGS AND GUINEA PIGS

I KNEW that I needed to improve my application, to show a greater breadth of experience, in order to impress the bigwigs at SFU. Bigwigs is a funny expression. I'm googling it. Well, the explanation is disappointingly obvious. It refers to the fact that back in the day, authority figures would wear powdered wigs. I wonder why they did that. Like, why would I take a judge more seriously if he was wearing obviously fake hair? Okay, I looked that up, too. Apparently, in the late 1500s, between outbreaks of syphilis and lice amongst the upper crust, healthy-looking hair was becoming an endangered phenomenon. So, someone came up with the idea that we could all just start wearing wigs. However, I wonder if being the first guy to wear a wig would not have just drawn more attention than a syphilis-induced bald spot. I guess it's just a classic case of, "if the people in power say it's cool, it must be cool." The next thing you know, all of the hoity-toity types started wearing powdered wigs made out of horse hair. It had to be horse hair or you were a loser. Poorer people used goat hair, but we don't really talk about them. Anyway, wigs became associated with being fancy and elite and, of course, that would definitely show up in places like courts of law and government, and ever since it came into fashion, it has never left, at least not in the UK. There you go. Now you know what I wanted to know about wigs.

The problem with trying to impress professors from a large, famous institution like SFU when you're coming from a small one like UFV is that you actually don't have the same breadth of experience as your competitors, simply because there aren't nearly as many opportunities for experience. I had maximized all of the opportunities that UFV had to offer, and I felt like it wasn't enough. The consequence of this was that I was forced to look outside of the school for chances to grow and impress. However, armed with only a bachelor's degree in psychology, which is probably only second to a degree in philosophy as an unemployable degree, these chances were very limited. And so it was that I was cutting grass, trimming trees, and pulling weeds for a living. One day when Jason and I were out driving around, trying to find our next job, we drove past a couple of buildings that had some shady-looking characters lurking and milling about. What do you guys want to do this afternoon? Oh, I thought we'd lurk for a bit, then maybe after that we'd mill. Some words just don't work out of the context that we usually use them in, even if it's grammatically correct. Can you tell that I forgot my Adderall today? I noticed a sign on the front of the property that included the words "treatment centre." I made a mental note of it, and when I got home from another long, hot, dusty day, I went online to look it up and found out that it was a residential drug and alcohol treatment centre for men. I didn't know anything about drug and alcohol addiction, but I figured that it would be as good as any place to broaden my horizons, so I emailed them, asking if there were any volunteer opportunities and explaining my background. I was surprised when they emailed me back, saying that they were actually exploring the idea of serving as a practicum site, and that if I was willing, I could be their guinea pig to see what that would look like. I was more than happy to be the pig, so I headed off to the offices for an interview.

The supervisor explained the program and asked what I wanted to get out of the experience, and I explained my situation. He said that the practicum would be about 30 hours total, which is really nothing at all, but it was only a trial run. I would just observe and report what I had learned to him. I readily agreed. I remember being intimidated by the clients and the staff and the program and just about everything, but I had also learned to pretend that I was confident, so it didn't shine through with obviousness. At least I don't think it did. I remember the first group session I sat in on. It was in a small, ancient office, overcrowded with about 12 guys in the room. We were seated in a circle, and the mood was low-energy. I could tell just by looking at these guys that they had been through some stuff. I listened as one of them talked about coming into some money back east and debating whether or not it was a good idea to leave treatment early to go claim it. Another guy offered the honest opinion that if he was in that position, he would leave and use the money to get as high as possible and that he was jealous of this other guy's opportunity. I appreciated his honesty. At one point, toward the end, the facilitator, who was also the supervisor that I had interviewed with, asked if I wanted to say anything. I started to say something about how impressed I was with the courage of these guys, when before I knew it, I burst into tears. I couldn't even speak, and I didn't know why. It caught me totally by surprise. In hindsight, I think I might have felt overwhelmed by the despair that was present in that room. I could sense the great pain that had brought them there and the pain that awaited them in the future. I could sense the disconnection from each other and the world. I could sense that I was sitting in a room with 12 wounded little boys. The tears came from a combination of sadness, empathy, and love. The men in the room responded really well. They reassured me that I was in the right place and doing the right thing. The support that I felt from that group of 12 wounded strangers was something that I had rarely experienced in my life. After the group ended and I was sitting alone with the supervisor, he asked me, "What was that all about?" I told him that I wasn't sure, that I just really felt for the guys who were there. Unlike the clients, those in a position of vulnerability and real-time pain, the supervisor just raised his eyebrows and said, condescendingly, "You might want to look into that." It didn't feel supportive or curious. It felt judgemental, as if there was something wrong with me for feeling these feelings toward these men. However, me being me, my own internal response was a mix of resistance and defiance and self-doubt. I resented him for talking to me like that but also wondered if he was right.

SIXTY-THREE

THE BABIES JUST KEEP COMING

THE PRACTICUM DIDN'T LAST the whole 30 hours, as the supervisor seemed to lose interest in giving me things to do and I lost interest in doing nothing, but the experience taught me that I wanted to learn more about addiction and treatment. I had also had a fun accident with a chainsaw while working with Jason that could have gone so much worse but that had left me temporarily with only one working thumb, so I wasn't able to be of much help to him. It turns out that chainsaws should be held with two hands, instead of one hand, while you're standing on your tiptoes cutting a branch off a tree. These elements combined led me to enrol in a 10-month substance abuse counselling certificate program at UFV, offered through the social work department. I had never taken a social work class throughout my education, and I'd had a negative view of social work students, since all I'd ever heard them do was complain about the system and drop out of psych classes because they were too hard and too much work. It turned out that my fleeting impression of the social work program was fairly accurate, and I was repeatedly shocked by how little was asked of us as students in the program.

A few months into the program, our family was blessed with the arrival of our fourth daughter, Holly. We had tried to find out the sex of baby number four, but she had been far too modest to reveal herself to us, so we were back to not knowing. By now I had resigned myself to never having a son, though, so it wasn't even really a thought anymore. Holly was just as beautiful as her sisters and just as welcomed by Amanda as the last two were. She didn't really register any feelings visibly about her arrival and was not interested in holding her. Becca was all over it and couldn't wait to hold her. Jill was also not sure. Her lack of certainty became more solidified into dislike over the next few months as she would often start out gently stroking Holly's head and quickly escalate into full-on clawing at her like an angry cat. We had to watch Jill like hawks to make sure she didn't gouge out Holly's eyes or bite a chunk out of her. My mom, somewhat melodramatically but also somewhat accurately, said that at times she feared for Holly's life. Jill was still the same sweet little girl we'd always known, but there was also a new side of her emerging that was aggressive, defiant, and stone cold. I know that she was also reaching the terrible twos, which is the most misleading title given to a development phase (though I'm not sure there are actually many entries in that competition), but this was more than that. It would be years before I would actually figure out what the issue was, and in the meantime, lots of damage was done by our ignorance. The fact is, Jill was experiencing the separation anxiety that comes with being displaced by a younger sibling. It's something that we take for granted as adults, that siblings will have a tough time, but we don't fully realize the extent of the trauma for some children. Especially in Jill's case, where she was weaned earlier than she'd wanted, had a mom who was sick and tired, and now a mom who was recovering from her fourth C-section. On top of that, I had what turned out to be a completely unnecessary knee surgery 10 days after Holly was born. It's a good thing that Holly was such an easy baby, because I was very little help to Tina for the first few weeks. I could barely hobble around, and I quickly abandoned crutches in favour of limping because the crutches were even more inconvenient. However, this wasn't the first time that I was out of commission with a young baby in the house.

SIXTY-FOUR

A REAL HEAD SMASHER

My family has a condition called postural hypotension, which means that when we stand up too fast, or after sitting or lying down for a while, the blood doesn't quite get up to our brains fast enough, causing the world to spin and go dark. Sometimes it only goes as far as a fuzzy tongue and ringing in the ears, but on a few occasions, it has led to some pretty brutal wipeouts. When Jill was still a nursing baby, I had gone downstairs to sleep on the couch when she had taken over my spot in the bed during the middle of the night. In the morning, Manda and Becca were making noise and demands of me, because how dare they be small children with needs? Couldn't they see I was trying to sleep? After the fourth time they asked me to get them some breakfast, I bolted up, threw the blanket off that I'd had over my head, and stood up quickly to stomp into the kitchen, having a little tantrum while parenting. However, the last thing I remember is leaning one arm against the back of the loveseat on my way. The next thing I knew, I was waking up, face down, with the wind knocked out of me and my face in incredible pain, with blood dripping from it onto the carpet. I had no idea what had happened. Talk about a terrible way to wake up from a nap. It was an interesting juxtaposition as--coming back to consciousness--I felt like I had been asleep for hours and felt very well-rested, but at the same time, I was in so much pain. I stumbled to the bathroom because my primary concern in that moment was not to get blood on the carpet. Once I reached the bathroom, I must have passed out again and immediately went into a dream where I was wrestling with a series of long hoses or snakes that were tangled up all through my arms and legs. In the real world, I was just thrashing around on the small bathroom floor, having what must have appeared to be an epileptic seizure. Eventually I came to consciousness again, once again feeling very well-rested and confused. Manda and Becca had witnessed the whole thing, but Tina had only heard the loud crash that was my entire body weight hitting the floor through the focal point of my face.

I had put my teeth deep into my upper lip and skidded my face across the carpet so hard and fast that to call it a carpet burn would be like calling ... so many comparisons are flying through my mind right now that I can't even grab one, and if I manage to do it, I don't like it. It doesn't hit the spot. But I don't know what I'm even looking for. It would be like calling the Grand Canyon a ditch. It would be like calling Bin Laden a big meanie. It would be like calling Arizona slightly warm. It would be like calling an amputation a scratch. None of those hit the spot. Oh well, the bottom line is that I learned that you can get second-degree burns from friction as my chin, upper lip, nose, and forehead all looked like when you leave your hotdogs on the grill for just a bit too long and they're all blistered and splitting open. Yeah, it was super sexy. I also hurt my neck when I tried to drive my face through the floor into the crawlspace, but the worst injury of them all was the major concussion that I suffered. As you might remember from way earlier in this long tale of disaster, this wasn't my first concussion. But it was my worst. I was still in school at the time, and I was surprised to find that I couldn't think straight. I remember trying to say the word kitchen in a sentence while talking with Tina, but I couldn't think of the right word for the life of me. I ended up calling it the place with the food. This was a sign to me that perhaps not all was well with my brain. I had headed off to the doctor the day of the incident, and he'd first chastised me for driving myself to the doctor and then made me call Tina to come get me. He'd also seemed much more interested in why I had passed out in the first place, and somehow lost in all of that was the damage to my brain. My emotions were up and down, my head hurt like crazy, I felt dizzy, and I was at a loss for words, which for me is a very serious sign. My professor at the time was very understanding, especially as my hamburgered face provided substantial corroboration of my story, and he gave me extensions on final projects and exams.

I debated whether to include this story because it isn't really ADHD-related except in a roundabout way. As I will get into later, if I haven't got into it already, one of the most prolific symptoms of ADHD in adults is doubting that you really have it. I don't mean doubting it in the sense that you don't think it's real, but doubting it in the sense that you think you are just making it up, using it as an excuse, or trying desperately to fit in with a group. There have been many times when I've wondered if my scatteredness, forgetfulness, and moodiness are just a result of banging my brain a few times. It can happen. I once met a man who had experienced a traumatic brain injury, a very serious one, and when he described his life after the injury, he was basically describing my life. However, then I remember that I've been this way my whole life, not just after I banged my head. Of course, smashing your brain like a boiled egg doesn't help things.... Why would someone smash a boiled egg? I guess to make egg salad. But that would be more like smushing or squishing, right? Smashing is aggressive. I don't think people typically make egg salad aggressively, but I suppose they might. Who am I to judge?

SIXTY-FIVE
IT'S FINE 2.0

AT THIS TIME, as I think I mentioned, I was back in school, trying to complete the substance abuse counselling program. The classes were held on the weekends, so during the week I split a few hours with Jason and his landscaping crew, filling my role as the academic coach and lab coordinator, and wasting a lot of time doing nothing. It was in this certificate program that I discovered a new way to get attention, a much healthier way. This new approach was to be quiet and only occasionally offer opinion or feedback, but when you do, make sure it's worth opening your mouth. With this new approach, my fellow students seemed drawn to me and would often approach me for help or insight. Contrast this with another student who was actually a medical doctor. He never missed the opportunity to make mention of this fact, even when it had no relevance to whatever else he was trying to say. It had the opposite of its intended effect, as his classmates avoided him like the plague. It was a good lesson for me in the importance of humility in making connections with people and letting things come to me instead of forcing them.

In the spring of the following year, one of the instructors of the counselling program mentioned to me that the treatment centre that I had stumbled upon was actually looking to hire a program support worker and that I should apply as I was more than qualified. I did so immediately and was given an interview by the same supervisor that had sat with me before. My duties were to run the orientation program, which were the first two weeks of residential treatment. I would need to do a ton of intake paperwork and make sure the clients did their assessments. I would need to run a group that was not therapeutic per se, but rather designed to prepare the guys for more in-depth group work after they had been assigned to one of the three counsellors. Even though I had exactly zero counselling experience and no education in the field beyond the few months of lightweight instruction that I'd received in the substance abuse program, which was not even over yet, I convinced them that I would be fine, and they hired me. I couldn't believe it. It was my first real job, making $18/hr, with benefits and everything! The supervisor assured me that my lack of experience wouldn't be a barrier, that he would be there to assist me and sit in on my group for the first couple of weeks until I got my feet under me. I remember my first day on the job, as I headed from my little shared office towards the stairs leading down to the area where I would meet the clients, I passed by his office to collect him and he looked up from his computer screen and absently said, "You don't really need me to come down there with you, do you? I'm kind of busy here." Instead of saying what I was thinking, which was, "Holy crap, are you kidding me? I have no idea what I'm doing! They are literally going to murder me!" I didn't miss a beat as I (fake) confidently said, "Sure, that's no problem, I'll be fine." As it turns out, I had internalized my dad's mantra after all. And at first, it was fine.

SIXTY-SIX

MYSTERIOUS WAYS

KEEP in mind that I had never had any interest in addictions or working with addicts. Working at this treatment centre had one purpose only, as far as I was concerned, and that was to make my application look more impressive so that I could have a better shot at getting into graduate school at SFU. This time around, I had also applied at the University of Calgary but no other places. To this day, it's interesting that I was willing to trade a shot at my dream career for the familiarity of being close to home and family. I guess that says something about how connected we are to each other and the degree to which I relied on them to bring some safety to my life. I did not re-write the GRE, though I could have. I figured that my math mark would not get higher, and my writing and verbal marks could only go down, so I just left it like it was and re-applied. Calgary didn't even consider me past the first round of cut-offs, which is interesting, because their program was not nearly as well-known or sought-after as SFU's. SFU once again passed me through the first cut-off and on to the interview stage. I interviewed with two different professors this time around, and I could tell that one of them needed some convincing. She was concerned about how I would manage the workload of graduate school while having a family and living so far from school (SFU is about an hour commute from Abbotsford on a good day). I told her that I was used to being really busy and working long hours because I had had so much on the go for so long. She didn't seem convinced. After the interviews, we all went out for lunch again, and this is where I really put the nail in my own coffin. While sitting at the table, trying to make light conversation, this same professor asked me what I liked to do for fun outside of my school and work hours. I responded with just about the worst thing I could have said to convince her, though at the time it seemed like a good idea. I answered, "I don't really have time for a hobby; I'm just too busy." The thing was, 1. It wasn't even true because I had a few hobbies that I engaged in on a regular basis, and 2. It pretty much confirmed her biggest reservation about me, that my life was too busy for me to commit to the program and all of its significant demands. When I said it, she made a little face and raised her eyebrows, and I felt sick to my stomach, but it was too late to back out. I couldn't unsay it.

Shortly after that, I was contacted by SFU and told that I was not going to be considered for admission to their clinical program that year. I wasn't put on the waitlist; it was just over. I felt like the life had been sucked out of me. I felt weak and then so angry. So ANGRY! How could this happen? I had literally done everything that I could do, crossed every bridge, gone every last mile and given it everything I had. Going to graduate school and getting my PhD in clinical sports psychology and launching my career at the 2010 Vancouver Olympics was my destiny! How could the stars have been so far off when they had appeared to be so aligned in my favor? I was used to dropping the ball and things falling through at the last second, but this was like a world-record disappointment. I was gutted. I stormed out of the house and went and sat in the car in the driveway for a while. I didn't want to talk to anyone or see anyone or listen to anyone. I just wanted to sit with my anger and rage and self-pity. The spell was finally broken when Becca, my once-colicky baby who was now a four-year-old full of love, came gingerly walking up to the car door, which I had left hanging open. She climbed onto my lap and gave me a hug and said, "I know you're sad, Dad. Sometimes we all get disappointed." Even now as I write those words, the emotions swell up in me. The pain of my loss juxtaposed with the sweetness of what was really important in my life. I had lost my dream of status and achievement and recognition but was reminded that I already had all of that from the people who really mattered. Later that day, I was talking to my mom on the phone and lamenting my situation to her. "I don't understand," I said. "Why would God give me all the ability to be a great psychologist and then not let me do it?" It didn't seem fair. Then my mom gave me some of the best feedback I've ever received in my life. She said, "Maybe you're missing the point of those gifts. All of the qualities that would make you a great psychologist would also make you a great dad." This was the final piece of the puzzle. After that phone call, I felt at peace with how things had worked out. I had been reminded of what my priorities were in the most loving of ways, and I set out to prove her right.

SIXTY-SEVEN
LIE TO THE NEW GUY

THE FACT that I was now working full time at the treatment centre also helped to soften the blow. I felt that my education had not been completely in vain as I was sort of working in the field that I had intended to pursue, although my client base was significantly different from what I had anticipated. The majority of the clients were mandated to be there in some way, either by a probation order, parole condition, or a family member who had had enough and delivered an ultimatum. Working in the orientation program, I often had to deal with the guys when they were at their worst. Many of them had not even gone to detox and were still experiencing serious withdrawal during their first days in the program but were still expected to fully participate, do their chores, attend all meetings and classes and follow the rules. I was in way over my head, but I really had no choice but to swim like crazy to make it to the surface, and I slowly gained my footing. I shared an office with another program support worker, someone who had been there much longer than I had. Like me, he really wanted to be recognized and valued, but he was just a bit too weird to achieve that dream. I think he resented me a little bit because the clients seemed to like me, and I had some education. In

the addictions field, it is not uncommon for staff to be mainly qualified for employment by having once been addicts themselves, and
this place was no exception. There was a lot of homespun wisdom
and old-school tough love, even though on paper it was supposed to
be based on a harm-reduction model of meeting the clients where
they were at.

I learned so much working in that orientation program, largely
because I was given so much leeway to figure things out on my own.
It's really surreal to think of the full spectrum of mental health issues
I had the opportunity to work with, despite my minimal training and
fictional experience. I worked with actively hallucinating schizo-
phrenics and narcissist, as well as people with bipolar disorder,
extreme PTSD, anxiety, depression, suicidality, homicidal rage, and
everything in between. Along the way, there were memorable experiences, like the time the federal inmate really didn't like the feedback
that I was giving him and got up from his chair and stood over top of
me, jabbing his finger at my face and screaming a warning about
something, or the time I overcame my hatred of being lied to. I always
hated being lied to. There are a few triggers in my life that can still
get me, no matter how much work I've done on myself. My kids
always find it hilarious how mad I get about someone tripping
someone else. It doesn't even have to be me that's getting tripped. For
some reason, it injects some sort of turbo boost into my anger rockets
and I blast off. How's that for a metaphor? It seems like it should be
delivered in the voice of Optimus Prime and be accompanied by
some 80s-style cartoon animation. Another trigger is being smacked
in the small of the back. The reality is that there are lots of nerve
endings in that region, so an open-handed smack will cause much
more pain than you would think. I already knew that's why it hurt so
much, but I wanted to be sure, so I googled it, and Google made some
pretty loose associations. Yes, it confirmed my answer, but it also
showed me some images of someone's teeth, took me to the online
support forum of a neurofibromatosis group, answered some questions about pregnancy, told me that I can't break my funny bone, and

helped me to define physical abuse in relationships. That's kind of how my brain works, too. No wonder google and I are such great friends.

Anyway, being lied to used to be one of these triggers, but then I had an experience that changed all of that for me. One afternoon, after group had ended, one of my clients came to my office. He was in tears. This guy was the classic downtown eastside homeless, crack-addicted lifer. He had few teeth, many scars, and was rail-thin. He told me that he needed to leave treatment, even though he had only been there for less than a week. I asked him why, and he said that his grandmother was dying in the hospital. He explained that she was the only caregiver that he'd ever had and that the thought of her passing away without being able to say goodbye to her was more than he could bear. I told him I understood and helped him to make arrangements to leave that evening, driving him down to the bus terminal and seeing him off. I felt like I had done the right thing in supporting him. When I got back to work, a client pulled me aside and told me, "His grandma's not in the hospital; he just wants to get out of here to go use dope." I denied that this was true, but the client made a pretty compelling case, and I realized that I had been duped. Just so you know, a dupe is a person who is easily fooled, and the word's use is believed to have been derived from the French *hoopoe*, described as an "extravagantly crested and reputedly stupid bird." How's that for a claim to fame? Anyway, when I realized that I had been tricked, I felt angry. How could he have manipulated me like that? He'd totally played on my sympathies and didn't care that my concern was genuine. He'd used me to get out. Then, in the midst of this storm of indignation, a few realizations landed on me, like beautiful hoopoes.

First, why had he lied? He was not required to be there. He had come of his own free will and had done so because he wanted to get clean. So why lie? I imagine it was because he knew the truth would be unpopular and probably even knew that the truth was not a great plan, and rather than have that argument, he just went for the efficient approach and came up with a cover story. Also, I was an authority figure, and he didn't want to disappoint me. That was not speculative, because I had gotten to know him over the week and knew of the horrific childhood he had experienced, the abandonment and abuse and neglect that had brought him to the lowest of low points. He didn't want me to see him as a loser, and so he created this elaborate story. The second realization was that it wasn't me he was lying to, it was the person in the chair. What I mean by that is that no matter who had been in the office that night, he would have been fed the same story, because that was the only story he had. He hadn't crafted this especially for me because he knew that I would fall for it. He lied out of desperation, and it wasn't personal. That might seem like a small thing to realize, but it was profound for me. I realized that the reason I was so triggered by being lied to was that I was interpreting it from a place of thinking that the liar thought I was stupid enough to believe the lie. So a lie was really an insult. It wasn't about a betrayal; it was about my own self-esteem. Somebody asked me one time about the connection between lying and ADHD. I had to think about it for a bit before it dawned on me. Why do most people lie? They do it for one of two reasons: 1. To avoid getting in trouble, and 2. To avoid looking bad (or to look good). What group of people is more likely to get in trouble, look bad, and feel bad about themselves than people with ADHD? None. So, if we look at it in that simple context, someone with ADHD simply has more opportunities to lie than the average person, which would make him or her much more likely to lie. We make impulsive decisions or, more accurately stated, take impulsive actions that make us look and feel stupid, and then we don't want people to see the truth, so we desperately try to cover it up.

SIXTY-EIGHT

CASUAL BUSINESS

THIS FEAR of being discovered as stupid showed up again during my time in the orientation program in another experience that significantly changed the way I understood behaviour. Because my shift was in the afternoon, I only overlapped with the other counsellors and supervisors for a few hours each day. I would come in to work just after lunch, do a little paperwork, run group for two hours, go to the counsellors' check-out meeting (it was the end of their day and thus a chance to debrief), and then come back to my office to kill the time until the end of the evening. I was very unsupervised and given minimal direction as to how to fill my time. I spent a lot of it doing intake paperwork and interviewing new clients, but when that was all finished (and sometimes before it was finished, not surprisingly), I would end up out on the grounds with the guys, shooting hoops or just sitting on a bench talking while trying to avoid the ubiquitous second-hand smoke. Because it was summer and I was unsupervised and my position was rather casual in nature, my clothes for work reflected these elements. That's a fancy way of saying that I usually wore shorts to work. Someone used the term "dress shorts" the other day, and I had to laugh because what a funny concept. These are my fancy shorts. I know they exist, but the thought of calling them that is just too pretentious for me. Anyway, I usually wore some khaki shorts or something like that, but one day, I wore a different pair, even more chill than usual. Like, surfer chill. Like, they were board shorts. Granted, they didn't have a wild floral Hawaiian print or anything like that. They were a solid dark blue, but they were essentially a bathing suit. This was pointed out to me by my favourite supervisor, who poked his head in the door of my office and said, "Hey, Ted, I'm all for casual Friday, but those might be a bit too casual." I said okay, and he left, and I had to work really hard not to follow him out the door and beat him to a pulp. The rage I felt was so intense that it could barely be contained. Almost immediately, however, the feeling transformed into shame, though it maintained its intensity. I felt waves of heat wash over me, with my face reddening and my stomach feeling like I'd been on the Tilt-a-Whirl too long. The emotion was so big that it caught me off guard; it was way out of proportion to what had triggered it. Because I was by myself, I opened a blank document on my computer and started to type out a counselling conversation with me. It was a dialogue, not a diatribe. I wasn't just venting, I was conversing. It was a very neat experience that I recommend to my clients all the time.

The dialogue went something like this:

Calm Me: What are you feeling right now?

Angry Me: I feel so embarrassed and angry that I just want to smash something.

Calm Me: What triggered these feelings?

Angry Me: When he told me that I was dressed too casually.

Calm Me: What was so triggering about that?

Angry Me: It's like he was saying that I was stupid or something. The way he said it so condescendingly.

Calm Me: But why does it bother you so much that he would say or think that?

Angry Me: I guess because I have felt like that so many times in my life. I have always doubted myself and now I'm here in this job and I had lots of doubts about whether I could do it and I was starting to think that I was doing a good job and that there were no problems and now all of a sudden, out of nowhere, I'm reminded that, in fact, I am stupid and I can't do anything right. It's like when he said that, it brought all of those feelings and memories and experiences right to the surface and they came exploding out of me.

Calm Me: So is it safe to say that these feelings aren't really about what he said or how he said it?

Angry Me: I guess they aren't. They're about all of those other experiences that I guess have had such a negative impact on me over the years.

It was really that simple. I sat at my computer and typed, and within a few minutes I began to understand the core of so much of my behaviour and emotional reactivity. Not just the feeling stupid thing but the idea that the past could be dragged into the present without us knowing about it. This revelation would go on to become the core of my counselling practice and further education, but on a deeper level, it began a process of self-discovery that I'm not sure would have happened if things had worked out the way I had planned them to all along.

SIXTY-NINE
OKAY, I'M GETTING BORED

AFTER I HAD BEEN at the treatment centre for some time, one of the counsellors left abruptly, creating a job opening. It turns out that his education was not even in the field of counselling or psychology, but he had attended a workshop with a well-known guru in the field of anxiety and brought many of the tools he had picked up at the conference back to his workplace. He was eager to try them out with his clients and see if he could take them to emotional places that they were not able to access before. His intentions were good, of that I am sure. However, his skill level was not adequate to handle the power of the tools he had been given. The methods and techniques succeed in unlocking previously unfelt emotions, unprocessed memories, and new levels of fear and self-discovery in his clients, but as he admitted during one of his last counsellor check-outs, once they got things out of the box, he didn't know how to put them back in. The unfortunate outcome of this misadventure was that several of his clients were left fighting for air in a sea of uncontrolled emotion, leading them to discharge from the program and relapse. It was a hard blow for this guy to handle, as it would be for anyone with a conscience. He was a genuinely nice and caring man who truly wanted to help, but he had unintentionally bitten off more than he could chew.

Anyway, because of his miscalculation, a counsellor position opened up, and I told the supervisors that I intended to apply for it. They were a bit surprised, I could tell, even though I had worked there for some time and was very qualified, on paper at least. They said I could apply and arranged a time for an interview. On the day of the interview, I came to work dressed a bit nicer than usual. No shorts and t-shirt but instead a button-down shirt with a collar and some dress pants and shoes. Roy, who shared an office with me and never got more dressed up than jeans and a sweater, asked what the special occasion was. I told him that I had a job interview, and he asked where. I joked that it was at the Dairy Queen, for a management position, and he didn't ask any more questions. About a week later, Roy asked me if I had heard anything. I asked him what he meant, and he said, "The Dairy Queen job." I laughed out loud and told him that I had just been joking. He said that he'd thought maybe because it was a management position I might have been serious. I felt bad about laughing at it because I realized that he probably would have been happy to have the Dairy Queen job, but I was also surprised that he'd thought I would be satisfied to take my psychology degree and go manage a fast-food restaurant. It was instructive to me, though, that what one person scorns, another adores, and I should be more mindful of the fact that different people have different expectations for their lives based on different experiences.

I didn't get the counsellor position that time, with the job going to someone else with the same amount of experience and education. I was surprised that I didn't get it, to be honest, as I felt like I had done a great job with the duties that I had been given so far. Instead, I continued filling out intake paperwork, driving to appointments, inspecting rooms, and collecting urine samples. After I had been in the position for about a year, I decided to start keeping an informal, top-secret poll, with myself as the only voter. As clients finished the end of their time in the orientation program and were assigned to one of the three small therapy groups for the remaining eight weeks, I would vote, based entirely on my gut, whether they would end up graduating or leave before the program was over. Over the course of several months I tracked this. I was careful to not vote until the day they left the program so as not to taint the outcome with my expectations. It turned out that after dozens of clients had gone through the program, I was right more than 80 percent of the time. I couldn't even tell you what it was with many of them that either gave me confidence or didn't, but it was a little project that I took on to break up the monotony of my job. I had a research brain, and I wanted to use it. I wanted to ask questions that didn't have answers and then see if we could find the answers. I wanted to ask questions that hadn't been asked and then see why they hadn't been asked before. The orientation program was not the right place for me to do this, though, and I became increasingly antsy with my position.

SEVENTY

COUNSELLOR TED

ONE OF THE unintentional themes that has emerged in the writing of this saga is that sometimes when a door closes, you have to kick it down or make your own. Waiting for opportunities can be a lonely vigil, but creating them can be exciting. So it was that I found myself in a unique position at the treatment centre, where the HR manager had taken a liking to me and happened to mention to me that the funding for the treatment centre actually had provision for four counsellors, not just three. He said that he would begin putting a bug in the ear of the executive director to see if maybe they could open up the fourth position for me. It's gross to think about putting a bug in you ear. Like a bug called an earwig. Please don't tell me those things actually go in people's ears. That was a great source of fear and disgust when I was younger, that an earwig would be in my ear. Anyway, the earwig must have worked, because the executive director called me into his office one day to tell me that they were going to create a position for me. The problem was that the treatment centre, which was very old, didn't currently have the physical space for me to have an office or meeting room. They were going to have to convert the weight room into an office for me. I knew that this decision would not be popular with the clients, as the weight room got lots of use. Probably a bit too much use, some might say. I remember one guy who came into treatment a hollowed-out heroin addict and left 70 days later having gained around 100 pounds, much of it muscle. His role on the street: debt collector. His transformation left some of us wondering if equipping people to become war machines was maybe not the best idea, so it was easy for us staff to do away with the weight room.

One of my great ADHD brainfarts happened in that weight room before it was replaced, however. In my day, I had been a bit of a powerlifter, but the muscles came and went as my dedication to fitness waxed and waned. Of course, any weightlifter has a fair amount of rooster in him, and when other roosters come around, it triggers the need to prove that you, too, are a rooster. It's really funny to watch, actually. So, one day I was the rooster. We had a particularly young cohort of clients at the centre at the time, and many of them were getting into weightlifting and feeling pretty good about themselves. I don't mean in a healthy esteem sort of way. More like a tough-guy, get-outta-my-way sort of way. So, out came my inner rooster. They asked if I wanted to join in a workout with them, and I obliged, with fake reluctance. Inside I was bubbling with excitement at the chance to show off, for these guys to see me as exceptional. I surprised them by lifting way more than they thought I could. We happened to be focusing on arms that day, no surprise, and I was a bit taken aback myself to see that I still retained much of my strength, even though it had been a long time since I had worked out at all. I not only was able to keep up with them but outperform them on every lift, every set, every exercise. This changed my standing with many of the guys because in certain populations, being able to move lots of weight carries more currency than being smart. The next day, however, was when the chickens really came home to roost. I used that one because I was a rooster. It fit together well. Usually after a good workout, you would expect the muscles that you had been training to be sore. There's a good kind of sore and a bad kind of sore.

The good kind is hard to explain, but if feels somewhat satisfying and you can still do all of the normal things you usually do, but they just hurt a bit, especially when the muscles are flexed or stretched. The bad kind of sore is the kind where you literally can't move your arms. At all. The kind of sore where you really think you tore something off the bone and you are panicking because how can a person live the rest of his life without arms? The kind of sore where you call to your wife from bed and tell her that you can't go to work that day because you can't move your arms and you need her to call in sick for you because you can't hold the phone and put it up to your ear, but also, it's just too embarrassing that you did this to yourself so you ask your lovely wife to cover for you. That's the kind of sore that I was experiencing the day after my short-lived rooster dance. Of course, in hindsight, this was entirely predictable. You don't go from no physical activity to extreme physical activity without paying a price. The problem is that the price is delayed. You really think you're getting away with it, that you've beaten the odds, and then the odds show up on your doorstep, drag you out into the front yard and stomp you into submission, and you remember for a fleeting second that this won't be internalized. Oh yeah, it's hard to beat the odds.

Eventually the renovations to the weight room were finished, and I found myself with a brand-new office and group room. My group was known for being a bit on the rowdy side, partly because I seemed to specialize in dealing with guys with anger problems. One way of thinking was to question the wisdom of putting all the angry guys in one group because that's the counsellor's specialty, and one way of thinking was to not think too much and just do it and see what happened. I was more in the latter group. It made for some interesting times, I will assure you, but I don't have time to tell even a small part of those stories. But a roomful of angry clients paled in comparison to the task of working with some of the other staff. We had clinical meetings in the morning, checkouts in the afternoon, and generally had a lot do with each other at the centre, which was a plus and a minus. When I first went there, I remarked to Tina that I couldn't believe how well everyone got along and supported each other, but the longer I was there, it became more apparent that the staff were just as troubled as the clients. That is not hyperbole; it is true. It was a struggle to apply the information and knowledge that I had gained in my education and other training opportunities because the staff seemed to be divided into two groups. One group was eager to learn more, eager to see things from a different perspective, eager to deliver more effective service and expand their horizons. The other group was eager to muzzle me and my crazy science talk, eager to force the clients to toe the line of tradition and to humble themselves into sobriety. I was never one to back down from an argument, and so in some ways, I became a bit of a torchbearer for the progressive side and a thorn in the side of the traditionalists. Then one day, in the midst of this increasingly hostile debate, an opportunity arose that changed my life forever.

SEVENTY-ONE

SKIP WORK. CHANGE YOUR LIFE

In the spring of 2008, I showed up for work as usual and took my seat at the computer for the start of our clinical team meeting. That name for the meeting is a bit misleading because the "clinical team" included the counsellors and support workers, but also the executive director, the HR manager, the janitor, and occasionally the cook. While many of them had been at the centre for years and had overcome addiction themselves, it would be misleading to call their input "clinical" in any way. Anyway, someone mentioned before the meeting that there was a workshop happening the next day in Abbotsford and management needed to know who was planning on attending. I asked what it was about and someone said something vague like, "Relationships or something and family stuff." That's the kind of sentence that was not uncommon at this place. Our HR director summed it up best, if not somewhat ironically, when he said with frustration one morning, "Our communication are ... suck." The truth is, it didn't really matter what the workshop was about because I was always down for the chance to miss work, just as I had always been down for the chance to miss school. I remember in Grade 8 arriving at school one morning to see some kids I knew getting on a school bus out front. I asked where they were going, and they said they were going to the track meet. I asked if they were going to be gone all day, and they said yes, so I joined the track team right there and then and missed a day of school. Since I had no athletic skill other than brute force, I signed up for the shot put, and Keith and I were the top two finishers and qualified for the Fraser Valley Championships. We were quickly eliminated, but once again we got to miss school, so it didn't really matter. So, when an opportunity to ditch responsibility came up, I was all over it. Especially when it involved learning something interesting. Kind of a weird paradox there. When I was in school I desperately wanted to escape it with fun, and now that I was working, I wanted to escape it with learning.

The workshop actually featured Dr. Gabor Mate, renowned expert on the origins and treatment of addiction. He had written a book called *In the Realm of Hungry Ghosts,* and this day-long workshop was basically a stop on his promotional tour. I won't go into great detail here, but the basis of his theory and approach is that attachment trauma, or disruptions in the building of secure attachment relationships between children and their caregivers, leaves the brain not only lagging behind in the area of self-regulation due to under-development of the prefrontal cortex, it also creates a chemical deficit in dopamine and endorphins, which are reward chemicals but also closely associated with loving and feeling loved. When people who cannot self-regulate and are starving for those chemicals are exposed to an activity that creates a rush of those chemicals, it is unrealistic to expect them to exercise self-control. Thus, the war on drugs is a war on traumatized children who have never learned another way to cope. His is very much a harm-reduction approach, designed to meet people where they are and see if we can't improve their quality of life in some small way, reducing harm to themselves and to society. His perspective was rooted in neuroscience coupled with philosophy, and it made so much sense to me that I couldn't even begin to capture it with my note-taking, so I just gave up and listened. He was very much the antihero that I had longed for in my life: someone who had issues and demons but had used those as a springboard from which he could make the leap from hurt to healer. His simple perspective challenged basic assumptions about who made the rules and why and his unassuming manner did not cloud his message behind the noise of self-promotion. I couldn't get enough.

Of course, carried by this tidal wave of excitement, I quickly bought the book, along with three other books he had authored or co-authored. *Hold on to Your Kids* was co-authored with Gordon Neufeld and described the disruption of attachment and the consequences of children being alienated from their caregivers and what to do about it. *When the Body Says No* was about the physical toll of suppressing emotion and how eventually the body gets to a point where it can't take it anymore and starts to let you know that you've reached that point by attacking itself. Like when I started having these little seizures that affected the left side of my body and increased in frequency at a rate that was very alarming to me. I had every test and scan completed that could be done, but they all came back clean. There was no identifiable biological cause for the seizures. It was after another MRI on my brain (most people get claustrophobic in MRI machines, but I find them cozy and actually fall asleep) that I was sitting with a neurologist at Vancouver General Hospital and he asked me if I could think of anything that could be causing it. Having read Mate's book, I suggested that maybe stress was a factor, and he asked me if I was under a lot of stress. At the time I was a father of five children, working full time at the centre, had a few private clients after hours, served in a leadership position at my church, and was in graduate school. As I made the list, I realized that I did have a lot on my plate and asked if he could write me a note saying I needed a couple of weeks off of work. At the time, I thought I was basically beating the system and getting a two-week holiday under the guise of stress leave, but as soon as I handed in the note, the seizures stopped. At first I didn't really make the connection, but when they asked me to come in a few days later to sign some paperwork, I had a seizure in the parking lot and realized I was allergic to working there.

This led me to do some introspection while I was off to try to determine exactly what it was about working at the treatment centre that was stressing me out so much. My conclusion was not that I was too invested, but that I was trying too hard to not be invested. The reality is that I had been drawn to this career and was good at it because I am naturally a caring person. I attach quickly and value relationships. In the world of counselling, we are constantly cautioned against bringing our "work" home with us and encouraged to have strong boundaries with clients. At the same time, we are taught--and I had personally done years of research--on the importance of the relationship and connection between client and counsellor as the single best predictor of therapeutic outcome. In addictions both of these positions are emphasized even more as the relapse rate is very high and poor outcome can be literally fatal. I realized that I was working so hard to stay detached that it was stressing my body out--to the point that it was revolting against me. I decided that it would be less harmful for me to embrace who and how I was and let myself care and attach and befriend the clients and hope that reducing this resistance would pay off for me. In the end, it did. Since the time I had that realization, almost 10 years ago as of this writing, I have only had two or three seizures, and they have always served as a reminder that I need to take care of myself. The reality is that that I owe it all to that workshop with Gabor Mate and the information he presented. Without his permission to care for others and myself, I never would have had the compassion to do it fully.

SEVENTY-TWO

THE MOMENT

As impactful as Gabor Mate's other books were for me, the biggest seismic activity in my life was the result of a book that was basically an afterthought. It was called *Scattered Minds* and purported itself to be on the origins and healing of ADHD. Up to this point in my life, what I knew about ADHD was probably about the same as everyone else. It was those hyper kids who couldn't sit still and kept interrupting. The ones who kept making the annoying noise even after the fifth warning. The kids who pushed the button that had the big label that said, "DO NOT PUSH." My younger brother Ben had been diagnosed with ADHD when he was little, almost by accident. He was really struggling in school, and my mom had taken him for a psychoeducational assessment, which uncovered a few serious learning disabilities but also this pesky little thing called ADHD. They put him on Ritalin for a little bit, but my mom said it just turned him into a zombie and he didn't even take it half the time. Instead, he hid it or they forgot to give it to him. Somehow Ben muddled along and managed to graduate from high school, along the way discovering that he is an amazingly gifted artist in all mediums. He is now a highly successful interior designer. Other than this exposure in the background of my life, I had never thought about, heard about, or read about ADHD, and my main reason for buying the book was that so many of my clients at the treatment centre were either diagnosed as children or seemed like they should have been. I thought it wouldn't hurt to become a bit more familiar with the issue if I was going to be effective at helping them overcome their addictions and other problems, so I started reading the book at the same time that I was reading Mate's other books. In retrospect, this was an indicator that I was about to discover something about myself.

To say that I found myself in the pages of that book would be an understatement by which all other understatements are measured. If that sounds like an overstatement, it probably is, but it also communicates the impact of seeing my own life in my own words, written by someone else. I had honestly never even once considered that I might have ADHD. It had never been suggested to me, not even in a joking way. This despite my report cards through the years reading like a virtual checklist of symptoms. Ted needs to be more organized. Ted needs to be less social in class. Ted needs to do his homework. Ted needs to hand in his homework. Ted needs to focus better. Ted needs to apply himself. When Mate described his daily routines of procrastination, forgetfulness, impulsivity, mood swings, insecurities and the constant flight from boredom, I felt like I was reading the journal that I had never been organized enough to keep. I did try to keep a journal on more than one occasion, but there are only a few entries that don't make me want to invent a time machine just so I can go back and smack myself. My first journal entry was penned by my mom when I was just a toddler. She asked me questions and wrote down my answers. Apparently, it was important to record for all future generations that my favourite food was bananas. I don't think it really was, but I had just eaten a banana before she'd asked me, and since the ADHD brain seems to be trapped in the moment, for better and for worse, it felt like the most honest and accurate thing I could say in response to the question. In high school, my journal entries were mainly about girls and bragging about myself. My journal during my mission was not much different. As an adult, I tried to fake maturity in sporadic journal entries, and eventually I just gave up.

I'm finding it really hard to sit down and write this portion of the story. This is where everything changed for me, where it began to become clear. I use that choice of words very deliberately, that it began to become clear. I do that to emphasize the very gradual nature of my self-realization. Absolutely it is true that the recognition of myself in those pages was monumental; it is also true to say that incorporating the meaning of that recognition has been very incremental. To quote Mate, "Beyond everything, recognition revealed the reason for my lifelong sense of somehow never approaching my potential in terms of self-expression and self-definition—the ADD adult's awareness that he has talents or insights or some undefinable positive quality he could perhaps connect with if the wires weren't crossed." This summed up my childhood and adulthood so well that I almost floated off the ground. I had always felt like there was something more I could do, that if people gave me a chance, they would see that I was smart and talented and funny and a good person, but because I had fallen flat on my face so many times in my attempts to demonstrate this, I also felt that my potential would always remain as such, something that could have been. To quote another section of Mate's description, "An adult with ADD looks back on his life to see countless plans never fully realized and intentions unfulfilled. 'I am a person of permanent potential,' one patient said."

I'm tempted to share many lines and sections from Mate's book to convey to you the realizations that it communicated to me, but instead, I am reminded of my mom's reaction when I began to discuss the issue with her. She told me that she didn't think that I had ADHD at all, that my younger brother Ben did, but he struggled in school, whereas I could have done well in school if I had really wanted to. I told her that I thought she was wrong, that not only did I have ADHD but, most likely, so did many other people in our family, not the least of whom was my dad. She again scoffed at this idea, mainly because my dad was so successful in so many areas. I know that I'm not alone in sharing how hollowing it can feel when you share an insight about yourself, something that you have found to be empowering, validating, and relieving, only to have that insight questioned, doubted, and dismissed. It left me feeling extremely frustrated. However, I was also locked on to this new piece of information and asked my mom if she would be willing to read the book anyway. She agreed to do so. The frustration melted away about a week later when she called me to ask a favor. She asked if I would mind if she made a little dot in pencil in the margin of the book when she read something that she felt she could relate to. I told her that would be fine. She then said, "I was initially copying out lines that I could relate to, but then I realized, I'm basically writing out the whole book." Once again, I felt like I could fly. Not only did I have an explanation for all of my "roads not travelled," another Mate quote, but I now had an ally in that understanding, as well as someone who could see that it was not just me who was wired this way.

The reality is that if you shake the Leavitt family tree, ADHD falls to the ground like apples in the fall. As I said before, I think it goes back in our roots for generations. The surname Leavitt actually comes from Northern France, and originated from the word *louet*, meaning wolf cub. When I say northern France, I mean the area known as Gaul. You know, like Asterix and Obelix, the Gauls with the magic potion? I know those guys aren't real, of course, but the Celtic tribes who lived there were known as fierce resisters of the Roman Empire and generally combative, aggressive, ruthless warriors. In other words, they kind of sound like our extended family at a reunion, except that we like each other. The modern strain of Leavitts that I descend from lived in Quebec, joined the Mormon church, and moved down to Nauvoo, Illinois, just in time for the Mormon leader, Brigham Young, to announce that they were all headed west. So they packed up their belongings into some covered wagons and travelled with that massive body of persecuted people until they reached Utah, which was then unsettled territory. Once they arrived, Leavitts were tasked with settling new areas and governing areas that had been newly settled. There were two brothers in particular, Dudley and Thomas Leavitt, who were both polygamists, as some Mormon men were at the time. After polygamy was made illegal in the state of Utah, Thomas headed north into southern Alberta, where he settled with one of his wives and their children. This is the kind of adventurous, rule-bending, determined, and antsy ancestry that breeds generations of people who have great potential but who face increasingly long odds to achieve that potential as the environment in which they were meant to flourish slowly disappears. The adventures become ones of learning and internet surfing. The rule-bending becomes bylaw infractions. The antsiness becomes business ownership because we don't want to work for anyone else.

My dad has always been successful professionally, but he has also gone swimming with his phone in his pocket on multiple occasions. He is a gifted speaker and teacher, but he has also run out of gas at least 300 times. I know that sounds like an exaggeration, but that might actually be on the conservative side. He has been a leader in every avenue that he has explored, but he once left his car running at a private airport for two days. Like, actually running. His car was a hybrid, and it was running on electricity when he got out to meet his plane for a short business trip. Because it was running so quietly, he forgot that it was turned on. Over the next two days, his battery drained down until the gasoline engine kicked in. This would then run until the battery was charged, at which point, the electrical component would take over. This process repeated itself until he flew back home the next day. When they approached the small runway, he saw his headlights were on in the parking lot and assumed that my mom had come to pick him up. It wasn't until he got off the plane and approached the car that he realized what he had done. Despite hundreds of these kinds of stories, my dad was always resistant about the possibility that he might have ADHD, saying that everyone is like that. I told him, "No, Dad. Not everyone. Just everyone in our family. And lots of our friends." After several years of being rebuffed, I had a momentous conversation with him in which I said, "I know you don't think ADHD is a real thing, but it is, and it causes me lots of difficulties in the basic areas of managing my life." He responded, "I never said it isn't real." I couldn't believe what I was hearing. Well, I actually could because he's kind of known for this sort of thing. I said, "Yes, you did. You've said it on more than one occasion." He answered, "No. I didn't say that it isn't real or that I don't have ADHD. I just said that if I do, it hasn't caused me any problems." Again, I could scarcely believe what I was hearing, but in the end, I decided to take the small victory and be quiet.

My siblings closest to me in age, Spencer, Mike, and Steve, almost certainly have ADHD in varying degrees and presentations. None of them can sit still for very long without having to look something up or get up and move around. As I said previously, Mike could have a whole series of books filled with his ADHD-fueled missteps and adventures. I remember Steve practicing piano as a kid, just sitting there staring at the piano keys, his hands distorted, looking slowly back and forth from his hands to the printed sheet music, seemingly in an endless pause until the next note was played. Both Mike and Steve were my partners through many of the adventures you've now read about and many more that didn't make these pages. My sister, Carrie, was always a high-stress kid (who wouldn't be with me, Mike, and Steve, as her next oldest siblings?), and in many ways, she is the poster child for ADHD in girls and women. She has amazing imagination, creativity and energy, a razor-sharp wit, and genuine curiosity, but much of the success that she has achieved in her life has come at the expense of serious anxiety. Ben was the first diagnosed in our family and has many of the same traits as Carrie, although his struggles in school were due as much to his learning disabilities (or differences) as to his ADHD. He is also a gifted artist and designer who cannot function without a team of dedicated people following him around turning his visions into realities. One of those dedicated people is my youngest brother Dave, who is the business Yin to Ben's creative Yang in their jointly-owned design company, Plaid Fox.

Dave is on a constant search for the next big thing, never content to own a car or house for very long before seeing the next opportunity on the horizon. Spencer is a computer programmer. I'm a therapist. Mike is a senior manager at Leavitt Machinery, my uncle's company, despite not passing more than a small handful of university classes. Steve is a forklift mechanic. Carrie is an accomplished pianist. Ben and Dave's company designs multi-million dollar homes and office spaces. We're all doing well, and certainly from the outside, it would seem accurate to echo my dad's statement that ADHD hasn't caused us any problems. However, to believe that is to judge the book by its cover, which we all know is a bad idea. Having said that, though, I think it's probably safe to judge romance books by the cover. It's unlikely that you would finish reading *Barely a Lady* or *Desperate Duchesses* and say to yourself, "Well, that was quite different from what I expected."

SEVENTY-THREE

THE MOMENTS AFTER

MONTHS after I'd woken up to realize that I had been reading the map of my life upside down, we were blessed with the birth of our fifth and last child, Luke. I couldn't believe it when the ultrasound revealed that we were finally going to have a boy. Tina felt afraid since she comes from a family of all girls and had no idea what to do with a boy. I assured her that I knew exactly what to do. Which, of course I did not. However, I did have a much better idea with him than I did with my other children, especially now that I had been informed about the importance of healthy, secure attachments between caregivers and children during those early years. I know that sounds obvious when I say it out loud, and many parents think they do understand the principle, but I can assure you that most don't understand the constant nature of attachment and the profound damage and influence that unhealthy attachment can have on the developing brain. We were seeing it first hand with Jill as she started school. She was so ready for school in so many ways, with her brilliant brain and curiosity. However, the trauma of being displaced by her sister Holly had left her quite a bit behind in terms of her ability to self-regulate appropriately. I add on that last word 'appropriately' because all acting-out behaviour is a form of self-regulation. It just varies by degree of social acceptability. If you think about it, getting angry and smashing something with a fist often reduces the intensity of that anger and can prevent it from growing into something even more damaging. In effect, the anger has been regulated but not in a way that is looked upon with favour in mainstream society. Jill regulated herself in much the same way as inmates do. She kept to herself a lot of the time, made unreasonable demands, and melted down when the demands weren't met. There were many times that I would leave her on the bathroom floor, not just crying, but roaring like a wild animal, teeth bared and eyes wide open. This would often be spurred by something innocuous and would go on forever. During that time, she was unreachable.

When she started school, this behaviour was even more intense, and to add to it, she was terrified of being left at her kindergarten class. She made some friends there, but every day, dropping her off was like in the movie *The Fox and the Hound*, when the old lady has to take the fox and leave him in the forest, but the fox doesn't understand what just happened and feels crushed with sadness as he watches her drive away. What is it with Disney movies and exploiting the tender emotions of children (and their parents)? That scene is among the hardest to watch out of all the heart-wrenching scenes I have ever seen. If you don't know what I'm talking about, just go to YouTube and search for "fox and the hound sad scene." Don't blame me for whatever you feel afterwards. But that's how Jill felt every day when we dropped her off at kindergarten. On top of that, she was getting picked on by a little demon who also told a girl in the class to go back to Africa because she was black. We weren't used to Jill getting picked on. In fact, since Holly had been born, Jill had become more often the aggressor than the victim. The teacher did nothing to stop the situation, so we met with the principal, who also did nothing. Finally, fed up with their inaction and the daily fight, but mostly because I now understood attachment in a way that I never had before, we decided to take Jill out of school and home-school her for the rest of the year. Of course, this meant she finished the last three months of kindergarten in about two weeks. We reasoned that what she really needed was her mom and more connection with her. In other words, she needed to be warmed by the fires of home. From the time we made that decision, it only took a few months before Jill was back to her former self: cheerful, happy, loving, and present (she retained some of her feistiness, but I don't think I would have taken it away if I could). Luke, in some ways, got the best parenting of the bunch, but he also has had perhaps the least amount of time with dad, since the others had me when I was in school and had a lot more time on my hands. Nevertheless, he was a good baby, meaning he wasn't too challenging, and I had matured to the point where I could handle a baby better than when I was younger.

I continued in my position as a counsellor at the treatment centre, becoming more and more aware of the prevalence of ADHD amongst my clients and taking on the role of advocate with management. Granted, it's a tough thing to hear that a crystal-meth addict might benefit from taking prescription amphetamine, but I felt that if I could just get the management team to listen to the data, the evidence and the science, then they would see the value in trying to get the guys the help they needed. One guy, in particular, stands out to me since his situation provided a major shifting point in my life, both professionally and personally.

Up to this point, I had always been opposed to medication for mental health problems. It left me with a metaphorical bad taste in my mouth to think that we were treating problems in thinking and belief by just throwing chemistry at them, and I gave my family members who were taking medication a hard time about it. Even after I realized that I had ADHD, I couldn't wrap my head around the idea of taking pills to be able to function, since I thought I was doing fine without them. It's really funny to think of that, in some ways, given the amount of evidence that I have described so far. I knew that my brain worked differently from other people's, but I figured that I could find a new way to think or come up with a strategy that would allow me to overcome or work around those differences and that I wouldn't need any stinking pills. Then I witnessed the case of a client, who I will anonymously call Jim-Bob.

SEVENTY-FOUR

FINALLY

JIM-BOB WAS a client at the treatment centre no fewer than 10 times. A handful of times he had even completed the 70-day program and received a graduation certificate. Many of the times he had self-discharged early, mainly to use drugs. A few times he had been kicked out for various infractions. He had lived in dozens of transition homes, recovery houses, shelters, and other residential programs of varying degrees of intensity, structure and accountability, along with different approaches. He had been exposed to religion, spirituality, the 12 steps, cognitive behaviour therapy, tough love and everything else under the sun. He knew the programs backward and forward and could recite the literature. What he couldn't do, however, was sit still. He was a perpetual motion machine. He talked non-stop, fidgeted non-stop, and when he wasn't in program, he worked around the centre doing repairs or driving people to appointments or organizing a support group, or anything that allow him to avoid the thing he couldn't do. He was intelligent, funny, and--at times--desperate to turn his life around. I remember one of the times he came through the centre, I met with him while he was still in the orientation phase, which was the first two weeks. He was feeling crushed with hopelessness and meaning-lessness when I sat down across from him at a picnic table. Along with sitting still, the other thing Jim-Bob couldn't do was stop using crystal meth. He had never managed to stay clean for more than a few weeks following his successful stints in treatment, and as the failures and setbacks added up, he began to believe that it was his destiny to stay addicted until he died. After listening to his concerns and feelings, I told him that I believed that his repeated attempts weren't for nothing, that one day he would be sitting in my seat, across from someone who needed hope because they had none, and who better to encourage that guy than someone who had once felt the same? He didn't believe me and self-discharged the next day.

The next time I saw him was a year or so later. This time he was more determined to have a different ending and stated that he was willing to do anything to stay clean. I have heard this same sentiment expressed by so many of my clients, but when they are asked, either by me or by life, to do things that make them uncomfortable or that they are unsure of, that's when the truthfulness of their commitment is revealed. Jim-Bob meant it, however. He was not assigned to my group but to the group of another counsellor who in many ways was very like-minded to me. His counsellor and I had had many conversa-tions about ADHD, brain development and function, attachment and all of the interconnections among these ideas and concepts. Despite having a degree in social work, he was very interested in the science of the brain and behaviour and learning. Because of this, he was open-minded enough to suggest to Jim-Bob one day that perhaps he might want to see a doctor about getting tested for ADHD. That's always a funny phrase for me, as if it's as simple as a blood test or something. If only it were that easy. Jim-Bob said he was willing to try anything, so his counsellor made arrangements for him to see a local psychiatrist. Sure enough, he was diagnosed and prescribed a medica-tion called Dexedrine, also known as dextroamphetamine. Jim-Bob felt very strange taking an amphetamine-based medication while he was in treatment for addiction to amphetamine but was willing to try anything, as he had stated.

After his first dose, the effect was incredible. Jim-Bob sat still in group. He didn't constantly comment in the class. He was able to listen and follow along and didn't seem to have the need to take over the conversation. Most impressively, following his group session that day, instead of finding a handful of chores to occupy his time, he went to his room and read a book. I couldn't believe what I was seeing. It was unfathomable to me that a single dose of medication could have such a profound impact. What was even more remarkable to me was that the changes stayed in effect. Until the end of his successfully completed program, Jim-Bob was a different person. He was still his outgoing, gregarious, helpful, intelligent self, but he was no longer driven. He was finally able to put into practice all the skills and knowledge that he had been exposed to over his years of trying and failing to leave his addiction behind. Following his graduation this time, things went very differently for Jim-Bob. Instead of relapsing and finding himself back in the street, he began to be more and more involved in the recovery community, and the last I heard of him, more than a couple of years after his graduation, he was sitting across from someone at a picnic table encouraging them to try just one more time.

After witnessing this miraculous transformation, I started to reconsider my long-held prejudice toward medication. I knew that the amphetamine had the effect that it did because the ADHD brain lacks dopamine, a reward chemical, in the prefrontal cortex, which is the home of self-control in the brain. Because it lacks dopamine, the self-control machine is either working sluggishly or completely unplugged, which leaves the rest of the brain in a state of unregulated chaos. That's the simplified version. When the PFC gets the appropriate increase in dopamine, it wakes up and then takes control of the rest of the brain. I tell my young clients that it's like the classroom when the teacher leaves and everyone starts breaking the rules and then the teacher comes back in and takes control of the situation. The medication is the teacher. This effect, where stimulants provide feelings of calm and focus, is called a paradoxical effect. I knew that this effect occurred with all stimulants, not just prescription amphetamines, and so I decided to try a little experiment.

As Mormons, we have a pretty strict health code known as the Word of Wisdom that proscribes ingesting all sorts of substances that are mainstays of modern culture, such as coffee, tea, tobacco, alcohol, illegal drugs, etc. It also prescribes healthy eating, but we don't pay as much attention to that part, unfortunately. Anyway, because I live by this code, I do not introduce stimulants to my body on a regular basis, other than pounds of sugar, but that's a little different. I reasoned that if my brain was truly an ADHD brain, then if I drank a bunch of caffeine, my brain should respond in much the same way that Jim-Bob's brain did. On the way home from work, I stopped at the gas station and bought the biggest can of Red Bull that they sold, and when I got home, I informed Tina of my plan. She was used to my weird ideas and didn't pay much attention to it. After dinner, I went downstairs to the rec room, sat on the couch, opened and chugged the entire can of Red Bull and pulled out a textbook and started reading. Oh, I forgot to mention that I was in graduate school at this time. That's another story. Anyway, not long after I started reading, I felt my eyes getting heavier and heavier. Eventually, I dropped the book beside me and flopped over on the couch and had a two-hour nap. After chugging a tall can of Red Bull. When I woke up, I felt great, and I realized that this whole paradoxical effect thing might just be real.

Soon after that, I saw my family doctor and was referred to a local psychiatrist, the same one who had diagnosed Jim-Bob. His name, believe it or not, was Dr. Saad. A psychiatrist named Dr. Sad. You couldn't make this stuff up. That's actually a pretty funny expression, because it's just so far from the truth. Are you telling me that no one could have come up with that from their own imagination? Tolkien not only came up with an alternate world with different races and history, he even created an entirely new language, just as part of the backstory for the main story about little people who have to drop a magical mind-controlling ring into a mountain of fire before a disembodied eye takes control of the whole place. Are you telling me that he couldn't have thought of an ironic name for a psychiatrist? Of course he could. Anyway, I thought it was funny. I was warned by Jim-Bob's counsellor that Dr. Saad was ancient and might even be narcoleptic as he was known to sometimes drift off during appointments. He was not inaccurate in this description.

On October 27, 2009, this was my Facebook status: "*Can't help but notice the irony. Today I have an appointment with an ADHD specialist, but first I have to renew the insurance on the van, which I forgot to do several times over the last couple of weeks. But no, it doesn't stop there because for the millionth time, I can't find my freaking wallet!!!! Thank goodness for Tina.*" As I sat in the waiting room, I didn't have any sense that my life was about to change drastically, but instead I sat there feeling sheepish. The self-doubt created by my life up to this point had convinced me that I was making a big deal about nothing, that my dad and everyone else was right, that I was just looking for an excuse and trying too hard to fit in with the people I worked with and around. I was sure that the doctor, after meeting with me, would dismiss me as faking it and tell me that I just needed to try harder to apply myself. Instead, he sat and listened to my long-winded answers to his questions. He looked like he was 150 years old and walked with such a bent spine that I wasn't sure if he was going to make it from the waiting room back to his office. He went through the standard questions, and I gave the universal answers, but he also went outside the box a little bit in his investigation. He even fell asleep on me once or twice. At one point, we had a funny little exchange. He asked me if I got much exercise. I told him that I liked to lift weights and play basketball, and sometimes was into running. He slowly shook his head and said, "No, you need to do something that is more peaceful. Have you ever done something like Tai Chi?" I told him that one time I had impulsively purchased a VHS tape on Tai Chi so that I could learn it at home but after getting lost and confused repeatedly in the first ten minutes I just gave up and never tried again. He looked at me without saying anything and then began to ask, "What do you mean you gave up? Why would you give up so...." Then a look of recognition and realization seemed to wash over his aged face. He nodded his head and wrote something down on his notepad.

At the end of the appointment, he told me that my symptoms were very typical but that they were also largely subjective. He explained that this meant that much of my experience of ADHD was internal and thus not easily observed by those around me, which would explain why it had taken 33 years for someone to finally say the words that explained my life up to that point. "You meet the diagnostic criteria for ADHD." As I write those words out this morning, tears come to my eyes as I relive the relief that came coursing through me. The validation for years of suffering and struggling. The alternative explanation for my "permanent potential." I felt forgiven, for lack of a better word. Dr. Saad's bedside manner was not what I would call textbook empathy, but his simple acceptance of the truth that I had told him and the gentle and simple way he proceeded, as if this was the most natural thing in the world, conveyed to me an acceptance that I had been searching for my entire life. He prescribed me a trial dose of Dexedrine and told me to take it early in the morning, then come back in two weeks to follow up. It was the first and last time I ever saw him. When I called his office a week later to schedule the appointment, I was told that he had retired abruptly. At the time, I was dismayed, but looking back on it now, he served the purpose I needed. He had unlocked the door to the next chapter of my story. Metaphorically. Also literally. Because that's the end of this chapter. The next one is about the medicine.

SEVENTY-FIVE

DEFOG

THE NIGHT before I took my first dose of ADHD medication felt like Christmas Eve. Dr. Saad had instructed me to take it at 6 a.m., much earlier than I was used to waking up, so I set my alarm to make sure I did it right. However, I couldn't sleep that night, tossing and turning, constantly looking at the clock, waking up and feeling antsy with anticipation. I was so excited to see what it would be like. I ended up getting up before my alarm and sitting on the couch, waiting for 6:00 to arrive. When it did, I did as I was told, took my medication and then went back to bed and slept for another hour and a half. When I woke up, I felt good. I felt really positive and cheerful. We had an exchange student living with us at the time, and I needed to leave early that morning to drop her off at school before heading to work. As I drove to the school, my mind was generating ideas at its usual pace, but something felt different about it. As I pulled away from the school, after witnessing the bedraggled mass of teenagers trudging to their scholastic doom, the thought occurred to me that it might be a good idea to offer to go to schools to speak about drug abuse and addiction. The thought, which ordinarily would have been quickly followed by a negative rebuttal, was able to grow, and I felt determined to actually call the principal and discuss the issue with him. The more I thought about it, the more realistic it seemed to be, instead of just some fantasy that would never happen. In the end, it didn't happen because the school system in B.C. is far more complicated than that, and you can't just call up and say, "I want to talk to your students about drugs," but the point is that I thought about it, pursued it, and followed it through. When I got home from my early morning trip, I noticed the garbage cans sitting empty at the end of the driveway, where they had been sitting for two days now because I would see them as I pulled in the driveway, tell myself to not forget to take them in, and then turn off the car and walk in the house, with the thought completely wiped from my mind no more than 30 seconds later. This morning, however, I saw them, turned off the car, got out and grabbed the cans and carried them back to the house. I know it seems like such a simple thing, something that real grownups do every day and don't get applauded for, but for me, it was those simple grownup things that always served as barriers and reminders of my innate deficiency. To be able to follow through on an intention was an incredible experience for me.

I have often described the impact of that medication as someone turning on the defog, clearing my view through a previously obscured window. Added to the thrill of finally being able to see is the realization that you didn't really know how foggy it was until the window was clear. It's kind of like when I tried a new pair of reading glasses and was complaining that everything seemed blurry still, even though the prescription was correct, only to notice that the lenses were covered in fingerprints. Now that I'm typing that, I'm noticing that my glasses are smudgy and I need to clean them, but the little cloth thing that you're supposed to use to clean them is down in my car and I'm in my office, and it's easier to just take them off, even though if I look at the screen for too long without them I might get a headache, but it's always hard to tell if the headache is coming from squinting or from the tension in my neck because I carry lots of stress in my neck and shoulders and clench my jaw sometimes, but I don't even notice until my teeth hurt, which means I might need to get a mouth-guard for sleeping at night because the dentist told Tina that if she doesn't get one, she might end up needing a root canal on some of her teeth because she clenches down so hard, but I've already had five root canals, so I guess the worry for me is that I'll actually clench so hard that I will break the tooth and then I'll have to get a crown, or even worse, a bridge, which is really expensive...

SEVENTY-SIX

AFTER THE FOG

WHAT WOULD you do if you finally found out the answer to a question you had been asking your whole life? Would you scream "Eureka!" and run through the streets naked telling everyone you saw about your discovery? Would you head straight to social media to share the news with your friends, both real and virtual? Would you fall on your knees and thank the heavens, universe, or flying spaghetti monster for the miracle that has occurred? Would you go and tell the people who are closest and most important to you about the importance of the discovery and the impact that it has had on you? As much as it isn't hard to imagine me doing the first one, luckily, I did the last one. Okay, I also did the second one, but I just couldn't shut up about the profound difference I was experiencing in how I felt and acted and thought. As I was going on and on in my excitement, describing to my mom the amazing impact of the medication and just the diagnosis in general, the validation that I had experienced and the hope that I now had due to the effectiveness of the medication, my mom's response was the same as Tina's, "That's good, but you sound like you're high." Uh, what? I just told you about this amazing thing that I had discovered and your answer is, "You might be wrong"? Because that's what if felt like. The reality is that I probably did sound high because, uh, ADHD. Also, I had just done the mental health equivalent of walking on water, so yeah, I was a bit excited and couldn't shut up about it. But when this was pointed out, what I heard was, "You're faking it." I don't know if that's what they meant or if they were just concerned because my over-the-top positivity was such a drastic change, but that's certainly what was engraved on my mind. It was such a juxtaposition between the completely nonchalant acceptance of Dr. Saad, who basically said, "Of course you have ADHD; why not?" and many of those around me, who said, "Of course you feel better on speed; who doesn't?"

Perhaps that's why I took to Facebook, to search for the validation that I was still finding very hard to obtain from my family. I don't blame them, because their knowledge of ADHD was the same as mine before I began this accidental journey of self-revelation, but that doesn't mean that their reception to my miracle didn't kill my buzz a little bit. In actual fact, it did more than dampen my mood; it gave a foothold for my lifelong companion, self-doubt, to creep back into my mind. I got defensive and irritated with people who questioned my realization, probably in no small part because I was terrified that they might be right. What if I was faking it? What if I really was just high and feeling great because of it. Even now, all these years later, all these seminars, workshops, and counselling sessions later, all of these research articles and books read and conferences attended, there is a core baseline that runs deep inside me that says I am a fraud, that I am Rachel Dolezal, that white lady who "identified" as black person and ran the NAACP chapter in her town and rejected people for membership because they weren't "black enough." I am just searching for a tribe that will accept me and my laziness and stupidity. Actually, let's go back to that whole fake race thing. Really? What kind of person would actually attempt something so brazen? Two answers come to mind: a) a narcissist who genuinely believes that he or she is smarter and more deserving than everyone else, and b) someone who is delusional. Not in the sense that they are out of touch with reality but in the sense that they have told themselves the same lie long enough that they have long forgotten it is not true. In many ways, my own self-doubt is the same, I suppose. I had told myself that I was lazy, dumb, etc. for so long that I actually started to believe it, despite all the evidence to the contrary.

One time, I was on some ADHD forum and someone posted the following challenge, saying, "You know you have adult ADHD if _____." with the idea that we would fill in the blank. Of course there were the predictable answers about showing up late for everything, forgetting the child at the mall, not paying bills, etc., but my answer was this: *You know you have adult ADHD if you doubt that you have ADHD at all.* If you are an adult with ADHD, especially if you have been diagnosed as an adult, you will know what I mean. The relief that comes with the explanation and the changes that occur as a result of the medication can quickly be forced to duel the long-held negative beliefs we have been trained and reinforced to accept. The secret to winning that duel is to see the whole picture. What I mean by that is that we are more than the sum of our parts, but we must also acknowledge those individual parts that combine to create that whole. It is incomplete and ineffective to say to yourself, "Yeah, I have ADHD, but I'm awesome and ADHD is awesome and a wonderful gift that has changed my life for the better." We must also acknowledge this statement's mirror to be true. "Yeah I have ADHD and sometimes I really suck at stuff and really underperform and disappoint people, and ADHD is a huge pain and a curse that has ruined many situations for me." I realize that you won't find the latter in *Chicken Soup for the Scattered Soul,* but trust me when I tell you that pretending that ADHD isn't hard doesn't make it easier. We must acknowledge the barriers that come with it, the things that are harder because of it, the limitations we experience and the dead ends that result from it. We can do this without becoming crushed by the weight if we counterbalance those truths with the fact that in many ways it frees us, makes certain things easier and much more natural for us, and has opened many doors and led to many experiences for us that we wouldn't have had otherwise. When we force ourselves to acknowledge and internalize the positive aspects of this brain we have, it is easier to acknowledge and adapt to the negative aspects. So often ADHD children and adults are resistant to accepting or even asking for help. We insist we can do it ourselves, even when it becomes clear that we are floundering. I remember this kid who lived around the corner from us in Salmo who joined us one day while we were doing bike maintenance. As part of that maintenance, we were adjusting the position and height of our seats. This required some basic tools, and an older kid who lived up the road was taking the lead on the project, providing the materials and supervision we needed to be successful. This other kid insisted that he didn't need tools and he didn't need supervision. As you might expect, our seats were soon perfectly adjusted, and his seat was literally smashed to small pieces with a hammer, the only tool that he thought would be useful.

In many ways, folks with ADHD are a lot like that kid, insisting we are fine while slowly self-destructing. It boggles the minds of those who are in a position to help but are rebuffed and even attacked when help is offered. What I try to get across to those would-be supporters is that the message you are sending is not necessarily the message they are receiving. If you offer input or ask a clarifying question or give a gentle reminder, the message we often receive is this: *You are stupid. You are inadequate. You don't know what you're doing and you can't do anything right because of it.* Now imagine that's what you actually said to your son or daughter as he or she struggled to complete a task. If you did, no sane person would be surprised to see a negative, even hostile reaction. It would be the appropriate and understandable response. However, since that's not what you actually said, that response seems inappropriate and confusing at best and downright crazy at worst. I've often used the example that a deep sigh from a parent, meant to invoke self-soothing and access reserves of patience, can communicate a very different message to a child who is struggling to feel anything other than stupid and worthless. That doesn't mean we don't do the deep sigh; it just means we do it around the corner, out of sight and sound of that person who is trying our patience to such degrees.

SEVENTY-SEVEN

THIS IS HOW I KNOW

ONE DAY, I needed to take Holly to a basketball practice. I backed my car out of the driveway and headed off down our street. As I got to the corner, I noticed and remembered that I was almost completely out of gas. Like, almost literally running on fumes. Since I was less than a block from my house, the logical thing would have been to turn around and go home and switch cars. Instead, I reasoned that I could probably make it the 20 blocks to the nearest gas station. I nervously pulled off our street and drove, careful not to press too hard on the gas pedal. I judged right, and just as I pulled into the gas station, the car sputtered and fell silent. I coasted right up to the pump. I couldn't have measured it better. As I congratulated myself for my estimating skills, I noticed that my car insurance had expired a week earlier and I had forgotten to renew it. Once again, I was at about the halfway point to the basketball practice, and the prudent thing to do would have been to go home and switch vehicles. Instead, I reasoned that I had gone this long without and it would probably be fine. Again, it was fine and I managed to make it to the practice, only a few minutes late. The next day I had a meeting in the evening at the police station, and I remembered on my way there that I still had no insurance on my car and it probably wouldn't be a good idea to park in the detachment parking lot with an uninsured vehicle, so I desperately searched for the closest insurance dealer. There happened to be one across the street from the police station, so I quickly pulled in there and explained my situation. The insurance agent literally had me out of there in less than five minutes. I pulled into the station parking lot and walked quickly from my car, through the front doors and into the meeting room with not a minute to spare.

One year, I swore that I was going to renew my driver's license on time. Because it only needs to be renewed on my birthday once every five years, it is very easy for it to slip my mind. This year, I was determined to be on time and avoid the risk of driving without a license, which had become a tradition. On my birthday, I made sure to include a trip to the licensing office in my plans and stood proudly in line as I prepared to do a thing that all grownups do without fanfare. When my number was called, I proudly strode to the counter to announce that I was going to renew my license on time for the first time ever. The kind lady behind the counter took my license and looked at it before handing it back to me with a patient smile on her face. She then informed me that not only was I not late this year, I was a year early. My license still had a year left before it needed to be renewed. Somewhat sheepishly, I took the license back and shuffled out of the office. The next year, I renewed it over two weeks after it had expired, as per usual. I'd had a brief and fleeting brush with adulthood and watched it float away.

One year I determined that for my birthday I wanted to get an action camera like a GoPro, because the idea of it was appealing to me. Instead of getting an actual GoPro, because we didn't have the money, I spent weeks researching different brands of cameras before settling on a Polaroid model. I ordered it online and was super excited when it arrived in the mail a week or so later. The first thing I did was fasten it to my steering wheel, because why wouldn't I? Not my dashboard, but my steering wheel, because I thought that would be more interesting to watch. The next thing I did was attach it to a broom handle and reach way up with the camera on the end to peek into a bird's nest that was attached to the side of our house. I could hear that there were young birds in there, and I was very curious to see what they looked like. Instead, what happened was that one of the young birds, frightened by the intrusion, came bursting out of the birdhouse and attempted to fly to safety. Instead, it was intercepted by a hovering crow and killed. I did get some good footage of the inside of the nest, but I felt a bit guilty for indirectly murdering the bird. That was the last time I used the camera. Not out of guilt but because I quickly lost the waterproof cover, the charger, and many of the attachments that were necessary to connect it to things like handlebars. The other reason was that I actually don't do a lot of things that could be described as "action" anymore. My days of jumping bikes into the trees were long over. However, hyper-focusing on something at the exclusion of everything else, only to quickly forget about it once I acquired it, that is something that may never be finished.

I have a private counselling practice and a contract with the city and township of Langley, which means I have two different work calendars. I also have five children who are all involved in extracurricular activities and a large extended family, almost all of whom live within 45 minutes of my home. This makes it a constant challenge to know where I'm supposed to be and what I'm supposed to be doing. I check both work calendars no less than 10 times every day and retain almost nothing from doing so (hence the repeated checking). One day, while checking ahead on my private practice calendar, I noticed that I'd booked an evening off, but I had no idea why I had done it. This often causes panic for me because I do so many speaking engagements and workshops that when I see a blank space like this, my greatest fear is that somewhere there's an audience waiting for me to show up. I asked Tina if she knew why it was empty, and she didn't know. I racked my brain to try to remember where I was supposed to be and what I was supposed to be doing. Finally, after a few days of mounting pressure, I resorted to a public appeal on Facebook, asking if anyone knew why I might have booked the evening off. I was saved not once but twice by two different people's replies. The first reminded me that I had bought a ticket to attend a lecture given by Gabor Mate that night in the nearby community of Mission. I had completely forgotten about it, other than a vague sense that it was coming up at some point in the future. Then another friend messaged me saying that while she didn't know why I had booked that evening off, she did know that the next week I was scheduled to speak at an event called Ignite Abbotsford. That one I hadn't blocked off on my calendar, and if she hadn't messaged me, I would have totally forgotten to show up. The title of my short speech that night was "20 ADHD Stories in Five Minutes," and the content featured a range of situations just like this.

I have missed mortgage payments more than once, simply because I forgot to transfer money into the right account. I pay late fees, penalties, and interest on my income taxes every year because no matter how much I want to, I just can't seem to file them on time. Over the years, I've had to replace several socket wrench sets and screwdrivers and hammers because the old ones ceased to exist, disappearing into another dimension, only to reappear after I've purchased and used the new ones. I've had so many items of clothing disappear that I'm starting to wonder if maybe somebody has been slowly enacting the world's greatest prank for the last 30 years. I've punched holes through doors and walls and broken porcelain countertops out of frustration. I've offended dozens of people with my mistimed comments. I've prepared countless talks, lessons, lectures and slide shows in the wee hours of the morning on the days before I was to present them. I've added countless slides to those presentations as the audience filed in to take their seats. I've started so many books that I've never finished, many of them lent out to others because I was so excited about what I was reading that I just needed to share it with someone else. I'm really good at imitating people's mannerisms and accents because I spend so much time observing people. My mood can go from happy and excited to sad and angry in less time than it takes me to forget what you just asked me to do, but it can also go in the opposite direction, just as fast. I've lost and gained the same 40 pounds four separate times, each time believing that this was the time that things had really changed, only to watch helplessly as I outgrew all of my clothes again. The pantry door in our old house didn't have a doorknob for 11 years and I only put one on two months before we moved to a new house. I've double-booked clients on multiple occasions, and one time I even triple-booked, but one of them no-showed, which saved me even further embarrassment. I can see how the little details may affect the big picture, which sometimes leads to overthinking—but then my impulsivity kicks in and I take the risk anyway, believing that the consequences will be an adventure. I need to be outside in nature, where I feel most at peace, but I often struggle with the motivation needed to actually get there. I can completely dominate conversations, even while I am self-consciously criticizing myself for doing so. I stay up way too late binge-watching TV shows or creating music but can still get out of bed early the next day and put in 12 hours of work. I interrupt people. I have 1000 good ideas, most of which will never turn into reality. I am prone to all kinds of addictive behaviour. I fidget so much that it's hard for people to sit next to me. I spend most of my time driving with my car almost out of gas. I hyper-focus and learn the *why* behind as many things as I can, but this is often at the expense of actually doing the things I'm supposed to. I once wrote a three-part blog post about procrastination, and after writing the first two parts in two days, I didn't write the third part until another month had passed, and I knew that's how it would go as soon as I started the first part. I once made a series of videos on my YouTube channel describing the diagnostic criteria for ADHD in detail and posted all but the last symptom, and I still don't even know why, especially since it's already recorded. I lost my train of thought in the middle of speaking to a group of school teachers and staff about helping kids with ADHD. The irony was so great that people thought it was intentional and part of my presentation. My brain can read a children's book out loud, substituting funny voices and accents while simultaneously figuring out how to fix the leak under the sink. I often say, "What?" when people say things to me because I don't think I was listening but then when they start to say it again, I realize that I did hear them, but I don't know if I should interrupt them and tell them I heard or if I should just let them say it again. Either way, they will be annoyed. I spend more time trying to think of an efficient way to do things than it would take to just do it the inefficient way. When I read, I often repeat the same line or paragraph without absorbing anything because I'm thinking about something else, usually triggered by what I'm supposed to be reading. I often meet people and within seconds of them introducing themselves, I've already forgotten their names, mostly because I wasn't really listening when they told me. Re-watching the same movie almost feels physically painful to me because of the boredom. So many times I sit at the computer, fingers hovering above the keyboard, poised for action, a Google search page glaring at me impatiently as I try to answer the question, "What was I going to look up?" When people hear this small sampling, they often say, "Well I do that too" or "Everybody does that." My practiced, patient response is to point out that of course, everyone has moments of forgetfulness, disorganization, impulsivity, and lack of motivation. Everyone has experienced the symptoms of ADHD at one time or another. However, when you experience most of the symptoms most of the time, that is something qualitatively different. I am qualitatively different.

SEVENTY-EIGHT

PEOPLE WHO JUST DON'T GET IT

AND PEOPLE WHO DO

IN THE YEARS that have passed since that eventful time in 2009, so many more ripples have spread across my life, their source being the realization of an alternate explanation. I have given numerous workshops on the subject, trying always to answer the why questions. Why does he procrastinate? Why doesn't she do what I ask her to? Why does he forget so easily? Why do I have a hard time getting motivated to do anything? Why can't I just pick a career and stick with it? Why does she get so angry? Why is he so sensitive? Why can't I stop eating these subpar rice crackers from Costco, even though they have hardly any flavour and may, in fact, be partly made from plastic and leave a coating on my tongue that makes me wish I had more self-control but not wish it hard enough to actually stop eating them? Okay, I added that last one in. There must be the perfect mix of salt and sugar in these things, and I am eating them robotically. Only if the robot was programmed to self-destruct. Okay, I put them away. The reason I spend so much time on the why is because if we don't have the real explanation, we are going to come up with, or accept from others, explanations that are, at best, inaccurate and, at worst, harmful. I try to teach people about dopamine and the prefrontal cortex and the reticular activating system and mirror neurons and the neurobiology of working memory because unless we can actually see the things that are different, it is very hard to accept the behavioural limitations that come with this brain we have. Even when it *can* be seen, it can still be difficult to accept.

When I was working at the treatment centre, I came into the morning clinical meeting one time, only to be told that one of my clients had verbally assaulted the cook the night before, cursing at her and acting rudely. I was told that I would need to address this behaviour with him and make sure that he understood that it was not acceptable. I told them I would talk to him but that it was important for everyone to understand that when this client was a young boy, he had wiped out on his bike and had his handlebars pierce the front of his skull so deeply into his brain that the firefighters just sawed the handlebars off and took him to the hospital with them hanging out of his forehead. After they were removed by the surgeons, what was left behind was essentially a large hole, specifically in the area of the brain responsible for self-awareness and self-control. As such, it was to be expected that this kind of thing might happen again. After this explanation, I was ready to move on to the next item when the janitor piped up, "Yeah, but still. He can't be doing that and he needs to know that." I couldn't quite believe what I'd heard, so I reiterated that the part of his brain responsible for self-control no longer existed and that this was going to be an ongoing issue. "Yeah, but still..." Realizing the futility of this conversation, I let it go, but it was the accumulation of moments like these that eventually led to the decision to leave the treatment centre behind. Management was happy to see me go, as I did not fit into the mold of "employee-who-takes-it-and-is-quiet-about-it," but I felt bad leaving the clients behind, knowing that they were now missing a staunch advocate for their rights, not only as clients but also as humans. About six months before I left the centre to pursue my private counselling practice full time, I had completed my master's degree in psychology, with a counselling specialization. It had been a long and difficult journey to get there, with about half of the course work being completed before I was diagnosed and treated for that pesky ADHD. Up until that point, and to be honest, even after that point to some degree, my style was very similar to that of university. In fact, graduate school was the scene of one of my greatest triumphs.

If procrastinating were an Olympic event, I would have a collection of gold medals that would make Michael Phelps jealous. Actually, now that I mention that, it's interesting that two of the most dominant Olympians ever were quite open about their own ADHD, meaning Phelps and Simone Biles, the tiny gymnast from the Rio games. I wonder how they got past the barriers that ADHD presents to become so disciplined and focused on a goal that was so far away. Anyway, I procrastinate with the best of them, and one time in grad school, I put off the writing of a final paper until the last three days of the semester, even though that paper was worth the majority of the grade in my Biology of behaviour class. I had been gathering research sources and reviewing them and essentially writing the paper in my mind but had yet to type even a single word of the actual document. When I reached that sweet spot where panic kicks in but has not yet overwhelmed completely, I sat down at the computer and began typing, reading, reviewing, researching and hyper-focusing like my life depended on it. I called in sick the next two days to work on the project and got only four hours sleep between the two nights, with every other waking moment occupied by the completion of the paper.

In the end, I finished and submitted it online with only 20 minutes to spare before the deadline, without even having time to proofread it. I was somewhat surprised, but not completely, when I got my course grade back a week later: 97 percent. I immediately called my dad to tell him about it, especially since, in his generosity, he was funding my graduate education. I wanted to let him know that his investment was a good one and, of course, I wanted him to be proud of me. It's funny, even to this day, that that's what makes me tear up more than anything, seeing or hearing about fathers telling their sons that they are proud of them. I didn't hear it very much growing up and that was probably partly because I made a lot of mistakes, but it was also because my dad handed out praise like Scrooge. He wasn't critical, but it took quite a bit to ripple the water, if you know what I mean. He answered and I told him the good news, and he responded by saying, "Okay, well, we're at Carrie's house right now, just pulled in the driveway, so we'll talk to you later." That was basically it. It felt like a punch in the stomach of my attachment and I sat down and wrote the following email:

HELLO MOTHER.

I have to say, I was a bit disappointed by your and Dad's reaction to my phone call last night. I guess it was just a repeat of the usual pattern. I come to you with something that I think is a wonderful achievement and inwardly wishing that I can surprise you with the accomplishment. Your reaction was underwhelming to say the least. I realize that this may seem like a baby-reaction, stomping my feet and demanding that you praise me, but that's how I feel emotionally. I worked my tail off and almost got 100% in a challenging course in graduate school and the reaction was "Well, good for you" from you and Dad's was, "Well, how did you get that mark?" as if there had to be some logical explanation for my success other than my ability. This is the kind of authentic directness you have to deal with when you have a therapist for a son, but I left the conversation feeling like it wasn't that big of a deal. It is a big deal.

Also, when I was talking to you about the troubles at work, I felt like I received no support, only "Well, don't make anyone mad." I felt a bit abandoned to be honest. Like, I was experiencing some emotional difficulty about my work situation and all I got from my home base was, "Well, don't do something dumb." Then you rushed me off the phone because you were in front of Carrie's house. I did not leave the conversation feeling very valuable. Maybe I'm overreacting, but emotions do not need to be justified, only described. I know you guys love me, and I think you are proud of me, but there is a hole in me that doesn't seem fillable.

Anyway, I just thought I would let you know my feelings, instead of holding it inside and holding it against you. Sorry for burdening you with all of this, but it's never too late to learn to do things differently.

Love, Ted

In this email you can see the pattern that has repeated itself so many times in my life, but this time was different. I was empowered by my career and educational success up to this point but mostly by the knowledge of my ADHD (this event occurred just before my official diagnosis) and the accompanying realization that I was worth something, that I was capable and valuable and deserving and that I wasn't going to just take it anymore. In no way do I want to paint my parents as bad people or bad parents. They, too, as humans do, get stuck in patterns of behaviour and feeling, products of their own experiences and of their own parents. All of that aside, I needed to let them know how I was affected by their responses, so I wrote the email. When working with couples, I often advise them to write letters or emails to each other to express their feelings about hard subjects because it allows the writer to take the time to reflect and process instead of just reacting to a lot of the nonverbal communication that triggers. I always say, "nobody can interrupt your email." Anyway, I figured an email was the best way to get my point across, and my mom, in her greatness, responded with the following:

TED, you were quite right. I thought about it afterward and thought, we kind of gave Ted the brush-off when he called us with his good news, just because we were about to go into Carrie's. And I asked myself why we did that. I think it would have been different if we had been home when you called. All I can think of is that we were otherwise mentally engaged. We were just about to step out of the car to go into Carrie's (expectation already firmly engaged) when you called. That must have been why we APPEARED so underwhelmed.

But we actually weren't as underwhelmed as you thought. We were delighted! Unfortunately, it just didn't come across. The funny thing is, Ted, we were happy for you and proud of you, but not surprised. I guess we expect that kind of thing from you because we know you are a really smart guy and that you were working really hard on your courses. We probably don't realize the magnitude of the work involved, either, and what a huge accomplishment it is to get marks like that in grad school. Poor excuses, though, and I'm truly sorry if we ruined your moment, as we clearly did.

I'm sorry, too, if you think you have to impress us. You are good enough just by being our son, but I know kids like to have their parents' approval. Especially with someone like dad, who is not emotionally demonstrative.

So, I apologize for our reaction, and in the future, because your parents are obviously denser than they appear, or maybe not, you might want to preface your next big announcement with, "Okay, I want you to listen because this is really important!" If that doesn't get our attention, we are truly hopeless.

I hope I have helped you feel a bit less dejected. This is obviously a long-standing concern of yours and not likely to go away with one email. You know that we love you a huge amount, and, believe it or not, we glory in all your successes, and feel your failures, too. If I came across disinterested about the work (time off) problem, I really wasn't communicating in that area, either, because I was very concerned about that. I guess I have been concerned that all your school work would take away from your job and 'they' would get mad at you. With so many people getting laid off these days, I worry about my kids' jobs and know how lucky you all are to have them!

THAT'S ABOUT ALL the excuses I can make for us. The very least we can do is go out to dinner to celebrate your success!

.   .   .

LOVE, Mommy

IS she a great mom or what? And she was right about my employer, too. They found out that I had called in sick to do my homework, and they were not happy about it, docking my pay for those two days. But I didn't really care; it was worth it.

SEVENTY-NINE

RELAX, YOU ARE AMONG WEIRDOS

Not long after my diagnosis, I attended a dinner event where a professor of psychiatry from the University of British Columbia was going to be speaking about ADHD. This was an event put on for doctors, probably sponsored by a pharmaceutical company in some way, and the psychiatrist who attended the treatment centre biweekly to work with mainly my clients had given me the heads up, passing his invitation on to me because he was unable to attend. I felt a bit out of place as a lowly counsellor, and my discomfort was only added upon when I saw one of my least favourite doctors in town come strutting through the door. The event was held at a restaurant, and he immediately ordered some wine, knowing that the dinner was being paid for by the organizers. He then loudly wondered what the event was all about, and someone told him that it was about diagnosing and treating ADHD. He then, much to my astonishment, asked, "What's that?" The incredibly patient person who was trapped in this nightmare then proceeded to give a brief synopsis of the main symptoms, to which Dr. Hyde responded, "Hell, isn't everyone like that?" While I wasn't shocked that he was an obnoxious freeloader and a condescending narcissist, I was shocked that

someone could finish medical school and have a booming family practice without even knowing what ADHD was. I'm sad to say that
since that day, the shock has worn off as I have heard so many frustrating stories from my clients of seeking help from doctors only to be
told, "You don't look that hyper to me," and that is the extent of the
assessment. One client, for whom ADHD seemed to fill in a lot of
gaps, like it had for me, was excited to see his family doctor and
explore treatment options, only to be told that he didn't have ADHD
and instead receive a prescription for antidepressants. I asked him if
the doctor had asked any questions about his childhood or school
experiences, all of which fit the bill quite seamlessly. He said that he
hadn't. I then asked if the doctor had, in fact, asked any questions
related to the ADHD symptom checklist that my client had taken to
the appointment. He said that he hadn't. I then strongly suggested to
my client that he go back to the doctor and insist that either he properly assess the condition or refer him to someone who would. My
client listened and came away from the appointment with medication
that began to help him immediately.

While attending this little information session where I felt
out of my league, I was pleased to learn about a doctor who lived in
the next city over who specialized in adult ADHD. I was also pleased
to learn about an organization called CADDRA, or the Canadian
ADHD Resource Alliance. I suppose it use to be called the ADD
resource alliance since that's what ADHD used to be called, but
when the disorder changed names, the organization didn't because
CADDRA is such an easy acronym, but I tell you, inconsistencies
like that drive part of my brain crazy. It's one of those places where
my brain needs symmetry. I find that I have a lot of those little things
floating around in my life that create aversive emotions for no
discernible reason. You'll notice that I didn't say "for no reason at all,"
because of course there's a reason; we might just be unable to explain
the reason. For example, you may or may not have heard of something
called synesthesia, where the different senses are interconnected in a
way that may cause a person to smell sounds, hear colors, taste

textures, or have emotional experiences evoked by inanimate objects. These interactions between senses are not based on past experiences or conditioning or anything like that; we seem to come into the world this way. In fact, some researchers believe that we are all born with this sensory interconnectivity but because it serves no survival purpose, the brain prunes these connections over time, dispersing the valuable energy resources in building and maintaining other, more vital, connections and networks. But then there's this group of us that believe that Wednesday is yellow or the color red makes us sad. The other thing about these synesthetic connections is that they are highly unique and personalized. For me, the number 8 feels very arrogant and the number 4 feels very low-key cool, like the kid who has self-confidence and doesn't need to brag but everyone still knows that he's the dude. For me, when I picture the year in my mind, it is shaped like a lopsided horseshoe with July and August prominently featured on the top and the last four months of the year squished into a small space on the right. I've had clients tell me that they felt sad choosing one article of clothing over another because it seemed unfair to the other clothes. I've had people tell me that they felt bad for their old microwave when it was left out in the rain. Why am I talking about this right now?

I sometimes describe these kinds of neuroanatomical oddities to my clients as allergies, especially to parents of kids whose behaviour seems hard to categorize. Imagine if the socks that feel scratchy actually have a synesthetic association that makes them not only feel scratchy but scary. What if making eye contact smelled like rotten eggs. Wouldn't it make it more understandable why the kid is so adamant about not wearing those socks or avoiding eye contact? What if we thought of the resistant, defiant, or overreacting kid as having an "allergic" reaction to tasks and sensations. Instead of their skin breaking out in welts or their throat swelling up, their central nervous system breaks out in anger or fear. Granted, this is just my own theory based on logic and neurophysiology, but it's the kind of thing that only someone who is on the inside, who lives with weirdness on a daily basis, might be able to understand and articulate to someone else. Whenever I found myself talking with a doctor who didn't need to be convinced that ADHD was a real thing, I felt like I was with my people. The presenter of the information session was a member of CADDRA, which is an organization dedicated to educating doctors, psychologists, counsellors, social workers and everyone else about the assessment and treatment of ADHD. I found out that not only was the annual CADDRA conference coming up soon, but it would actually be held in Vancouver that year. I quickly applied for membership, was accepted, and registered for the conference.

I was so excited to be surrounded by like-minded people and medical and helping professionals who were past the stage where they needed convincing and had moved on to the "how can we help?" phase. I learned about all different aspects and wrinkles having to do with ADHD symptoms, causes, treatments, and mindset paradigm shifts that are necessary in our world. While it was exciting to be learning so much about something so important to me, it was the acceptance and absence of skepticism that probably impacted me the most at the conference. It reminded me of a documentary I'd watched one time called *Teenage Tourette's Camp*, where these British kids with Tourette's got on a plane and flew to the U.S. to attend a week-long camp with other kids in the same situation. It was a week of twitches, tics, cursing and yelling, and the greatest part of the show was that the Tourette's quickly faded into the background of the story as it became more about one girl ditching the group to try to fit in with the cool kids at the camp (I mean, they were teenagers, after all) instead of the shame and anxiety that they all lived with on a daily basis due to their very noticeable differences. At the CADDRA conference, I kind of felt like those kids (minus the cursing and shouting, though I do have some significant tics), as if I was allowed to walk around with my mask off. It was quite exhilarating to be freed from the prison of self-doubt for a temporary reprieve.

One of the other things that stood out to me from the conference was the lack of understanding that many professionals seemed to have about the impact of living with ADHD. They were all quite well-versed in the symptoms of ADHD but not in what I call the symptoms "because of." I'm not talking about the distractibility, impulsivity, fidgetiness, boredom and questionable decision-making skills. I'm referring to the impact of living like that in a world that can't accept it, isn't built for it, and doesn't want to understand it. I'm talking about accumulating failures, near-misses, and shame-filled moments. I'm talking about evaporating self-esteem, self-confidence, self-worth, and self-identity. I'm talking about the hopelessness that comes from believing you are helpless. I'm talking about the self-soothing that comes in the form of a multitude of addictive vices, the opportunities missed, the second-chances squandered, the confirmation of your greatest fears and the dashing of your greatest hopes. These are what I and many others with ADHD experience on a regular basis, and they are what I experience *because of* ADHD. As the doctors and other professionals joked about distracted patients, those who showed up late, missed appointments or forgot to take their medication, I chuckled along with them, but I began--for the first time in earnest--to really be aware of the pain those chuckles were covering up. I began to see ADHD as more than a collection of symptoms and behaviours, explained through neurochemistry and neurophysiology. I began to see it as a collection of definitions about myself and the world around me, things that I had always accepted as facts but may simply be masses-produced fictions. I began to see that the pain I felt was not from the ADHD itself and all of the complications it brought to my life. I began to see that the pain came from the gap between how I was and how the world expected me to be, and as the process of revelation unfolded, I began to see that I needed to make some changes. Not just in the way I saw the world, but in the way the world sees us.

EIGHTY

YOU ZIG, I ZAG

Interestingly, when I googled the question, "Are some people not built to read?" Google asked me if I meant to ask if some people are not built to run. So unacceptable is this idea that the only article that came up on the subject was arguing that the notion is a silly one and should be dismissed. The author argues that while there are some positive traits that seem to come along with dyslexia, there are "foundational academic skills" that are missing and this should therefore continue to be classified as a disability. It is strange to me that what appears so obvious is apparently quite obfuscated. How's that for a word? It means to make something unclear. All we need to do to see the crack in this argument is to change the arena of the missing skill. Consider the example of LeBron James on skates. In the case of this fish out of water, this would be a true statement: "Although James is able to literally jump over defenders and shoot the ball in the hoop from 40 feet away, there are some foundational hockey skills that are missing. Therefore, it is accurate to conclude that James has a hockey disability." Anyone who made that argument, or hot take, as it is known in the annoying world of sports talk radio, would be laughed off the air. If I'm skilled at building car engines but not at reading, I have a reading disability, but if the reverse was true, you wouldn't say I had a mechanical disability. What is the difference between these two? It is simple, and it finds its roots in the history of education. I don't have time for a detailed review, but oh man, I want to dig into it so bad. I will resist and give you the short version.

First, let me say that I am not anti-literacy. That would be pretty dumb considering I'm hoping that you are reading this. I'm using literacy as an example of how an idea can spread until it becomes so ubiquitous that it appears to be self-evident, simply because we have all stated it to be true for so long. While it can be argued that literacy allows for education to be possible, it is also true that this is the case because education is built around literacy. An analogous argument would be that basketballs are round because the hoop is round. Are we to understand that before the advent of the written and read word humans simply wandered around, bumping into things and wondering what to do with themselves? Of course they didn't. For the societies that existed at the beginning of literacy, reading and writing were a luxury. Survival and progeny were the main focus of existence. As reading and writing developed, they became not only a way to store and convey information, but also a way to distinguish those who had to work to survive from those who had the luxury to sit around and read about it. In other words, literacy became a status symbol. As such, the rise of literacy is inextricably linked to the desire of the majority of humanity to rise above their station in life, to be seen as noble and special. Luckily, the vast majority of humanity possesses the required brain anatomy to be able to read and write, so bringing the children in from the family farm and plunking them in a desk with a slate was not traumatic. The reality is that for many of them this was probably a welcome change. I know I'd rather sit and read than plow the field or bale the hay. But what about that kid who loves baling hay and plowing the field? The kid whose brain is built to understand the subtleties of the seasons and the soil. The kid who was born to farm. We didn't invite him in out of the field; we mandated that he come. We didn't rescue him from the field; we tore him from the field. Not only that, but after we did, we told him that there was something wrong with him because he couldn't learn to read and write. Never mind that the teacher probably couldn't grow a carrot to save his life; the kid is the one who is seen as broken.

For years there has been debate in the field of ADHD research and treatment regarding the question, "Is ADHD a gift or a curse?" It's weird that after literally thousands of years of scientific inquiry, humans are still stuck asking binary questions, locked into false black-and-white arguments in which neither polarized side can ever fully capture the truth. This is because the answer to that question is highly situationally dependent. I once spoke to a group of teachers about working with students with self-regulation struggles and gave them a hypothetical situation to consider: Imagine that you are in university and your entire grade in the course is dependent on two assignments. The first assignment is to be reading at least three to four books at the same time. The second assignment is to not finish any of them. When I posed this to the group, one teacher, sitting at the back of the room with a notepad full of notes, jokingly began to hyperventilate, saying, "I think if the syllabus said that, I would have a panic attack!" I pointed out that those same feelings often occur in people like me when the assignment is to just read one boring book all the way to the end. It feels like a wall that is too high to climb over. In high school, I didn't even try. In university, I learned to get lots of information from the chapter summaries, glossary of terms, and chapter subheadings. The point of this thought experiment is two-fold. First, it gives some insight into what we are really asking of some of these ADHD brains when we want them to do seemingly simple tasks such as working on a project, reading a boring novel, or keeping their binder or desk organized. Second, it points out that the expectation that we are foisting upon them is, in fact, somewhat arbitrary. It is agreed upon by the masses that this is the correct way of doing things, when in fact, it is only the consensus way of doing things. The reality is that the consensus way works for most people; that's why it's the consensus way. If we look at a bell curve of the distribution of characteristics in a given population, we know that the biggest portion, the middle part, accounts for only 68 percent of the data. On either end, there is another 32 percent each. Of course, I'm no math genius, but it seems to me that the consensus way excludes, in whole or in part, almost one third of the participants. When you then take someone from either side of that curve and expect them to function in the same way as the middle 68 percent, problems arise.

Can we not accept that at times ADHD is super convenient and at other times it is definitely not? Russell Barkley, professor of psychiatry at a few different universities in the United States and leading researcher in the field of ADHD, seems to have a very bizarre sense of mercy when it comes to this question. At the beginning of almost all of his lectures that I have watched, he makes sure to dispel, in the most condescending way possible, the notion that ADHD is a positive thing. He says that if someone with ADHD has succeeded, it is despite their ADHD and not because of it. He says the notion of a hunter-gatherer brain is a fantasy and the reality is that ADHD is a debilitating disorder that must be taken seriously because the data indicate that it can literally be deadly. Not only does he lead off with this dismissal of our hard-fought-for silver lining, he says that to do so is the merciful thing to do. That for people with ADHD to believe otherwise is to be delusional and to set themselves up for failure. Really, that's merciful? Is he the kind of dad who says to his kid, "Don't try out for the team; you're too short and fat and probably won't make it. Also, I tell you this because I love you." The thing is, the data he is referring to does, in fact, exist. We do drive more carelessly, fall into addiction easier, make impulsive financial and relationship decisions, and accidentally injure ourselves far more than the average person. How could something that is behind these statistics ever be considered a blessing? It's a question that's actually not that hard to answer.

The D on the end of ADHD stands for disorder, but that is not what ADHD is; it's what ADHD can cause. There are symptoms and signs and differences in processing and wiring and chemistry, but only when those differences cause significant impairment in functioning in important areas of life is it referred to as a disorder. The issue is that those areas are not omnipresent, but situational. For example, being more social than average might work very well for someone who has the responsibility to greet customers entering a store. Having an insatiably curious mind might produce endless research ideas and insights into how things work and can be improved upon. Being extremely sensitive is very useful when empathy is needed to connect to another person or animal. Being forgetful is useful when the thing to forget is unpleasant, such as another failure or mistake. Being easily distracted is only an issue in distracting environments. Working memory problems are only an issue when the individual is presented with a list of things to accomplish while in the midst of doing something else. Saying what is on your mind without a filter is only problematic when the situation calls for conformity and, believe it or not, the norms to which we are expected to conform are arbitrary and entirely dependent on the population in which we exist. In other words, in a different environmental and social context, what appear to be impairments and deficits become assets and advantages. I often tell kids with ADHD that back when they were building big ships and sailing off into the horizon with no real idea where they were going or what they would find, we would have been first in line for the adventure, and once we had come back victorious, full of tales of adventure, we would have been celebrated and venerated. Unfortunately, someone already did most of that, so we just have to go to our social studies classes and listen to the teachers talk about it and then read boring textbooks about it and then write essays about it when we really just want to go get on the ships and see what is out there. The different place and time is what has created the disorder, not the traits and tendencies.

In many ways, Russell Barkley is right: ADHD is a lifelong issue and must be taken seriously. If left unattended, ADHD can contribute to many unpleasant complications across the lifespan. Having said that, the case can be made that even the symptoms "because of" ADHD are situationally driven. Shame is only present if we are shamed. Depression is only present if we are led to believe that we are fundamentally inadequate and that the world is not built for or accepting of us the way we are. Anxiety is only present if we are not adequately supported in our shortcomings and forgiven for our mistakes. Addiction is only present when the pain of isolation and detachment drives us to find a way to block the pain and escape the misery of hopelessness, rejection, and futility that is experienced in a world that is not built for us. To quote Gabor Mate, in the final chapter of *Scattered Minds*:

ALTHOUGH THE SOUL-DESTROYING fear of being different is shared by many in North American culture, conformism is less a painful struggle for those who really do fall in with social norms. Those who do not consciously experience themselves as different may also shrink from any temptation to be themselves, but they are not compelled to live every day aware of the mask they are wearing, tense for fear it will slip. The irony is that the energy ADD adults expend on their attempts at sameness is wasted, as is the anxiety parents generate over their child's differentness. The world is much more ready to accept someone who is different and comfortable with it than someone desperately seeking to conform by denying himself. It's the self-rejection others react against, much more than the differentness. So the solution for the adult is not to "fit in," but to accept his inability to conform.

EIGHTY-ONE

THE GREATEST WORK

ONE TIME MY SON, Luke, who was probably seven or eight years old at the time, was struggling with some homework, which is a ridiculous sentence, if you think about it. Why would he have homework in Grade 2? Anyway, Luke, like me and all of his sisters and probably even Tina and all of my brothers and dad and several cousins and my uncle and maybe my aunts and probably my grandma, has ADHD. As such, his long-term recall of movie quotes, comics and books he has read, and conversations with friends is incredible, but he struggles to remember what I just asked him to get from the fridge. After being reminded for the third time, he will finally get his socks from the laundry room, but instead of putting them on, he will carry them around with him as he goes from distraction to distraction until he finally loses track of them. In other words, he is just like me. Anyway, this particular day, his homework involved memorizing something, and he was really struggling with it. Finally, he put his head in his hands and dejectedly summed up the ADHD experience of so many in such a simple but elegant way when he sighed, "It makes me ashamed that I can't remember things." When I heard him say that, my heart hurt. I knew how he felt--the feeling of inadequacy and stupidity, the feeling that there was something wrong with him, that he wasn't as good or smart as the other kids and that we must be disappointed in him. I wanted so badly to shield him from those feelings and that self-perception. However, rather than rush in and encourage him, telling him that he shouldn't be ashamed or that he was smart and to just keep trying, I told him about an experience that had left me feeling the same way, not just as a kid, but recently. I told him how I felt and what I thought. I knew it was important that he not only know about my historical struggle with the same thing but my current struggle. He looks up to me and has said on more than one occasion that I am his hero (no pressure), so he needed to know that his hero was quite the Forgetful Jones as well. He needed to know that it was okay to be forgetful instead of denying that he was. Then we started to talk about all the things that he is good at remembering, and I pointed out that one of the reasons he is bad at remembering some things is probably because he's so good at remembering other things and that most people aren't good at both kinds of remembering. I recall from that conversation the feeling of pride that washed over his face as we talked about his strengths and the feeling of relief that allowed his shoulders to slump, not in shame, but in relaxation as he realized for a moment that he was okay.

My children are my lab. They are spread out in age but close enough to be friends. In them, I have been able to observe the brain and emotional development of ADHD across the span of over 19 years now. Somebody once said that once you've met one kid with ADHD, you've met one kid with ADHD, and my family is such a clear demonstration of that idea. Manda is an overachieving perfectionist who tries hard to be organized but struggles with time management, takes a long time to do tasks, struggles to find things to occupy her very active mind, gets bored easily, and can find it hard to be still and quiet unless she is in a very uncomfortable social situation, like a new class. She's a straight-A student and has been through her entire education. She shows incredible dedication to pursuits that she is interested in, but she is easily distracted and quick to feel hopeless.

She experiences synesthesia in weird ways, like a physical aversion to small holes like those found in a sponge or Swiss cheese.

Becca is an underachieving procrastinator, a minimalist when it comes to effort. She has a hard time retaining information or even maintaining eye contact during a conversation without becoming distracted by either internal or external stimuli. She is a very talented singer and actor who doesn't believe that she is talented at either. She taught herself to play the guitar over a summer, and she is hilarious, but she is also prone to really big emotions, both pleasant and unpleasant. She has dealt with tics when she was younger, along with severe separation anxiety. She struggles with motivation and lack of interest in things and spends long periods of time bored out of her mind, but she is extremely sensitive to the needs and emotions of others and will go out of her way to help someone who is suffering.

Jill told me recently that her life is like a sneeze that never happens--a bunch of pent-up energy looking for release, lots of good ideas that don't turn into reality--something to which I can relate. She has sensory hypersensitivity, can get easily overwhelmed in crowded, noisy environments but can also be the loudest part of that environment. She, more than any of my kids, is the most likely to say the inappropriate thing, to ignore propriety and the expectation of a social filter. She is brilliant and underachieves, then gets hyperfocused on a goal and obsesses until she accomplishes it. At the age of 14, she had already written two novels, generated completely from her own imagination.

Holly is a sweet girl who has no end of friends but struggles to pay attention for even a minute at a time. Her lack of working memory is the stuff of legend and she overcompensates for her inner scatteredness with outer OCD and cleaning, tidying, and sorting. She is also probably the biggest litterbug in the family, leaving a trail of dishes, clothes, and granola bar wrappers in her wake as she tours the house. She gets bored incredibly fast and has a hard time entertaining herself. She has been known to say, with no self-aware hint of irony, "I LOVE Netflix!" speaking of it as a friend who really understands her needs. She is hilarious and has many hidden talents but also struggles with anxiety to the degree that she could barely attend the first half of her first year of middle school, a challenge she overcame and then used to help her friends who struggled with the same problem.

Luke, as I mentioned, has an incredible memory unless you ask him to go and brush his teeth, clean something up, help carry something in from the car, or get his shoes on. It's not out of stubbornness or defiance; he simply gets lost on the way, absorbed in an imaginary pursuit, like the time I asked him to carry my walking stick in from the truck on the day we moved into our new house. A few minutes later he hadn't returned, and I peeked into the living room to see him practicing his ninja skills with the stick. He worries about fairness and rules and would play video games until his thumbs fell off if we didn't exert some control and boundaries. He has so many incredible talents that we keep discovering, as well as tendencies to be easily wounded, to hyperfocus on people making annoying sounds, and to beatbox in church.

Tina is the glue that holds us all in place, but only barely. She was often described as a space cadet or an airhead growing up, leaving her feeling chronically dumb. She is loved by everyone who meets her but struggles to see in herself even a shred of the person we can all recognize. She is talented in many areas but sees mainly her shortcomings and weaknesses. She is very sensitive, creative, and has the most amazing work ethic of anyone I have ever known. She will also hyperfocus on a project, whether it is preparing a Sunday School lesson (where her public speaking phobia is tested on a regular basis) or finishing a jigsaw puzzle, and I often have to physically stop her from doing chores around the house, insisting that the house won't get any messier overnight. She has the most incredible talent for knowing where stuff is that I've lost. She can remember the location of a small slip of paper that has been buried underneath a pile of clothes in a closet. She is as stubborn as I am, which makes for some interesting discussions, but she loves me more than I could ever ask for, something that is of ultimate value when facing my demons and ongoing struggles.

Together, we are an interesting, heterogeneous bunch, and I have tried as hard as I can to daily reinforce the beauty of our uniqueness. I don't sugar-coat things and readily live by the motto that I proclaim to my children and my clients: "It's okay to suck at stuff and not know stuff." I know that motto doesn't exactly roll off the tongue, but I also know that it's the truest, most honest way I can share that message. When we moved into our first house, we needed to do some major renovations, a job for which I had no skill whatsoever, other than a willingness to be curious and learn. I had no experience with a hammer other than smashing my Hot Wheels, and keeping track of my tools was like tracking down fugitives on the FBI's most wanted list, only with less success. If I ever needed to go to Home Depot to buy tools, equipment, or building supplies, I would do hours of research on YouTube and various DIY websites so that I could walk into the store and talk as if I knew what I was talking about. I desperately wanted to avoid being seen as I was, an amateur who was in over his head. One day it dawned on me, I *was* an amateur who was in over his head. Why should I pretend otherwise? I began to go to Home Depot with no advance research at all. When the highly elusive Home Depot helper would approach and ask if I needed help, I would essentially tell them, in slightly different words, "I suck at this stuff and I don't know how to do stuff." I would tell them that I was no handyman and was in over my head and that I needed to buy a thingy for the thingy that attached to the thingy. Their eyes would light up at the prospect of providing their expertise, and not only was I shown exactly what I needed much quicker than I could ever have found it on my own, but there was virtually no pressure on me to pretend. This is my goal for my children, to not have to pretend that they've got it together. I often ask myself, in the midst of a challenging parenting situation, "How will my kids describe me to their counsellor?" While this may seem like a defeatist attitude, assuming someday they will need therapy, I see it as a reality fueled by permission to acknowledge areas of weakness and a desire to find more strength. If I can effect no other change in this world than for my own children to rise up with healthier self-esteem, with the knowledge that they are loved and lovable--not despite their uniqueness but because of it--that they have boundaries that keep the wolves at bay and the confidence to repeatedly fail, I will have done my job.

EIGHTY-TWO

THE POWER OF RELATING

I've GOT to be honest with you, the closer I have got to the end of this story, the more anxiety I have felt. All of my familiar feelings come back in waves, sneak-attacking me with thoughts that alternate between nobody cares and people expect too much of me. I wonder if my stories trail off into loose endings, if they are coherently attached to each other, if they convey the point. I wonder what I was thinking in putting myself out there, whether I have been too open and honest, whether the people who say they are looking forward to reading it will follow through and read it. I try to tell myself that I really just wrote it to prove that I could do it and that it doesn't really matter if no one ever reads it, but of course it matters. I drift in and out of fantasies of book tours and television interviews and book signings where no one shows up and I have to make some self-deprecating jokes and then go home. I criticize myself for making it too long but then argue that everything is important, even if it just gives context to the stuff that's super important. In the end, I doubt whether this was all worth it and wonder if people will read it and see the person I am and be drawn to me or repelled by me. This is the lifelong impact of being the kid who's standing when everyone else is sitting, of being the grownup who can't help his kids with Grade 7 math despite having a master's degree, of feeling the pressure of permanent potential, of....

There's currently a car alarm going off in the parking lot outside my office and it's very distracting. Maybe distracting isn't the right word. It's more annoying. I guess it's both. I wonder how far away the person must be parked that they can't notice their car alarm going off for five minutes. Now they've turned it off, which reminds me that throughout the afternoon, whenever I've looked out my window, I've seen a rough-looking guy, driving a rough-looking van, parked in the parking lot. He is standing with a well-dressed, nice-looking woman, who appears to be talking to someone in the backseat of the van through the open sliding door. I have no idea what they are talking about, but each time I've looked out over the course of three hours, the actors in the scene are all there, though their blocking looks different. I wonder what the heck they are talking about. The guy has a slight smile on his face, but I don't know if that's because of what she is saying or because of how she looks and he can't believe she's hanging out at his van. My stomach is gurgling, even though I just ate, so it's not because it's hungry but digesting, I guess. My shoes are too tight. I keep having this a capella religious song playing in my head, but not the whole thing, just one line over and over again in which the singer mispronounces the name Israel, and it really bothers me because the rest of the performance is so good, but how could no one have mentioned somewhere along the way that he was saying it weird?

We recently moved into a new house, and our cat, who I often refer to as the worst pet ever, discovered an inaccessible (to humans) little closet under the stairs which led to Tina referring to her as Harry Potter for a few days. When the last *Harry Potter* book came out, I read the whole thing in one day, and then when I finished it, I immediately regretted it because the characters had come to feel like real people in my life. Finishing the book meant saying goodbye to them, and I wished I had dragged it out a bit longer. In truth, though,

Harry Potter was very annoying to me because so many things could have been easier or avoided if he'd just been willing to ask for help. One of the most annoying things in the world is when a character in a movie or book needs to leave on a quest and insists that this is something he or she has to do alone, because it almost never is. I feel like I already wrote about this, but if I did it was probably a long time ago and no one really remembers it because most people probably aren't going to sit down and read the whole thing through in one shot the way I did with *Harry Potter*. In fact, most people won't really read it at all, let alone all the way through.

Since discovering my own ADHD, I've had the pleasure of helping countless people make sense of what previously felt like nonsense. I've watched as the realization dawned on them that there was a reasonable explanation for the things they had struggled with their whole lives. I've seen people before and after they have started medication and marvelled with them at the difference, the clarity, the motivation, the focus that has been evoked. I have watched as ADHD parents embraced their ADHD kids and found a commonality that was previously missing. I have seen teachers put things into perspective and meet kids where they are at, working together to adapt learning environments, modalities, and expectations. I have sat with people as they have gone through the mixed emotions of adult diagnosis. I've felt their shame and their sorrow and their relief and their anger. I've ached when a person who has a chance to make a difference in someone's life by deepening their understanding has refused to go down that path and instead insisted that the other person is the one who needs to change. I've explained and taught and demonstrated and joked and even cried--in every way I have thought of so far--the important principles that are crucial to arriving at a different meaning for the experiences that we accumulate, both positive and negative. For all the positive feedback that I've received about my speaking, my writing, or my counselling, the most impactful is when someone says to me, "you really get it."

In counselling, much research has been done on what factors

influence successful outcome. These include the counsellor's age, sex, theoretical orientation, years of experience, education, ethnicity and a host of other factors. Time and time again, the results reveal that the single greatest influence on outcome is the quality of the relationship between the counsellor and the client. What does this finding tell us, other than that therapists ought to pay attention to it? To me, it tells us that the true healing power lies not in the words, but in relating. How can there be relationship without relating? There can't be. It has been my intention all along, through this collection of disasters and triumphs and painful lessons and missed opportunities that some of you will have found yourself or someone you care about in these pages. I hope you will have seen your own thoughts expressed, your own fears articulated, your own pain shared. I hope that if you have found value in these words, it is the value that comes from knowing that you are not alone, that others can be there for you, and that it is worth it to share your own story, to connect, and to build a community that is so desperately needed.